GRATITUDE:

AN EXPOSITION

OF

The Hundred and Third Psalm.

BY THE

REV. JOHN STEVENSON,

AUTHOR OF "THE LORD OUR SHEPHERD," "CHRIST ON THE CROSS," ETC.

NEW YORK:

ROBERT CARTER & BROTHERS,

No. 285 BROADWAY.

1854.

STEREOTYPED BY
THOMAS B. SMITH,
216 William Street.

PRINTED BY
JOHN A. GRAY,
97 Cliff St.

Contents.

Psalm ciii.

1 BLESS the LORD, O my soul: and all that is within me, *bless* his
holy name.

2. Bless the LORD, O my soul, and forget not all his benefits:

3 Who forgiveth all thine iniquities; who healeth all thy diseases·

4 Who redeemeth thy life from destruction; who crowneth thee
with loving-kindness and tender mercies;

5 Who satisfieth thy mouth with good *things; so that* thy youth is
renewed like the eagle's.

6 The LORD executeth righteousness and judgment for all that are
oppressed.

7 He made known his ways unto Moses, his acts unto the children
of Israel.

8 The LORD is merciful and gracious, slow to anger, and plenteous in
mercy.

9 He will not always chide: neither will he keep *his anger* for ever.

10 He hath not dealt with us after our sins: nor rewarded us according to our iniquities.

11 For as the heaven is high above the earth, *so* great is his mercy
toward them that fear him.

12 As far as the east is from the west, *so* far hath he removed our
transgressions from us.

13 Like as a father pitieth *his* children, *so* the LORD pitieth them that fear him.

14 For he knoweth our frame; he remembereth we *are* dust.

15 *As for* man, his days *are* as grass: as a flower of the field, so he flourisheth.

16 For the wind passeth over it, and it is gone; and the place thereof shall know it no more.

17 But the mercy of the LORD *is* from everlasting to everlasting upon them that fear him, and his righteousness unto children's children;

18 To such as keep his covenant, and to those that remember his commandments to do them.

19 The LORD hath prepared his throne in the heavens; and his kingdom ruleth over all.

20 Bless the LORD, ye his angels, that excel in strength, that do his commandments, hearkening unto the voice of his word.

21 Bless ye the LORD, all *ye* his hosts; *ye* ministers of his, that do his pleasure.

22 Bless the LORD, all his works in all places of his dominion: Bless the Lord, O my soul.

ANALYSIS

OF THE

HUNDRED AND THIRD PSALM.

PART I.

INTRODUCTORY ADDRESS.

CALL TO PERSONAL GRATITUDE, v. 1, 2.

PART II.

CAUSES OF GRATITUDE ENUMERATED.

I.

SPECIAL BENEFITS

ENJOYED BY THE BELIEVER.

First.—The Pardon of Sin, v. 3.

Second.—The Healing of Disease, v. 3.

Third.—The Life Redeemed from Destruction, v. 4.

Fourth.—The Crown of Loving-kindness and Tender Mercies, v. 4.

Fifth.—The Mouth satisfied with good, and the Strength thereby renewed, v. 5.

Sixth.—The Lord Executing Judgment for the Oppressed, v. 6.

Seventh.—The Lord making known His ways to Men, v. 7.

II.

MANIFOLD BENEFITS

FLOWING OUT ON THE CHARACTER OF GOD,
THROUGH CHRIST,
IN SEVENFOLD FULNESS AND PERFECTION.

THE LORD IS (1) MERCIFUL, AND (2) GRACIOUS,
(3) SLOW TO ANGER, AND (4) PLENTEOUS IN MERCY,
THE LORD (5) DOTH NOT ALWAYS CHIDE,
(6) NOR KEEP HIS ANGER FOR EVER,
(7) NOR DEAL WITH SINNERS AS THEY DESERVE, v. 8, 9, 10

THESE TRUTHS AMPLIFIED AND PICTORIALLY EXHIBITED
IN THE 11TH, 12TH, AND 13TH VERSES, BY

III.

IMMEASURABLE BENEFITS

SURPASSING COMPREHENSION IN HEIGHTH
AND BREADTH, IN DEPTH AND LENGTH: THEREFORE
INDESCRIBABLE; AND ONLY ATTEMPTED TO BE ILLUSTRATED
BY COMPARISON WITH NATURAL EMBLEMS:—

THE HEIGHTH OF GOD'S MERCY—IMMEASURABLE, v. 11.
ITS EMBLEM—THE HEIGHTH OF HEAVEN ABOVE THE EARTH.
THE BREADTH OF GOD'S FORGIVENESS—INCOMPREHENSIBLE, v. 12
ITS EMBLEM—THE DISTANCE OF THE EAST FROM THE WEST.
THE DEPTH OF GOD'S PITY—UNFATHOMABLE, v. 13.
ITS EMBLEM—THE PITY OF A FATHER TO HIS CHIDDREN.
THE LENGTH OF GOD'S LOVE—EVERLASTING.
ITS EMBLEM—NOT TO BE FOUND ON EARTH: COMPARISON FAILS; THEREFORE CONTRAST IS EMPLOYED TO EXHIBIT.

IV.

EVERLASTING BENEFITS

CONTRASTED WITH THE BREVITY
OF HUMAN EXISTENCE, v. 12 to 19.
EVERLASTING MERCY, v. 17.
EVERLASTING RIGHTEOUSNESS, v. 17.
THE EVERLASTING AND PREPARED THRONE, v. 19.
THE EVERLASTING AND UNIVERSAL KINGDOM, v. 19.

PART III.

CONCLUDING ADDRESSES.

CALL TO UNIVERSAL GRATITUDE

UPON ANGELS, v. 20.
— ALL THE HOSTS OF THE LORD, v. 21.
— ALL THE WORKS OF THE LORD, v. 22.
-- THE PSALMIST'S OWN SOUL, v. 22.

I.

Call to Personal Gratitude.

Bless the Lord, O my soul: and all that is within me, bless His holy name.

Bless the Lord, O my soul, and forget not all His benefits.—Verses 1, 2.

The hundred and third Psalm is an exquisite song of thanksgiving. It is the outpouring of a heaven-taught gratitude. It is the "spiritual hymn" of a redeemed sinner, "singing and making melody in his heart to the Lord." It is the inspired address of the Royal Psalmist to his own soul, which so powerfully affects also the souls of others, that multitudes in every succeeding age have felt its appropriate and inspiriting words to be addressed to themselves.

The hundred and third Psalm is an universal song. It is suited for all ages, appropriate to all persons, and applicable to all conditions. Every nation under heaven may equally adopt its language. With the single exception of the seventh verse, it might have been written by the first Adam, to be sung by him and by all his descendants to the days of David, by whom it was written with that verse, to be sung by the second Adam and all His posterity to the end of Time. Jesus used this Psalm in the days of His flesh. The Spirit of God inspired it, and the Son of God employed it, to express the gratitude of the whole family of the redeemed. The Head of that family is the chief singer on this well-tuned instrument. He leads the prayers, He leads also the praises, of His household. The only pure and perfect thanksgivings, ever uttered in our fallen world, issued from the lips of Jesus of Nazareth. His human heart beat high with holy gratitude. He was the High Priest of the Church, not only to intercede, but also to offer thanks. He has acknowledged in our name, all the known and unknown mercies for which we stand indebted to the God of love. Our debt of sin, He has not more surely paid, than our debt of gratitude. Christ abounded in thanksgivings. We read that He "gave thanks," Matt. xxvi. 27, and that He "sang an hymn," v. 30. Such we believe was His constant habit. In solitude, we doubt not, He spake often "to Himself," and in company with His disciples, He and they would speak often "one to another, in psalms and hymns and spiritual songs," Eph. v. 19. This joyous Psalm, we cannot but conceive, would be specially delighted in by Christ and His disciples, as it is, and has been, by all true Christians. Jesus thanked God for the forgiveness, not of personal, but of imputed sin. As Luther, to this effect, remarks on similar expressions in other psalms, "The Lord Jesus so identifies Himself with His bride, taking all her debts upon His own head, that He speaks of her sins as if they were His own, confesses them, bewails them, entreats for their forgiveness, and gives thanks for their full remission." The hundred and third Psalm becomes hereby consecrated to every disciple, because his

Master used it. And that Master ever lives, as grateful now as when He dwelt on earth. Jesus still praises God, and calls on all His disciples to join their praises with His. As our prayers ascend only through His prayers, so our praises ascend only through His thanksgivings. It is in Christ that we pray. It is in Christ that we praise. The High Priest is expressly " ordained to offer" both " gifts and sacrifices," Heb. viii. 3—" gifts," the visible praises, and " sacrifices," the visible prayers, of the Church. When we use this, or any other psalm, in public or in private worship, we can do so, with acceptance, only as members of Christ's body. The action of one member is regarded as the action of all, that there may be no schism in the body. We take part in Christ's praises ; and He takes part in ours. He feels a sympathy with the gratitude of the lowest member of His body. And oh ! what a relief and consolation is it to know that our poor praises become enriched and harmonized by the perfect thanksgivings of our Lord, and that our unworthy acknowledgments are presented before the throne as His praises and our praises—as His acknowledgments for what He has received in us, and our acknowledgments for what we have received through Him !

So elevated, however, is the strain of holy gratitude in this Psalm, that we essay in vain to reach its height. Every emotion we feel seems too cold, every thought too weak, every expression too tame, when we read these glowing words of David. Oh, God our Saviour, how wanting are we in this most needful grace of gratitude to Thee We long to praise Thee with the Psalm, and also with the spirit of David. We long to be one in gratitude with those who love Thee most, who praise Thee best, in earth and heaven. Oh Thou blessed Spirit, who didst attune the heart and harp of David, waken our souls to gratitude and praise! Forgive their mute and miserable state. Their loose and broken strings set right,—yea, furnish new. Then deign to be our Teacher. Strike the key-note, and bid us learn. Touch every chord within our breast, and make it vibrate to Thy will. Help us to catch the note of every mercy as it flies. Let the varied harmonies of temporal, spiritual, and eternal benefits, rise full and strong upon our ear, that new songs of gratitude, fresh themes of praise, may daily cheer our earthly pilgrimage; and, by our meditations on this Psalm, prepare our lisping souls to join the happy choir above of saints and angels, who cease not day nor night their holy strains of gratitude; singing the praises of the Father, and of the Son, and of the Holy Ghost, one God, forever, Amen.

We cannot now determine with precision either the particular time when the hundred and third Psalm was indited, or the circumstances which called it forth. Every successive line, however, discloses to us the intense and varied emotions by which its utterance was prompted.

The son of Jesse appears, at the period of the composition of this Psalm, to have been specially impressed with a joyful consciousness of the Divine goodness. The love of God was shed abroad in his heart, and kindlings of unusual joy and gratitude were awakened within him, by the Holy Spirit. Under the impulse of these glad emotions, he would fain draw nigh at once to God with the most fervent praises;

but suddenly he appears as if arrested by a deep sense of his own sinfulness. He feels that he is altogether unworthy to lift up his eyes unto heaven, much less to speak to the High and Holy One that sitteth on its lofty throne. In unfeigned humility, therefore, he presents his adorations indirectly, like the cherubim and the seraphim on high. Veiling their faces with their wings, these blessed beings, in profoundest reverence, as all unworthy to address the Divine Majesty, cry one to another, Holy, holy, holy, is the Lord of Hosts. So David, in like manner, does not here address himself, as in other Psalms, directly to the glorious Jehovah; nor does he begin by calling upon any of his fellow-creatures to magnify His name: he addresses his words to his own soul, and stirs up every spiritual affection, every inward faculty, to praise and bless his gracious Benefactor. He places himself in lowliest posture and position before the footstool of the throne of grace, and there, "speaking to himself in this Psalm and spiritual song," he breathes forth the spirit of praise in the sublimest strains.

It is observable that no petition occurs throughout the entire compass of these twenty-two verses. There is not a single word of supplication in the whole Psalm addressed to the Most High. Prayer, fervent, heartfelt prayer, had doubtless been previously offered on the part of the Psalmist, and answered on the part of God. Innumerable blessings appear to have been showered down from above in acknowledgment of David's supplications; and, therefore, an overflowing gratitude now bursts forth from their joyful recipient. He touches every chord of his harp and of his heart together, and pours forth a spontaneous melody of sweetest sound and purest praise.

In many of his Psalms, David had called on others to celebrate the mercies of his God. Their hearts he had often thus incited to grateful praise: "Rejoice in the Lord, O ye righteous: for praise is comely for the upright." Psa. xxxiii. 1. "O give thanks unto the Lord: call upon His name: make known His deeds among the people. Sing unto Him, sing psalms unto him; talk ye of all His wondrous works." Psa. cv. 1, 2.

So full and overpowering also, at various times, was his sense of the Lord's goodness, that we find the Psalmist calling in the aid, not only of other believers, but also of every instrument of music, and of all the different members of his body, and of all the various faculties of his soul, to assist him in its utterance: "O come let us sing unto the Lord; let us make a joyful noise to the Rock of our salvation." Psa. xcv. 1. "Praise the Lord with harp; sing unto Him with the psaltery, and an instrument of ten strings." Psa. xxxiii. 2. "I will also praise Thee with the psaltery, even Thy truth, O my God: unto Thee will I sing with the harp, O Thou holy One of Israel. My lips shall greatly rejoice when I sing unto Thee; and my soul, which Thou hast redeemed. My tongue also shall talk of Thy righteousness all the day long." Psa. lxxi. 22—24.

It is, however, in this hundred and third Psalm, that the personal gratitude of the "man after God's own heart" stands out most vividly to view. Here his own duty, as an individual to praise his God, is at once personally pressed, and personally discharged. He sets his mind on the contemplation of the Divine mercies,—and instantly spiritual, temporal, and everlasting benefits crowd on his remembrance. Full and fervent, therefore, does his gratitude become. His whole soul glows with love to his Redeemer,—he appears wrapt in an ecstasy of spiritual joy. The bond of holy, heavenly affection, has made him one in heart with God. He believes that his Lord loves him, and he feels that he loves his Lord; overflowing, therefore, with the blessed sense of this mutual love, he addresses his own happy spirit, and thus incites it to attain the utmost height of gratitude and praise: "Bless the Lord, O my soul: and all that is within me, bless His holy name. Bless the Lord, O my soul, and forget not all His benefits."

What a proof is here of the sincerity of the Psalmist's heart, and of the reality and the fervor of his gratitude! The state of his soul formed the grand object of concern to David. He watched over its feelings. He diligently examined into its position as before God. He was jealous over himself with a godly jealousy, and he suffered not his spirit to continue in a listless and lukewarm condition. On the contrary, he pressed it forward to attain higher and still higher degrees of love, and thankfulness, and joy. He called in every faculty, he summoned every emotion of his soul, and he suffered not a word, nor a thought, nor a feeling, to remain unemployed in praising his Redeemer. As if one term were not enough, he redoubles his soliloquy,—he repeats and amplifies the terms of his address: "Bless the Lord, O my soul: and all that is within me, bless His holy name." It is as if he would say, "Whatever may be my natural and my spiritual endowments, 'all that is within me' shall love, and laud, and magnify the Author of my being, the Finisher of my salvation, and the Sanctifier of my nature. Not a thought, nor a feeling, not an affection, nor a sentiment within me, shall draw back from this blessed occupation. Every faculty of my nature, every emotion of my soul, shall be consecrated unto God."

Who is there among us that would refuse to follow this example of the Psalmist? Who does not feel his constant need to imitate it? Our hearts within us are dull and selfish by nature. They require to be continually roused to activity and zeal in the Lord's service, and to be effectually stirred up to grateful celebrations of the Divine goodness.

Alas! how prone are we to forget the mercies of our God. Day unto day uttereth speech of the liberality of the Lord: night unto night showeth forth knowledge of His long-suffering: year after year proclaims aloud the vastness, the freeness, and the excellency, of His love toward us. Oh! that day unto day uttered speech also of our devotedness: that night unto night showed forth knowledge of our gratitude; and that one year after another proclaimed aloud the sincerity, the intensity, and the continual increase, of our love to our Redeemer. Surely the burden of every renewed heart is this, that its praises are so cold and lifeless, and its gratitude so grievously inadequate.

Intelligent thank-offering is the honorable employment, and the peculiar prerogative, of angels and of the Lord's redeemed. All creation, indeed, should celebrate the praises of the Great Creator. In either world, the animate and the inanimate, all things, all beings, should show forth His praise. The lower animals in their measure, equally with men, are recipients of the blessings of the Most High, and are, like them, dependents upon His bounty. They partake of His universal provision, and they lie sleeping under His almighty protection. But, so far as we can tell, they know not the God that made them, neither do their instincts raise them to their unseen Benefactor. They possess, however, earthly benefactors whom they see and know, and the gratitude of these dumb creatures towards their masters, not unfrequently presents a striking contrast to the ingratitude of men towards their God. In His own unerring word, He thus puts His people to shame by the comparison: "Hear, O heavens, and give ear, O earth: for the Lord hath spoken, I have nourished and brought up children, and they have rebelled against me. The ox knoweth his owner, and the ass his master's crib: but Israel doth not know, my people doth not consider." Isa. i. 2, 3.

Ingratitude is no light sin. Its guilt increases in a four fold proportion, for it must be estimated by the greatness of the Giver, by the unworthiness of the receiver, and by the number, and by the excellency, of the benefits bestowed. Ingratitude from man to man is odious. Ingratitude from man to God is base and horrible in the extreme. To accept a benefit and to return no acknowledgment, is altogether without the shadow of an excuse. In the sight of God and men, the ingrate is most justly despicable.

Who shall describe the Egyptian blackness of ingratitude?

It is "a darkness that may be felt." It is the "midnight" of the soul. It is the death-stroke on every "first-born" hope, every noble aspiration, of the human breast. Ingratitude is satanic. The first foul spirit that rebelled, was the first ingrate in creation. The type, the personification of ingratitude, is the "Dragon, that old Serpent." Rev. xx. 2. Nursed in his first estate of happiness and glory, he kept it not, but turned against the gracious Lord that had created him. No bosom is proof against the entrance of ingratitude; and when once admitted, no created being can of himself resist its transforming, and demoralizing, power. The angel who first entertained it in his breast, became thereby the first fiend. Pride has been called the father, and ingratitude may be denominated the monster-mother, of iniquity. The whole brood of our transgressions display the lineaments of their descent. So "exceeding sinful" is this sin, that there is not a single thought, or word, or deed, against the Universal Benefactor, but bears the impress of their ingratitude upon its front. Every sin is not envious, nor false, nor malicious, but every sin against our God is certainly *ungrateful.* Anger is an ingrate. Envy is an ingrate. Falsehood is an ingrate. Examine every form and species of transgression against the Most High,—idolatry, disobedience, self-righteousness, blasphemy, pride, malice, self-will, and every other sin that can be named—these, all these, not only render us guilty in express terms of law, but also prove us to be a "generation of vipers," who sting the very bosom in which they have been nursed.

Ingratitude is the arid desert in the region of the human

heart, warmed by the sun and watered by the rains, yet continuing as bare and unproductive as before. It exhibits the sluggard's garden in our soul, bearing disgraceful testimony both against its owner and itself. It is like the barren fig-tree in our profession, which after years of watching and of cultivation, brings forth no fruit. The dark mine yields ore, and the hard rock gives gold; from the worthless shell we gain a pearl, and from a poor mean worm we are supplied with silk; but from ingratitude we get no return. It is darker than the mine, and harder than the rock; it is more worthless than the shell, more mean and ungenerous than the worm. Some sins have a specious appearance in the eyes of the world, whereby men's minds are oft beguiled to call them virtues; but ingratitude possesses not a single redeeming quality. It has no specious appearance, no fair color, no bright side whatsoever. It is unmixed evil—essential evil—"only evil, and that continually." Historians have not recorded it in any single instance with approbation. Moralists have made no exceptional case in its favor to admit it amongst the virtues. Poets have not been heard to sing its praises in any nation or language under heaven. Philosophers may have pandered to almost every vice, but none have pandered to ingratitude. Merchants have made gains of innumerable sins, but no man has turned ingratitude to account. It is an unstamped coin of the kingdom of darkness. None acknowledge it in earth or hell. It is a vice so base, that even the vilest of men will turn with indignation when denominated ingrates. Ingratitude is robbery, for it deprives the benefactor of the acknowledgment that is his due. Ingratitude is rebellion, for the King of Heaven has commanded us in everything to give thanks. Ingratitude is cruel, how many a heart has it not broken? Ingratitude is a monster which, wherever it appears, obtains universal execration, standing unrivalled in its own peculiar turpitude, alike unexcused and inexcusable.

How revolting, therefore, how "exceeding sinful" is ingratitude towards God. It deepens the guilt of all our other sins against Him, and imparts to each of them its own hateful character.

But oh, how good, how pleasant, how comely, is gratitude! How just is it, how reasonable! Next in blessedness to giving gifts, is the consciousness of giving thanks. Gratitude is a noble return. It is the highest which man can render either to his God or to his fellows. It is the response of the heart—that very response which God requires, and in which His soul delights. Why has the Lord made this world of ours so fair—adorned the earth with flowers—and crowned the year with goodness? To draw forth our gratitude! Why did he preserve our infancy, guard our youth, and sustain our manhood? To draw forth our gratitude! And why, in addition to all these temporal mercies, has the Lord loaded us with spiritual benefits, so great, so suitable, and so precious, that neither heart can conceive, nor tongue can express them? Why, we ask, has the Lord poured forth upon us all the blessings of redemption? Surely, amid other gracious reasons, this is not the least,—that He might draw forth from our hearts a full and everlasting gratitude.

Oh gratitude, gratitude!—What amount of thankfulness can ever equal infinite obligations? "Who can utter the mighty acts of the Lord? who can show forth all His praise?" Psa. cvi. 2. Surely "it is a good thing to give thanks unto the Lord, and sing praises unto Thy name, O Most High. To show forth Thy loving kindness in the morning and Thy faithfulness every night." Psa. xcii. 1, 2.

Gratitude adorns the believing soul. "Praise is comely for the upright." A thankful heart must needs be a happy heart. Let us, then, cultivate gratitude. It is one of the fairest and most useful flowers in the garden of the soul. It should be the first to blossom, and the last to fade, in every believer's breast. Its presence is always pleasant, and its odor sweeter than the richest perfumes. Gratitude gladdens the heart in which it dwells, and imparts its gladness to the hearts of others. It dispels melancholy. It dissipates care. It begets cheerfulness, and it throws a charm over all the little incidents of life. A grateful man is sure to be a contented man. No fretful thought, no murmuring disposition, can remain long in the breast of a grateful Christian. Whatsoever his lot in life may be, he will neither envy the position of others, nor repine against his own. He will look around him with a contented mind, because he looks upward with a thankful heart.

Holy gratitude is an assemblage of graces—a combination of virtues—the gathered honey of the choicest flowers —a moral constellation of the brightest stars. Examine it steadfastly by the glass of the Word, and you will observe in it the collected lights of faith and love, of humility and contentment, of obedience and temperance, of meekness and goodness, of peace and hope, and joy. Gratitude is a mirror in the soul, reflecting the image of its several benefits. It is as a bright rainbow in our spiritual atmosphere, displaying the various colors of the rays that call it into being. It is as the "apple-tree amongst the trees of the wood," Cant. ii. 3, dropping its ripest fruits upon the earth, which gives existence to itself and them. It has been likened to a verdant willow, bending gracefully her boughs to kiss the waters that refresh her roots. Gratitude is like a tidal wave returning with all its gatherings to the ocean whence it flowed. It is like a sunbeam sparkling on the waters, and then darting a bright ray to heaven ere it dies. It is like an infant with its joyous countenance smiling back a mother's look of love. It is like an awakened echo in the heart, responding to the voice of its gracious benefactor.

Gratitude is a noble and ennobling virtue. It glorifies the Lord and enriches the believer. It elevates its possessor, and inspires him with joy. Who shall describe the happiness of a believing grateful heart—

> "When o'er the soul a pleasure steals
> Sweet as the gentle breath of even;
> Making the bosom that it fills
> A little heaven?"
>
> H. V. T.

Yes, sanctified gratitude is heaven begun. The city of the living God abounds with worshippers, it resounds with hallelujahs. The voice of angels is praise. The language of the saints is adoration. The anthems of the Church below, are her responses to the symphonies of the Church above. Gratitude is the music of heaven in the soul. The full swell of the benevolence of the Most High, meets a most perfect concord in the everlasting gratitude of the redeemed.

Let gratitude then abound on the earth. Let it continually actuate every believer's breast. Let us set ourselves diligently to prayer; let us also set ourselves diligently to praise. "Pray without ceasing," says the apostle; and immediately adds, "In everything give thanks: for this is the will of God in Christ Jesus concerning you." 1 Thess. v. 17, 18. Obey this command, O believer. Look around you for causes of thankfulness. Be eagle-eyed to discern your mercies, rather than your miseries. See how many they are in the house, and in the street—in the country, and in the city—in your own person, and in your family—among your relatives, and throughout your friends—in your native country, and in the world at large. Look not always at the dark spots in every picture, lest your mind be darkened like them. Fix your eyes also on the bright and the beautiful, that your mind may reflect your image. Let the one teach you to pray. Let the other teach you to praise.

Stir thyself up, O Christian, and be not slothful. Call home thy wandering thoughts; be not ungrateful. It is the will of God that thou shouldst be thankful, and He has given thee innumerable reasons to be so. Search the two worlds of matter and of spirit, with which thou art closely connected in soul and body. Behold how they abound with tokens of the beneficence of thy God. Thy creation is a marvel. Thy preservation is a miracle. Thy redemption is a theme of love and joy unspeakable and full of glory. Who called thee out of nothing, and gave thee being?—The God of love. Who preserved thy being in its frailest hour, and fed and nourished thee to thy present strength?—The God of love. Who gives thee health and raiment, and friends and fortune, encircling thee with His zone of blessings?—The God of love. Who bears with thy waywardness, and forbears with thy provocations, the coldness of thy affection, and the short-comings of thy gratitude?—The God of love. Who gives thee "means of grace" for the well-being of thy soul, and sets before thee the "hope of glory" for the encouragement of thy fainting spirit?—The God of love. Who spared not His own Son, but freely delivered Him unto death for us all?—The God of love. Wilt thou not, then, most fervently say with David, "Bless the Lord, O my soul; and all that is within me, bless His holy name. Bless the Lord, O my soul, and forget not all His benefits?"

Yes, O believer, it is the Lord Jehovah who "performeth all things" for thee. Psa. lvii. 2. Give Him then the honor which is so justly due; and let not even affliction hinder thee from praising God. His name is holy. His nature is holy. All His ways are holy and just and good. Whatever may have been the trials of thy past life, believe that the Lord is holy in every thought of His mind, in every feeling of His heart, and in every act of His hand, towards thee. And whatever may be the burdens that now press down thy soul, believe that the Lord is holy in laying them upon thee. Yea, seek to rise higher than this. Seek with the apostle to glory even in infirmities, and to bless God unfeignedly for afflictions. Those burdens by which he bows thee down are blessings in disguise. Those burdens are benefits. Despise them not. The drag upon thy chariot-wheel saves thee from destruction. The time is coming when each afflicted believer shall be enabled to say of the Lord, "Bless His holy name, all my bitterest sorrows have worked together for my eternal good." Anticipate, then, this song of gratitude. If thou art to bless God in heaven for all things, bless Him also now for them on the earth. Stir up thy heart. Call loudly on thy slumbering soul. Invoke continually the quickening Spirit to rouse up "all that is within thee" to this angelic work of praising God.

Remember, O Christian, for thy encouragement, that it is the blessed office of the Spirit of God to fill thy heart with thankfulness. It was not from mere natural disposition that David here praised God. Of ourselves we should never exhibit true spiritual gratitude to our Maker. Our lips are closed, because our hearts are dead in spiritual insensibility. God is not regarded as the Giver, and the Doer, of all things. In our sleep by night, and our food by day, in the light we see, and in the air we breathe, we behold not the Lord, and therefore we give Him not the tribute of special thanksgiving. The natural heart takes all these mercies as its right, and as matters of course; therefore it must be quickened and instructed by the Spirit of Grace. The cold, ungrateful soul, must be warmed by the fire of a Saviour's love, and then will the closed lips be opened; then will the voice of gratitude be heard saying,

"I love Him, because He first loved me." It is the Divine Spirit alone who kindles in the human breast the consecrated flame of holy gratitude. That gratitude sweetly constraining us to think, to speak, and to act, for the glory of God, converts the whole life of the believer into a continuous thank-offering. On Jesus only for acceptance, as the true Christian altar, will that thank-offering be placed. He also is our great High Priest, by whom alone it can be presented unto God. "By Him, therefore," says the apostle, "let us offer the sacrifice of praise to God continually, that is, the fruit of our lips giving thanks to His name." Heb. xiii. 15.

Let us ever, therefore, remember that our praises, as well as our prayers, must be offered only through Christ. Our most fervent thanksgivings require both an atonement and a Mediator. Let this truth be strongly and continually impressed upon our minds. Amid much that is of an opposite character, there is still to be found a great deal of natural gratitude in our fallen world. It is so right, so amiable, so acceptable, between man and man, that we are ever prone to conclude that it is acceptable also with God. If naturally you possess a cheerful, contented disposition, and, as men speak, "feel thankful for everything," be thankful for such a disposition, but be not mistaken regarding it. In and of itself, it is indeed lovely and pleasant before men; but it is not, in and of itself, acceptable before God. Bear constantly in mind the following important distinction which the Psalmist made when speaking of himself, "My goodness extendeth not to Thee; but to the saints that are in the earth, and to the excellent in whom is all my delight." Psa. xvi. 3. Nothing is acceptable with God—"nothing extended to Him"—unless it is offered through Christ, perfumed with the incense of His sacrifice. Men say, "It is right to be thankful; and if we are only thankful, what more can be demanded? Do we not all delight to hear men say, 'Thank God for my mercies?'" So far, indeed, as the mere words are concerned, the Pharisee himself may not be blamed, and all of us ought to pray thus with ourselves, "God, I thank Thee that I am not as other men are." If we have not personally gone all lengths in wickedness with others, we certainly must not take the credit to ourselves, but ascribe the praise to God, and thank Him for it. No doctrine can be more correct. But while this is the character of the words, such is not always the character of their offerer. The Pharisee conceived that his thanksgiving must needs of itself be acceptable; but we are informed that he went down to his house not accepted—"not justified"—before God. His gratitude was a mere natural effusion of selfish satisfaction. It was not true thankfulness. Let us beware of selfish gratitude, which loves the gifts more than the Giver; which congratulates self on their possession more sensitively than it blesses God for their bestowment; and which prizes temporal mercies above those which are spiritual and everlasting. Natural gratitude may also lead us further than mere words; it may constrain us to do much, and to give largely. After some great experience of blessing, some remarkable deliverance vouchsafed; or providential mercy bestowed, we may look around us for an altar already erected, or at much cost and labor we may construct one for ourselves, whereon to offer a liberal gift unto the Lord. All this may be done in a right spirit, and will be certainly accepted in Christ, when it is truly presented through Him. But as Scripture informs us that there is "a repentance that needs to be repented of," so we must declare that there is also a thank-offering that needs to be again offered. Cain is an affecting example of a rejected thank-offerer. The eldest son of Adam, instructed by such a parent, must needs to some extent have been sensible whence his mercies flowed. Grown to manhood, and reaping of the fruits of his labor, he appears to have been the first of the two brothers to prepare an offering unto the Lord: "And in process of time it came to pass that Cain brought of the fruit of the ground an offering unto the Lord. And Abel, he also brought of the firstlings of his flock, and of the fat thereof. And the Lord had respect unto Abel and to his offering. But unto Cain and his offering He had not respect." Gen. iv. 3. And why?—Because he had sinned even in his thank-offering! The Lord informs him of this by the interrogation, "If thou doest well, shalt thou not be accepted?" And wherein had Cain not done well?—Because he conceived that his thanksgiving must be in and of itself acceptable to God. Cain presented his thank-offering without a sin-offering. He had no respect to an atonement and a Mediator, and therefore the Lord had no respect to him and to his offering. Let us take warning by this example. Let us not substitute a natural, for a spiritual, gratitude. Let our praises always be offered through Christ.

"All things are by the law purged with blood." Our gratitude must be sanctified on the altar of Christ. The flame of our profession may be bright, but it must also be pure. A lamp of the most luminous brilliancy is rejected amongst men, if it emit an offensive odor. Everything is offensive to God, that comes not before Him perfumed by His Son's merits. Apart from these merits, every oblation is vain: "Incense is an abomination, our Sabbaths," and "appointed" festivals of thanksgiving, "God hateth." Isa. i. 11–15. Look, then, continually to Christ. By Him, and by Him only, offer the sacrifice of praise. Let your gratitude be kindled at the altar of Jesus; then will it never be rejected by God. The light thereof will "extend" to Him, as well as to your fellow-men: neither by the clouds of adversity shall its lustre be dimmed, nor by all the power and violence of Satan shall its flame be extinguished.

Is this hallowed fire, let us seriously ask, burning within our breasts? Are we mindful of the many, nay the innumerable mercies of our God towards us? Do we constantly acknowledge that we owe them all to the sacrifice of Christ? And do we return our thanksgiving only through Him as our Great High Priest? Do our lives testify to the purity and to the intensity of our gratitude? And do we diligently call upon our souls, all that is within us to bless and praise His holy name? Had we conferred one-half the number of benefits upon a fellow-creature, which the Lord our God has bestowed upon us, we should feel satisfied with that small amount of gratitude which we ourselves have shown to the Most High? Assuredly not. Let us, then, like David, rouse our languid affections. Let our souls, and all that is within us, be stirred up to bless our God through Jesus Christ. And never, oh! never, may we be so unjust, so criminal, so base, as to forget any of His benefits.

II.

The Pardon of Sin.

Who forgiveth all thine iniquities.—Verse 3.

HAVING roused his soul and all its powers, to celebrate the goodness of his God, the Psalmist proceeds immediately to set before it many signal proofs and instances of that goodness. His grateful mind could not feel satisfied with general expressions of thankfulness. The mercy of the Lord had exhibited itself in special acts of kindness; David, therefore, testifies his thankfulness in special terms of acknowledgment. Anxious that not a single blessing should be overlooked, he makes up a list and catalogue of the various benefits which he had received. Delighting to expatiate on the loving-kindness of his Saviour, he occupies the whole body of this Psalm with a glad summary of the tokens of His love. From the beginning of the third verse, and onward to the end of the nineteenth, one blessing after another is specified. He rehearses their several names and natures, that he may the more readily and indelibly impress them upon his remembrance. Thus the Psalmist enjoys his mercies over again by a thankful enumeration of their exlencies, and makes himself doubly blessed by this joyous recapitulation.

The first benefit for which David calls upon his soul to bless the Lord, is the "forgiveness of sin." Pardon is the blessing which the son of Jesse places at the head of his list as the greatest of all the mercies which he had received from his Redeemer. Such, indeed, it is. The greatest amount of temporal benefits is but of little avail, if this one grace be wanting. What are health and wealth, when the wrath of God abides on their possessor? What are honors and the pleasures of the world, when the poor sinner that enjoys them lives and dies in his sins? John viii. 24. But, on the contrary, to have our iniquities forgiven—to have the great debt blotted out from between us and God—to have the full remission of all our sins in the blood of atonement; this is happiness indeed—this is the foundation and the earnest of all true blessedness—it is the soul's sweet foretaste of heavenly bliss.

David had bitterly felt the exceeding sinfulness of sin. "Mine iniquities," he says, "have taken hold upon me, so that I am not able to look up: they are more than the hairs of mine head, therefore my heart faileth me." Psa. xl. 12. These were not hasty expressions of inordinate and morbid sorrow; they were the deliberate declarations of a conscience enlightened by the Word and Spirit of the living God. It was not a mere article of knowledge, and of bare belief, to David, that he had broken the holy law:—it was a matter of painful, self-abhorring consciousness. He possessed not only a conviction of the guilt, but also a painful sense of the pollution, of sin, and he therefore loathed himself as unholy and defiled in the sight of Infinite Purity. Job exclaimed, "Behold I am vile," ch. xl. 4.; and again, "I abhor myself," ch. xlii. 6. Isaiah also declared, "I am a man of unclean lips." Isa. vi. 5. And again the same holy prophet testified, "We are all as an unclean thing, and all our righteousnesses are as filthy rags." Isa. lxiv. 6. David, in like manner, gives frequent utterance to his soul's deep sense of sin; "Have mercy upon me, O Lord, for I am in trouble. My life is spent with grief, and my years with sighing: my strength faileth because of mine iniquity, and my bones are consumed." Psa. xxxi. 9, 10. And again he confesses, "There is no soundness in my flesh because of thine anger; neither is there any rest in my bones because of my sin. For mine iniquities are gone over mine head: as an heavy burden they are too heavy for me." Psa. xxxviii. 3, 4.

Those who have thus most bitterly felt the guilt and the loathsomeness of sin, will be most ready to welcome and to celebrate its forgiveness. So does David in this Psalm. He had felt sorely grieved that he had sinned, and now he felt truly joyous that he had been forgiven.

Forgiveness of sin is one of the Lord's marvellous methods to turn us from its commission. A frank and unexpected pardon makes an appeal to the best part of our nature. The generous declaration touches us to the quick with a deep sense of our transgression. We are made to feel that we cannot forgive ourselves for having offended a Lord so gracious and so forgiving. This principle is recognized by the Lord Himself; for He thus describes the effect which His intended mercy to Israel shall have upon their minds in the latter day: "That thou mayest remember, and be confounded, and never open thy mouth any more because of thy shame, when I am pacified toward thee for all that thou hast done, saith the Lord God." Ezek. xvi. 63. "Then shall ye remember your own evil ways, and your doings that were not good, and shall loathe yourselves in your own sight for your iniquities and for your abominations," Ezek. xxxvi. 31.

David understood this principle, and felt its power: "There is forgiveness," he says, "with Thee, that Thou mayest be feared." Psa. cxxx. 4. In this Psalm he gratefully acknowledges that forgiveness, and exhibits the reverential "fear" and love, with which it had inspired him. "Being forgiven much, he loved much," and therefore he hastens to celebrate the pardoning mercy of his Redeemer, with the earliest note of his awakened lyre.

Oh what a change! to pass from the gloom of guilt into the sunshine of the Divine favor—to be delivered from the convictions and the forebodings of conscience, and to be introduced into the liberty and the peace of acceptance with God—to have the gnawings of remorse done away, the burden of sin removed, the fear of death dispelled, Heb. ii. 15, and the dread of judgment dissipated, 1 John iv. 17. Well might David, and every believer who partakes with him of the same blessed faith, burst forth in the joyous thanksgiving of this Psalm, and say, "Bless the Lord, O my soul: and all that is within me bless His Holy name.

Bless the Lord, O my soul, and forget not all His benefits: who forgiveth all thine iniquities."

The knowledge of forgiveness is regarded by many as one of the most exalted and remote attainments of religious experience. Not clearly understanding the Divine method of forgiveness, and hindered by what they conceive to be a becoming humility, they say, "Such a state can never be ours in this life. It is high; we cannot attain unto it." But did they rightly understand salvation by Suretyship, as revealed from heaven, they would perceive that pardon is not directly a matter of religious experience, but of religious faith. Pardon is not a state to which the believer raises himself by a long and holy course,—it is an act of God's free mercy and grace in Christ Jesus. A full and free forgiveness is granted unto us the moment that we believe in Jesus. Even the "little children," to whom St. John writes in his first epistle, enjoyed this blessing from the commencement of their Christian course, 1 John ii. 12. All other Christians are equally welcome with these youthful believers, and with the Psalmist before us, to the immediate enjoyment of this privilege.

The forgiveness of sin flows from the death and sacrifice of the Son of God, as our Surety: "It is the blood that maketh an atonement for the soul," Lev. xvii. 11; and, "without shedding of blood there is no remission" of sins, Heb. ix. 22. The Psalmist was well acquainted with this law. He had learned it in his childhood, he had obeyed it in his manhood, and he had constantly believed that the blood he offered in sacrifice was doubly typical, first of his own blood as a sinner, and secondly, of the blood of the Great Redeemer as his Surety. "The Gospel before was preached unto Abraham," Gal. iii. 8: and not unto him only, but unto David also; yea, to Abel and to all believers from the beginning of the world. They received the forgiveness of their sins from the very same source that we receive it, that is, through the shedding of the blood of Jesus. "It is not possible," says the Apostle, "that the blood of bulls and of goats should take away sins." Heb. x. 4. This truth David fully understood; and at that very moment of his life, when, more than at any other period, he would have been ready to double his sacrifices, if necessary, and to give or to suffer anything by which he might obtain forgiveness, he deliberately places on record this most remarkable statement (so apparently contradictory and heretical for a Jew to utter), "For Thou desirest not sacrifice, else would I give it: Thou delightest not in burnt-offering." Psa. li. 16. David, therefore, with other true believers, discarded all reliance for forgiveness on mere material sacrifices; and Christ Jesus was to him, and to them, as He is to us, the alone spiritual and acceptable sacrifice on which are fixed the eyes and the hopes of God's people, from the beginning to the end of time: "Behold the Lamb of God, which taketh away the sins of the world." John, i. 29.

The "taking away of the sin of the world," signifies its removal out of every sinner's way in returning to his God. Sin had excluded us all from the Divine presence. The only light that met the sinner's eye, searching for an escape from death, was the gleam of that "flaming sword which turned every way, to keep the way of the tree of life." Gen. iii. 24. The only law which meets the sinner's case is that unchangeable enactment, "In the day thou eatest thereof thou shalt surely die." Gen. ii. 17. The sinner's penitence and tears, his prayers, and his professions of amendment, can make no alteration of this condemning law. Its awful sound falls still upon his ear, "In the day thou eatest thereof thou shalt surely die!"

But lo! salvation by Suretyship is revealed. The Son of God comes down to bear the sinner's curse. He places Himself in the sinner's stead, and suffers for him the penalty of death: "He was wounded for our transgressions, He was bruised for our iniquities: the chastisement of our peace was upon Him; and with His stripes we are healed." Isa. liii. 5; "All we like sheep have gone astray, we have turned every one to his own way; and the Lord hath laid on Him the iniquity of us all." Isa. liii. 6.

Behold the Lord's amazing method of forgiveness. Sin is "taken away," by being "laid upon" the Surety's head. No more offering for sin is to be made thenceforward forever: and we are all commanded to draw near by the new and living way which is thus opened for us into the presence of God by the blood of Jesus. Heb. x. 19.

The offended Lawgiver has graciously given His own Son to be an able, willing, and all-sufficient Surety,—that Surety has already suffered and died in our stead, and our sins are already atoned for by His blood: to reject that gift, and to dishonor this Saviour's work, by our unbelief, is to commit the greatest crime, and to ensure our own condemnation,

John iii. 19, and cause us to die in our sins. John viii. 24. But he that believes in this Saviour passes from condemnation to acquittal, from death to life, obtains a full and free forgiveness, so that he shall neither live, nor die, nor rise again in his sins. Unspeakable and undeserved as is so great a blessing, the fact is certain, the truth is undisputable. Not one, not two, but "all the prophets give witness" to this joy-inspiring doctrine that "whosoever believeth in Jesus shall receive remission of sins." Acts x. 43.

When in human affairs a surety has stood in our place, has obeyed every law in our name, has suffered every penalty in our behalf, and has paid every debt in our stead, not to believe in him and rely on what he has done, is to reject and disown his representative character, is to repudiate his obedience, to despise his sufferings, to dishonor his payment, to annul his suretyship work, and to cast from us all the benefits he has acquired. To refuse to believe in Jesus as the author and the finisher of our salvation, is virtually to assert that we put Him aside as a Surety, from between our souls and God, in order that we may stand in our own name, and in our place, before the bar of the Almighty to undergo every penalty in our own persons, and to pay every debt out of our own resources. It is to trample under foot the Son of God, and to count the blood of the covenant an unholy thing, and to do despite unto the Spirit of Grace. Heb. x. 29. But, on the other hand, to believe in Jesus, is to acknowledge His representative character, is to accept His obedience, to honor His sufferings, to accredit His payment, to ratify His suretyship work, and to appropriate to ourselves all the benefits He has secured. There is not a single prophet, apostle, or evangelist, that insinuates a doubt on this important subject. Where is the text to be found, in the whole compass of the word of God, which declares that though a sinner believe in Jesus, his iniquity shall not be forgiven? No. Never can it be. If we believe not, yet He abideth faithful to the threatening. God cannot deny Himself, 2 Tim. ii. 13. If also we believe, He abideth faithful to the promise. God cannot deny Himself. He that believeth *shall* be saved. He that believeth not *shall* be condemned, Mark xvi. 16. The covenant in Christ is ordered in all things and sure, 2 Sam. xxiii. 5. He is the Surety of this covenant—this "better covenant"—this best of covenants, Heb. vii. 22; viii. 6. His own declaration is, "Him that cometh to Me, I will in no wise cast out." John vi. 37.

It is in continually thus "coming to God through Christ," that our safety consists. It is in continually believing and confessing, that we obtain continual remission. Virtue flows from Christ, whenever, with the hand of believing prayer, the true penitent touches but the hem of His garment. David expresses this truth by the use of the present tense, "who forgiveth all thine iniquities." God forgives as man confesses. We are thus kept near to God in Christ, by receiving present supplies according to our present circumstances. There is no stock of grace given to be enjoyed at a distance from the Giver. The sins of to-day are not pardoned by the grace of yesterday. The sweet communion we then enjoyed is no atonement for our present coldness and alienation of heart. We must go with these to Jesus the instant that we feel them. No sins are pardoned till they are confessed to Him. And no sin is confessed to Him that is not freely pardoned for His sake. "Let God be true and every man a liar" who negatives the promises of the Lord, or who questions His readiness to forgive according as He hath said. Through the abundant righteousness of the Surety, God "multiplies to pardon." David believed firmly in that blessed Surety, and therefore unhesitatingly testifies to his soul, "He forgiveth all thine iniquities."

Understand, then, oh Christian! the gospel of suretyship clearly, that thou mayst give thanks joyfully. God the Father has laid all thy sins upon His own Son as thy surety. Isa. liii. 6. And He is now, therefore, not imputing them to thee as a cause of exclusion from His presence. 2 Cor. v. 19. Believe in Jesus as the Surety who has procured these two great blessings for thee, and so draw near, just as you are, to this gracious God, as in Him thy reconciling and forgiving Father. Oh! glorious and everlasting Gospel,—how simple is thy message,—how efficacious is thy devised suretyship,—how direct and immediate is the believer's entrance into the joy of forgiveness.

Such was the position of David in the Psalm before us. Jehovah appointed the blood of atonement for the remission of sins, and David simply believed what his Lord declared. With every sin that he committed he drew near to the atoning blood, he offered sacrifice, and he returned persuaded that he was forgiven.

That sacrifice was typical of the blood of Christ; let

David's obedience, and David's faith, be also typical of thine, oh Christian! God has announced to thee this gracious truth, that the Lord Jesus is the Surety on whose head He has laid thy sins. It is thy duty to believe simply as David did, what thy Lord has plainly declared; and when any sin that thou hast sinned comes upon thy conscience, then immediately in secret prayer draw near with thy sin-offering, that is with Christ Jesus, the Lamb of God, in thy hand of faith, confess over Him that iniquity, believe in thine heart that God laid it on His head as thy Surety, and return from the throne of grace persuaded that for His sake thine iniquity is forgiven thee. Compare Lev. iv. 28 and xvi. 21.

"Coming to Christ" and "believing on Him," "trusting in Christ," and "fleeing to Him for refuge," "eating Christ's flesh" and "drinking Christ's blood," with other similar forms of expression in Holy Scripture, are designed to denote that one grand act of faith by which the poor sinner, the bankrupt debtor, "receives the atonement," Rom. v. 11; that is, accepts and ratifies what his Surety has accomplished in his name. There must be an open consent and agreement on the part of the debtor, as well as on that of the Creditor and of the Surety, before the reconciliation can be completed. Reader, thou art the poor debtor for whom the Divine Surety has already paid, and the Divine Creditor has already accepted a full and matchless ranson. And now thou art called to be at one with Them, in that which They have done on thy behalf. Hear thy God Himself beseeching thee to be reconciled to Him, and assigning this as the mighty reason, for He hath made Him, who knew no sin, to be sin for thee. 2 Cor. v. 21. If thou hast confessed thy transgressions over thy Saviour's head, if thou art thus daily laying there every sin that rises on thy conscience, then by all that is true and faithful in the promises of God, be entreated to believe with an undoubting mind that they are all forgiven thee in Christ. The declaration of the Scripture is express and positive,—Whoso confesseth and forsaketh his sins shall have mercy. Prov. xxviii. 13. See also 1 John i. 7.

Enter, then, with David by faith into the joy and gratitude which he here expresses. Give God thanks for the forgiveness of thy sins in the blood of the Lamb. Say often within thyself, "I never can sufficiently praise Him for such an inestimable benefit." Hasten therefore to stir up thy soul and all that is within thee to endless and unceasing gratitude. Be perpetually praising God. Being forgiven much, love much; serve much; praise much. Bear the sanctifying knowledge of thy forgiveness about in thy heart continually. Keep it as thy companion-thought for all seasons and situations of thy life. Let it lighten thy gloom in adversity, and elevate thy soul above the seductions of prosperity. Let the remembrance of thy forgiveness be a joyous bond uniting thee to God and to thy fellows—to the One in all gratitude and obedience, and to the other in all readiness and cordiality of forgiveness. Let this blessed truth, that in Christ thou hast redemption through His blood, even the forgiveness of sins, Col. i. 14, gladden thy going out and thy coming in. Let it cheer thy rising up and thy sitting down. Let it be the last thing in thy thoughts every night, and the first thing in thy grateful recollections every morning, to say with David from thy very heart, "Bless the Lord, oh my soul, and all that is within me bless His holy name. Bless the Lord, oh my soul, and forget not all His benefits, who forgiveth all thine iniquities."

III.

The Healing of Disease.

Who healeth all thy diseases.—Verse 3.

MAN is twice diseased, and the God-man alone possesses the double cure. Could our two natures, the flesh and the spirit, speak individually for themselves, they would each testify, "There is no health in me." Medical science, with its long catalogue of diseases, bears testimony alike to the multiplied and to the multiform maladies to which our flesh is heir. The revelations of Scripture, the records of history, and the experiences of all men, attest the presence and the power of unnumbered maladies also in the human spirit. The world in which we live is a vast hospital of distempered patients; and when the Good Physician came to visit it, He put forth His power to heal alike the sick and the sinner.

The restoration of the body is a simple act of omnipotence; the restoration of the spirit implies a twofold exercise of the Divine prerogative. The soul requires pardon for the past committed sin, and purgation for the remaining inward corruption. There is no guilt in sickness, neither also is there any merit. Disease is not disobedience. On the contrary, it is the working out of God's righteous law of chastening. In bodily disease man is passive and reluctant. In spiritual disease man is an active and a willing agent. In the former he naturally and cordially hates his sickness. In the latter he naturally and cordially loves it. A fever makes no man a destroyer of the law, but a corrupt desire entertained in the breast constitutes him a wilful transgressor of the commandment. To emancipate the sinner from the position in which a single sin has placed him, he must be both acquitted from condemnation, and rendered free from pollution. These two blessings are vested solely in the God-man. He dispenses them as He pleases. By pardon He imparts health to the conscience of the sinner, and by sanctification He infuses health into his affections. Pardon and purity are the medicines of the Gospel. They are the freely-proclaimed and the inseparably-united blessings of the Good Physician.

The word of God comforts every penitent with the assurance of this twofold blessing. "If we confess our sins," says St. John, (first) "God is faithful and just to forgive us our sins, and" (second) "to cleanse us from all unrighteousness." Here the apostle includes himself. He says not "If you," but "If we," classing himself with his readers, showing them that he too felt his doubly-diseased state, that he too needed forgiveness and cleansing, and that he too had recourse to confession, coming daily as a sinner to the throne of grace in the name of Jesus, to obtain pardon for the past, and grace to help for the future. Observe the high and amazing argument which the apostle uses to prove this delightful and all-important truth. He does not say, as we should have expected, God is merciful and gracious to forgive, but, "God is faithful and just to forgive"; by which he teaches us that those very attributes, which, before our confession of sin, were directly against us, are thereupon directly for us. To whom, then, is God faithful and just? We answer: First, to Himself, to His own promise, and to His own oath; those "two immutable things in which it was impossible for God to lie." Heb. vi. 18. Secondly, He is faithful and just to His own Son, who came into our nature to fulfil the righteousness of the law, and to die under its penalty, that as the perfectly righteous Man He might enter into covenant with God, and obtain a right to all the blessings which God would have bestowed upon unfallen man. It would be unjust, therefore, to Christ, to withhold any blessing asked in His name. He himself said to His disciples, "Whatsoever ye shall ask the Father in my name, He will give it you." John xvi. 23. Thirdly, He is faithful and just to His believing people who come to Him through Christ, with penitence and prayer. They rely on God. They confess their sins, expecting His forgiveness; and He will never dishonor their confidence: "Whoso trusteth in the Lord, mercy shall compass him about." God will not disappoint the hope that is truly fixed on Him.

Mark again, that St. John assures himself, and all believers, of both blessings equally. Where God vouchsafes forgiveness, He bestows sanctification. The former is a mean to the latter. The one without the other would be incomplete, unavailing, and impossible. And it may be because so many desire the former more earnestly than the latter, that God withholds even both from their sensible enjoyment. How many professing Christians do we hear declaring "I cannot say that my sins are forgiven; if I only knew that, I should indeed be happy." Yet it is too evident, from their life and conversation, that they are not equally anxious to obtain the greater blessing—purity of heart. Instead of "cleansing themselves from all filthiness of the flesh and of the spirit, perfecting holiness in the fear of God," they indulge in the follies and gaieties of a "world which lieth in wickedness." Such persons do, indeed, desire to be saved from the punishment of sin, but not from sin itself as their greatest punishment. It is safety, and not sanctification, which is uppermost in their thoughts. It is pardon, and not purity, which they mainly seek. It is deliverance from hell, not meetness for heaven, which they are most anxious to obtain. If there be no real penitence and confession toward God in the heart of such persons, we must declare that from Him there is neither forgiveness nor cleansing granted toward them.

When, however, the eye is spiritually opened to discern the disease within, to look into the hidden workings of the breast, and to behold corruption festering in every part; the whole inner man one mass of disease, from the sole of the foot even unto the crown of the head, "no soundness in it, but wounds, and bruises, and putrifying sores," Isa. i. 6; it is then that we confess, like the apostle, "I know that in me, that is in my flesh (my fallen nature) dwelleth no good thing," Rom vii. 18; it is then that we cry, "Heal me, O Lord, and I shall be healed;" "Create in me a clean heart,

O God, and renew a right spirit within me: then it is that we look upon hell as our just desert, and regard deliverance from its burning flames as a far inferior thing to deliverance from the burning hell within our own breasts. Oh, it is then that we long for victory over our besetting sins, for freedom from our enslaving passions, for sanctification from our polluting lusts, for superiority to our continually recurring infirmities. It is then that we sigh for purity of heart, for conformity to God, for renewing after Christ's image, for the full and continual in-dwelling of the Holy Ghost. Then it is that we "abhor" ourselves, and say, "Behold I am vile." Then it is that we "would not live alway," that we long to be "absent from the body, and to be present with the Lord," and that we earnestly "look for the Lord Jesus Christ from heaven, to change our vile body, and make it like unto His own glorious body."

Blessed be God, this is also His own desire respecting us. It forms His first, and last, and strongest desire. Again and again does He say, "Be ye holy, for I am holy." His own spirit, also, conveys this desire from the heart of God into the hearts of all His children. David was His child; and, therefore, we here see that he is taught to congratulate his soul not only that God "forgiveth all its iniquities," but also that He "healeth all its diseases."

The diseases of the soul are far more deadly than the diseases of the body. Murmuring, stubbornness, and self-will, are as opposed to spiritual peace, as the most virulent distempers are to bodily repose. God in Christ is the alone healer of both soul and body. And infinitely does the health of the former exceed that of the latter in desirableness. Holiness is spiritual health. Cry, therefore, earnestly to obtain it. Prayer here cannot possibly be mistaken. No importunity after holiness can ever be displeasing to the holy God. Conformity to the likeness of Christ Jesus, is the standard of spiritual health. He was always thankful. Pray to be like Him, and to be altogether cured of ingratitude. Discontent is a mental cancer, and eats into the very vitals of the spiritual man. Its roots spread wide and deep. They carry death wherever they advance. Pray, therefore, to be healed. Bring every disease of thy soul to this Great Physician in earnest prayer. A sick man must not conceal any of his symptoms. Confess all the pains and maladies of thy soul to Christ. Unbosom to Him without reserve thy hidden failings. Lay bare thy sins, thy tempers, thy backslidings, thy coldness and waywardness, thy pride and worldliness. Keep nothing back. Tell all to the Good Physician, and He will cure thee. Thy poor, sin-sick soul shall be made strong. Thy spiritual diseases shall be healed. Health and thankfulness will spring up together within thy breast.

David, in this Psalm, as elsewhere in other Psalms, uses the term "soul," as expressive of the entire man. And in this verse he is not to be considered as exclusively referring to spiritual healing. That gracious Lord who cares for the soul, cares also for the body of man. Jesus, when here below, not only forgave sin, but likewise healed disease. He had compassion on both soul and body. David believed God to be, in both, his good Physician. In another Psalm he says, " He is the health of my countenance, and my God." And in this verse we are to consider him as offering special thanks, also, for the healing of his bodily diseases.

The Psalmist, on several occasions, had experienced severe attacks of sickness. His wonted health had fled. His strength had waxed feeble, and his fair and manly frame had pined under disease; but now he was enabled to testify that the Lord had healed him. And whether the deliverance were granted at a former or at a more recent date, he is determined to retain it continually in the most grateful remembrance.

Recovery from sickness is a joyful cause for thanksgiving. We arise, as it were, to a new life. The couch had seemed to be the shadow of the tomb. Dissolution appeared to have begun its gradual work. But it may be, that in the very hour of greatest apprehension, the Lord manifests His compassion. At the momentous crisis He speaks the word " be still," and the raging fever becomes a " great calm;" the sleepless eye-balls close in gentle slumber, and the peaceful countenance indicates that the first process in recovery has commenced. How fervently do we congratulate the anxious relatives, the friendly physician, and the watchful attendants, on the auspicious change. But more deep and holy is the emotion with which the devout believer looks upwards and says, " I thank Thee, oh my God! for this deliverance."

If there be one truth more plain and indisputable than another, it is this, that the Lord is the great healer of disease. Never, amidst human efforts and instrumentalities, never let us lose sight of His gracious and over-ruling hand: "The help that is done upon earth, He doeth it Himself." Ascribe not your recovery to the potency of this remedy, the suitability of that medicine, or to the skill and the care of your kind and experienced physician. Give not the honor of your restoration to their varied and united influences; nor to some happy combination of circumstances; nor yet to your own care and prudence. Ascribe it entirely to the kindness and the care of your heavenly Father, who has condescended to use some, or all, of these, as successful instruments in His own healing hand.

When a friend sends you a present from a far country, by the hand of his servant, it is to the friend that your gratitude is due, and not to his messenger. Doubtless you will acknowledge the care which the latter has displayed to bring that present into your possession; but you will never for a moment lose sight of your friend amid these just encomiums upon his servant. God is this Friend, and all earthly medicines, circumstances, and physicians, are his servants, by whom he conveys to you His own precious gift of restored health. Your acknowledgments and your thanks are not the less justly due to the means and to the instruments. Give each of these the full credit that belongs to them in their proper place, and in their just measure; but ever remember that the first place of praise, the highest measure of acknowledgment, belongs to Him who has blessed them to your benefit. Give God the glory, therefore, as David does. Stop not short at second causes. Rise not from thy sick bed with a mere worldling's gratitude. Act not the infidel or the atheist, excluding an omnipresent God from the circle of thy acknowledgments. Remember that men and things are nothing to thee but what God pleases to make them. See, then, His hand in them all. Recognize Him in their operations,—acknowledge Him in their successes. God is the God of means. He acts by human instrumentalities.

Most interesting and instructive is it to observe how the Lord, by this gracious arrangement, binds men together in society, and causes them too feel their mutual dependence, by making them, in His providence, mutual benefactors. The physician occupies his true position, when he regards himself, and is regarded by others, as an instrument, under God, for the benefit of his fellows. Honorable and blessed is the office of the Physician. He is called of God to assuage the pain, and to heal the maladies of men! How gracious is it of the great Creator to bestow His benefits upon us by our brother's hand, and to blend the skill and the wisdom needful to our recovery, with the tenderness and the sympathy of a member of our common family!

Too many, alas! under sickness and disease, act like Asa rather than like Hezekiah. It is recorded regarding the former, as a warning to all others in their maladies, that "in his disease he sought not the Lord, but to the physicians." 2. Chron. xvi. 12. How different was the conduct of Hezekiah. Though the prophet had solemnly declared to him "in the name of the Lord, that he should die and not live;" yet we read that he prayed earnestly for the prolongation of his life. God was not displeased with that importunity. He never regards with indifference the distresses of His creatures. He turns not away from His people in their misery. The Lord, being full of compassion, said to the afflicted monarch, "I have heard thy prayer, I have seen thy tears. Behold I will add unto thy days fifteen years." Isa. xxxviii. 5. And how did the Lord fulfil this mercy? By the use of means; for Isaiah had said, "Let them take a lump of figs, and lay it for a plaster upon the boil, and he shall recover." Isa. xxxviii. 21.

Look, then, in all your diseases to the Lord; and, as you look, use every available means that lies within your reach. Employ all means and instruments, but depend on none. Depend alone on that God whose blessing is necessary to give them success. If thou disregardest food for the nourishment of thy life, and medicine for the healing of thy maladies, thou disregardest Him who has commanded thee to use them both. Neglect not, then, this plain duty, under the plea of looking to the Lord; and, again, neglect not the Lord, under the plea of attending to the necessary duties of the sick bed. No case can possibly be so urgent as to prevent thee from calling upon Him. No disease can be so desperate as to justify despondency of mind, and neglect of prayer. What case has ever exceeded that of Hezekiah? Was he not worn under a "pining sickness"? Had not all remedies proved unavailing? And had not God himself declared that he should die? Yet even in such circumstances he did not refrain from prayer. He cried earnestly for recovery, and recovery was vouchsafed.

It is not prohibited to the believer to ask for bodily health. The Scripture expressly assures us that "the prayer of faith shall save the sick, and the Lord shall raise him up." James v. 15. "The prayer of faith" is, in its very nature, a prayer also of acquiescence and submission. No temporal blessing should be sought from God, without this Christ-like addition, "Nevertheless not my will, but Thine be done." So gracious is our heavenly Father, and so tender is He to the feelings of His children, that there is not a single subject, or condition whatsoever, that He has forbidden them to Him in prayer. On the contrary He invites, yea, He commands them to unbosom their whole hearts to Him without reserve. His word expressly says, "trust in Him at all times; ye people, pour out your hearts before him: God is a refuge for us." Psa. lxii. 8.

The more desperate the case, the more urgent should be our appeal to God. Does a beloved friend lie sick and ill? Is a wife, or a husband, or a child, at the point of death under some alarming malady? Have you scarcely a day or an hour to depend upon their life? Submit, but do not despond. Pray, wrestle, agonize in supplication, but be not dumb with despair. While there is life, there is hope. All things are possible with God. For aught that you can tell, He may be waiting to give the blessing as soon as you have earnestly importuned him for it. Compare Luke xi. 8, and Gen. xviii. 24—32.

Remember, however, at all times that we must never set our hearts inordinately either upon our own recovery, or upon that of others. Life and health are in the hands of God. He gives, and he retakes them, when and how He pleases; and who dare say to Him in either case, "What doest Thou?" We must not even feel, much less declare, that unless recovery and life be granted, we shall not be satisfied. This is not submission, but opposition, unto God. It is a positive rejection of His will, and a guilty preference of our own. Such conduct can only defeat our own object—blast our wishes—and provoke the Most High to withhold from us the very blessing which we so rebelliously demand.

It is the prerogative of faith to recognize God in all things. Like Moses, we are called to endure "as seeing Him who is invisible." Heb. xi. 2. And never is that far-seeing eye of faith more needed, than when the natural eye is dimmed by the influence of disease. Bodily maladies have too often a depressing influence upon the believer's spirit. The anxieties and the necessary duties of a sick chamber, occupy and distract the thoughts. When suffering and danger are present, it is often difficult to believe that a gracious God is equally present also. Yet the God of love is in the sick man's chamber. Faith asserts that He is present there. It does so, because God himself declares it: "Fear thou not, for I am with thee." Isa. xli. 10. When thou passest through the waters, I will be with thee." Isa. xliii. 2. And hence, even in the valley of the shadow of death, Faith says, "I will fear no evil, for Thou art with me." Psa. xxiii. 4. The presence of God is the sunshine of the believing soul, and the joy thereof is its strength.

Great is the difference between the submissive believer, and the self-willed infidel under the fatal influence of disease. Dark and dismal is the death-bed of the man who knows not God. The utmost service that human ingenuity can effect, may be rendered to his malady. Wealth may command whatsoever seems necessary to his cure, and no expense may be spared by which his comfort can be promoted. Science may employ her abundant resources, and men of skill and of experience may unremittingly devote their best energies to his relief. Still, day after day, it may be that, baffling all appliances, the disease gains ground. One physician is called in after another, and the dying man looks wistfully to each as he enters—but looks in vain. The unseen, the unknown, the unthought of Physician, is present in his room; but, alas! he neither believes in His presence, nor implores His aid. He addresses not a single petition for recovery to Him who alone can cure. All his thoughts are fixed on the various ineffectual remedies, and on each successive earthly physician. His feeble voice is heard saying, "Call in another." There is another, "the Physician from Gilead," Jer. viii. 22, who can change even death itself into a sleep; but not one individual, perhaps, around that dying bed prizes His balm, or advises to have recourse to Him. Even at this, the eleventh hour, it may be that the book of God is not opened for consolation; nor does a single voice, in friendly and fervent intercession, offer up a final supplication on his behalf. Friends weep around him because there is no hope. His own heart sinks within him because there is no remedy; his eye wanders in vain from relatives to attendants, and from attendants to physicians. He casts a last look imploringly around him, and closes his eyes in despair upon a helpless and a disappointing world.

But how different is the case of the man who confides in God through Jesus Christ. Bright and comforting is the death-bed of the believer. Poor or splendid may be the circumstances that surround his sinking frame. His heart is raised above them all. Wealth he knows cannot prolong his existence, neither can poverty hasten his dissolution. Friends, attendants, and physicians, he firmly believes can avail him nothing without the blessing of his heavenly Father. His first act, therefore, is to place himself in the hands of the wisest and the best Physician, and by earnest and believing prayer to commit his case implicitly to His care from first to last. He receives with gratitude the remedies supplied by human skill, and he regards with satisfaction the prompt and persevering efforts that are made for his restoration. He fervently prays also that they may be crowned with success, saying to his unseen but ever near Physician, "Have mercy upon me, O Lord, for I am weak; O Lord heal me, for my bones are vexed." Psa. vi. 2. During the progress of his malady he gives way to no anxious thoughts or desponding fears. The peace of God, which passes all understanding, keeps his heart and mind through Christ Jesus. His soul reposes through unerring wisdom, and in reference to whatsoever may be the ultimate issue, he feels that he can be both thankful to live and willing to die. Remedies may prove unsuccessful, and the resources of science unavailing. Friends may weep around him, and attendants wail. Physicians may lament that they can do no more, but still he an answer, "All is well, everlastingly well. There is no danger to the Christian whatever may happen." Having expected nothing certain from mere earthly instrumentalities, he feels no bitter disappointment at their failure. Neither sullenness nor gloom overspread his mind. Despair and terror find no place in his breast. "The hour of his departure is come. He hears the voice that calls him home." He looks around upon relatives, attendants, and physicians, with gratitude and affection; he commends them with fervor to the care of his long-tried and never-failing Friend; and he invites them, with a smile, too meet him in the abodes of glory. Then yielding his spirit into his Saviour's hands, he casts a last look of love around him, and closes his eyes in peace, with a "hope full of immortality."

None can fully know the blessedness of health, but those who have experienced the ravages of disease. None, therefore, can be truly thankful for healing mercy, but those who have endured painful chastening. Nor even these universally. Such only of their number will be truly thankful, as have received the spiritual benefit of their chastening. We can never rightly, that is, adequately and spiritually, bless God for the removal of disease, till we have learned, in some measure, by divine grace, to thank Him for the disease itself. Strange contradiction—marvellous gratitude! The believer can thank God both for sending him affliction and for taking it away!

Health is a great blessing, but sanctified affliction is a still greater blessing. I knew an intelligent and pious man who carried an affliction with him from his birth. "You observe, Sir," he remarked, "I can but creep upon the earth." Then looking down and pointing to his limbs, he added, "I was born with these club feet; but since the time that I was born again, I have not ceased to give thanks for them unto God; for, with my light and joyous spirit, I think had I had feet like other men, they would have carried me headlong to destruction."

Health is a great blessing, but sanctified affliction is a still greater blessing. "Visit for me a parishioner," said a brother clergyman; "she has been bowed together on her bed for these sixteen years." On entering her chamber, I beheld a countenance radiant with intelligence, and beaming with Christian joy. Her sufferings were constant, she said, and at times almost insupportable; but then she added with a smile, "they are nothing to my Saviour's love. Sometimes I think that the time is long; but I check myself and say, 'Forgive me, Lord; thy will is best, not mine.'" Unlike many other long-tried sufferers, her thoughts and feelings had by no means become morbid or selfishly contracted. On the contrary her heart appeared to be filled with generous and universal sympathies. Every work that was going forward for the spiritual and temporal benefit of her fellow-creatures, obtained immediately her thoughts, her contributions, and her prayers. "I lie here," was her remark, "and bless my God for everything." Never shall the sight be forgotten of that long-tried but cheerful sufferer, that weak but thankful prisoner of disease. So fair and lovely was her countenance, so joyous, and lively, and energetic was its expression, that she seemed like a bird of paradise with half-expanded wing, watching and waiting for the opening of her cage, that she might soar away to her desired heaven; and thither her sainted spirit is now flown.

Reader, hast thou enjoyed uninterrupted health? How grateful shouldst thou be; more grateful, in one sense, than David. He blessed God fervently for having taken away his diseases. Thou shouldst bless Him still more fervently for not having sent thee any. Be doubly thankful, therefore, for thy freedom from disease. Use thy unbroken strength solely to the glory of the Giver. See that thou do more than others in His service. Let not the outward blessing of a robust frame bring an inward weakness upon thy soul now, and an everlasting blight upon thy soul and body in the last judgment.

Reader! art thou a sufferer? Few of thy fellow-men are altogether whole. Suffering, debility, or disease in some one or other of their varied forms, are common to men. A thorn in the flesh is part of our inheritance from Adam: "Man is born to trouble as the sparks fly upward." And has thy trouble, Reader, come to thee by chance? Job had greater experience of sorrow than thou, and he declares that "affliction cometh not out of the dust, neither doth trouble spring out of the ground." Job v. 7. Therefore say instantly NO, emphatically NO, to every insinuation of the infidel, and to every suggestion of the tempter—NO TROUBLE COMES BY CHANCE. Whether it be that through the hostility of man the possessions of the believer are swept away; or that by the fire of God falling from heaven his flocks are burnt up, and his servants are consumed; whether it be that a great wind from the wilderness buries his whole family in one night amid the ruins of their habitation; or that a virulent disease breaks forth upon his own person from the sole of his foot unto the crown of his head; whether it be that his dearest friends, and his nearest relatives, turn against him in his calamities, yet will the believer look above all these second causes, and recognize in each event and circumstance the hand of God. He will not say, "the wind happened to blow; the house to fall; the lightning to strike; and the enemy to despoil." On the contrary, his language is, "The Lord hath taken away." Say, then, with Job in all thy sicknesses, "Shall we receive good at the hand of God, and shall we not receive evil?" Job ii. 10. Yea, say with thy suffering Saviour in every affliction, "The cup which my Father hath given me" to drink, "shall I not drink it?" John xviii. 11.

Diligently consider thy diseases, oh believer! that thou mayest thankfully consider thy deliverances. Regard God's hand in the one, that thou mayest acknowledge His hand, also, in the other. How many sicknesses hast thou seen? Of what nature were they? How violent? And of what continuance? Let all these several inquiries be distinctly answered in thy remembrance, that with the deeper gratitude thou mayest bless thy good and great Physician. Each sickness has made thee a debtor to thy God; and each deliverance has doubled that debt. Defraud not, then, thy Lord of the glory that is His due. He condescends to accept through Christ the poor payment of thy praise: "Whoso offereth praise glorifieth Me, saith the Lord, and to him that ordereth his conversation aright will I show the salvation of God." Psa. l. 23.

Art thou as one of the ten that were cleansed? Be not as one of the nine that went away. The moment thou perceivest that thou art healed, turn back, and give glory to God with a loud voice, Luke xvii. 15. Be not ashamed to proclaim thy obligations to the good Physician. Amidst thy family, amongst thy friends, and within the house of God, declare alike His healing power, and thine own fervent gratitude. Again and again return to give glory to God. Offer thy praises unceasingly, like David. Peruse this hundred and third Psalm frequently in thy closet. Close up thy weekly account with praise, as each week closes upon thee with mercy. Yea, let not a single day of spiritual or temporal health pass over thy head without saying, in most fervent gratitude, Bless the Lord, O my soul, and all that is within me bless His holy name—who healeth all thy diseases.

IV.

The Life redeemed from Destruction.

Who redeemeth thy life from destruction.—Verse 4.

From his earliest days the Psalmist was the child of Providence. Many were the hair-breadth escapes, and the wonderful deliverances, which he experienced. Dangers of various kinds presented themselves as his years advanced. The paw of the lion, and the paw of the bear, at various times threatened to terminate his existence, and at others the ruthless hand of man. The same God who delivered him from the sword of Goliath, rescued his life from the javelin of Saul. That almighty Friend who had covered his head in the day of battle, delivered him, at one moment, from the lords of the Philistines, saved him at another out of the hands of the men of Keilah, and again preserved to him his life and throne from the unnatural rebellion of his own son. Well, therefore, might the Psalmist stir up his soul, and all that was within him, to bless the Lord with most fervent gratitude, who, by so many signal deliverances, had "redeemed his life from destruction."

The term "redeemed" is of high and holy import. It

leads the mind far above the mere fact of preservation, and sets before it the wondrous means, the glorious reason, why any sinner obtains deliverance from destruction. Few of us sufficiently realize the position in which Adam's sin and Christ's redemption have placed us. Our lives are forfeited. The transgression of our first parents brought them, and all their family, under the attainder of the curse. Every sin we commit deserves our immediate condemnation and death. The original law under which our race was created, pronounced this sentence, "In the day thou eatest thereof thou shalt surely die." And why was this decree not executed upon our first parents? and why is it not executed upon ourselves? The only true answer that can be given is this: Because of the gracious interposition of that Redeemer, who is emphatically declared to be "the Lamb slain from the foundation of the world." Rev. xiii. 8. The Son of God caught up our falling world. The second Adam offered himself as a substitute to die for the first Adam. And by virtue of His blood, shed for our guilt, the blood of man flows not for his own guilt. The original law was express and universal: Die through sin. The redemption law is also express and universal: Live through righteousness. Because the *first Adam sinned*, we have all fallen under the sentence of that original law. Because the *second Adam sinned not*, its execution is stayed, and we are all spared under the power of this redemption law. The suretyship of Jesus is the only legal ground on which mercy can be shown to an attainted race. His redemption is the just and righteous cause of the prolongation of our forfeited existence. It is, therefore, with peculiar and expressive fitness that David here applies that term to himself as a sinner obtaining mercy, when he thus addresses and instructs his soul to bless the gracious God "who redeemeth thy life from destruction."

The statement of this truth might thus be drawn in parable. There was a wise and gracious monarch of a mighty empire, whose subjects lived upon his smile, and placed their supreme delight in giving obedience to his will. There was but one law promulgated in his kingdom—it was the law of love. There was but one sentence published throughout its vast extent—it was the sentence of death. Love and live: disobey and die.

Throughout the whole of this great king's dominions, loyalty and harmony prevailed. But suddenly the inhabitants of a distant province, seduced from their allegiance by misrepresentations of his character, revolted against this gracious Sovereign, repudiated his authority, and formed an alliance with the enemy of their King and country. Every faithful subject rose with indignation at the tidings of their rebellion, and demanded that the sentence of the law should be enforced against the rebels. The royal mandate was issued for their immediate extermination. But before the execution of that decree, the Prince approached his Royal Father with a counsel of peace. "These rebels deserve the death decreed. I offer no apology for their crime. The laws of the empire must be maintained inviolate. But if the lives of so many may be spared, I will lay down my own. Let them live. Let me die. Thus thy mercy and thy justice will be alike displayed. Every shadow of misrepresentation and of pretence for rebellion will be done away forever. My heralds will proclaim thy clemency to the guilty, through my death in their stead. Those who believe my dying love, will return to Thee in allegiance. Those who believe it not, will continue in their rebellion. The one will prove themselves to be devoted friends: let them be regarded with favor as thy children for my sake. The others will prove themselves to be irreconcilable enemies; let them be given over to condign punishment."

This counsel was followed. The Prince died to maintain the law, and yet to spare the guilty. Heralds were sent forth to the inhabitants of that rebellious province with this gracious proclamation—"The King against whom you have rebelled, has given his own son to die on your behalf. Your forfeited lives are now spared through his death in your stead. The last entreaty—the dying command which he left—is this, that you return to his Father. Your rebellion shall be no hinderance to your acceptance. The King is not now imputing it to you as a cause of exclusion from his presence. Believe in his mercy. Lay down your arms. Let the dying love of the Prince prevail with you all to return to your allegiance. Whosoever continues in rebellion, shall assuredly be condemned."

The message of the Prince was variously received in various parts of the rebellious province. Some denied that any rebellion had existed, and maintained that their province was as loyal as any other in the empire. Some declared that the slight rebellion which had arisen, did not deserve so severe a sentence as had been decreed against it, and that consequently, the death of the Prince was uncalled for, and altogether unnecessary. Others doubted whether the Prince had really died on their behalf, and refused to credit the fact that they were indebted to him for their deliverance from immediate destruction. Others professed delight at the intelligence of their Sovereign's clemency, but yet retained a secret wish for the success of the rebellion. Some listened eagerly to each successive herald, but questioned whether they would be accepted if they laid down their arms, and passed their time amid doubts and fears, that perhaps, after all, they should be condemned. Others again there were, who heard the proclamation with deep emotion. They were pierced to the heart by the goodness of their Sovereign. The death of his Son displayed to them at once the greatness of his clemency, and the foulness of their own rebellion. Self-condemned, they knew not how to forgive themselves for having taken up arms against so good a King; and when they thought of his Son's sufferings and death in their stead, they wept, they cast away every weapon of opposition, they renounced all association with their rebellious companions, and in the face of every risk and peril, they openly espoused their sovereign's cause.

It is obvious that the Prince is immediately the preserver of the life of all the rebels, and particularly and finally of those who return to their allegiance. In like manner, it is said of Jesus, that "He is the Saviour of all men, especially of those that believe." 1 Tim. iv. 10. Every human being that has ever lived, or that now breathes, or that shall hereafter exist upon the earth, owes his life to the death of Jesus. He is the immediate Saviour of all men, otherwise every man in the first day that he sinned must have surely suffered death. But He is particularly and finally the Saviour of those who believe in His dying love, and return to His Father through Him. The past sin and rebellion of men, is at present, no hinderance to their acceptance. Whenever a rebel presents himself before God, acknowledging his guilt, and supplicating forgiveness in the name of Jesus, he is admitted to favor. The death of the Son of God, our own present existence in consequence of that death, and all the mercies and benefits with which our spared lives are crowned, are conclusive arguments to assure us that as certainly as we confess and renounce each act of rebellion, so certainly does the Lord forgive it. To doubt the clemency of the Sovereign, to regard the death of the Prince as of no avail to their benefit, and to entertain the opinion, that though they confessed their guilt, laid down their arms, and supplicated pardon, they should yet, after all, be condemned, would be a grievous aggravation of the original sin of our rebellious province.

It can never be sufficiently impressed upon our minds that every sin forfeits the life of the sinner. The law of sacrifice affirmed this solemn truth. For every sin, blood—which is the life—was commanded to be shed. Innocent, but representative, blood, was accepted for the blood of the guilty. The life of a surety was taken for the life of the principal. To the sacrifice of that surety, the sinner ascribed his redemption from destruction. So likewise to the redemption in Christ's blood, every human being should attribute his daily, and hourly, preservation. Every sin, but for the Lord Jesus, the Redeemer, would be visited on the spot with immediate condemnation. The continuance, therefore, of our race upon the earth, and the prolongation of each individual's natural life, though a sinner, is entirely owing to this gracious Daysman between us and God. Ever since the fall, the world has been given into His hands as the Mediator. God the Son is the Conservator and the Governor of our rebellious province. Therefore free Mercy, by reason of satisfied Justice, now sways the sceptre over this sin-laden world. Therefore is it that our every sin meets not with instant vengeance, because Jesus is the Saviour of all men, and especially of them that believe. In this sense we are all "redeemed from destruction," as were the children of Israel from Egypt, and the Red Sea, and yet, because of unbelief, we are not all brought into the promised land. In this sense we are all being continually "redeemed from" deserved "destruction," every day we live; and therefore, our daily preservation, notwithstanding our daily sins, should awaken within us the grateful emotions of the Psalmist when he said, "Bless the Lord, O my soul, who redeemeth thy life from destruction."

Do we really believe that our natural life is forfeited, that our body is legally dead because of sin—that in the eye of God, and of the original law of our world, our soul is actually dead, having by nature no union with God, who is our spiritual life? And do we realize that being thus dead in law, all our works are "dead works?" Heb. ix. 14. We stand before God, as an outlawed man stands before society. He is dead in the eye of the law. He can, therefore, occupy no office, he can hold no trust, he can perform no act, he can execute no deed, recognizable and commendable by the body politic from which he is outlawed; so are we before God. All our natural amiableness and good deeds, one to another, are "dead works" before God; they are the works of men under sentence of outlawry, who are dead in the eye of the law. The vivid and continual remembrance that we have by nature, the sentence of death in and upon our persons, will make us prize highly that Suretyship, by the grace of which our life is prolonged, our sins pardoned, our prayers and our persons accepted. Thus gratitude will be kindled deep and strong within our breasts. We shall increase in thankfulness at every fresh advance we make in the knowledge of our great deliverance. We will look back with more intense wonder to the rock whence we were hewn, and more horror-stricken to the hole of the pit whence we were digged; and we will praise, and bless, with increasing and unceasing fervency, the name of our gracious Surety and Deliverer.

The omnipresence, the omnipotence, and the benevolence of our God, are often strikingly displayed in the sudden averting of impending dangers. Those marvellous escapes, which we occasionally experience, plainly testify that the Lord is nearer to us than the nearest calamity, and that His power is stronger than the strongest enemy.

It is not only in rare and remarkable occurrences that we observe the providential care of God. Our daily life is encompassed with daily dangers. Our going out and our coming in, our rising up and our sitting down, expose us to a variety of accidents. So frail are the materials of our earthly fabric, that the movement of a limb, the stretching of an arm, the displacing of a muscle, may cause instantaneous sufferings—sufferings which cannot be moderated by the skill of man, and which can only be terminated by the hand of death.

> "Our life contains a thousand springs,
> But fails, if one be gone:
> Strange, that a harp of thousand strings
> Should keep in tune so long!"

Our existence hangs upon a brittle thread, which the slightest breath may snap asunder. It is the mighty power of God alone that can preserve that thread unbroken to His own appointed time. And many and marvellous are the gracious interventions of His providence, by which he effects that preservation.

Appropriate and necessary for every human being is the prayer to be delivered "from battle, and murder, and from sudden death." To the true believer sudden death is, indeed, sudden glory; but to him it should not be merely on that account, the more desirable. Believers from the beginning of the world have generally been privileged to glorify their God in their departing moments: sudden death is an exception to the general rule. Even the most advanced believer should hesitate to express a desire for sudden removal. The cowardice of our nature too frequently conceals itself beneath this specious wish. Through fear of death, many are all their life-time subject to that bondage, from which the Saviour came to deliver us, Heb. ii. 15. Why should we be afraid to know that we are drawing near to the close of our earthly journey? An escape from this knowledge, and its accompanying sorrows, is all that can be really gained by sudden death. Glory is as sure to him who pines, as to him who drops in death. "Rather," should the Christian say, "Rather would I face the last enemy, than not be privileged to know that I am going so soon unto my God." The wish for sudden death is far too selfish in its character, to be indulged in by any true Christian. This wish is not in harmony with this thanksgiving of the Psalmist; and, though he will avoid, indeed, a conscious personal conflict with his last and dreaded foe, yet he will lose the opportunity to glorify his God, while his family and his friends will be overwhelmed with deeper grief. Be not selfish then, O Christian, but rejoice when thou art preserved, and thank God, like David, when thy life is redeemed from destruction.

Review thy various deliverances. Consider the consequences to thyself, if thou hadst not been snatched from destruction. Had death surprised thee in an unprepared state, where now should be thy soul? Was not, therefore, the redeeming of thy life, at that moment, a twofold deliverance in one—a deliverance both of soul and body?

Review thy various deliverances. Recall the expected shipwreck which was averted, the deadly battle where you fought unhurt, the alarming pestilence which raged around thee, and passed away. Remember the far distant land where death threatened thee amid a world of strangers

—or the hospitable board, where the very food thou wert enjoying well-nigh deprived thee, in a moment, of all vital power. Canst thou not recall a day to memory when thou hast left a house, a room, a chair, and speedily some accident occurred, which, but for that removal, had crushed thy limbs, if not destroyed thy life?

A party of relatives and friends, had assembled in an ancient baronial mansion. A fearful storm had raged throughout the night, and the various details of its devastating effects, cast a gloom, in the morning, around the social board. As they were conversing, the proprietor, glancing toward one of the windows, vehemently exclaimed, "My favorite tree—my favorite tree!" Instantly he rose, and his friends followed him. The lady of the house was left alone at the head of the table, in the distant end of the room. Suddenly a high stack of chimneys fell heavily through the ceiling, and carried everything before it, sweeping the table and the centre of the floor, in a moment, to the lowest story of the house. A margin of floor, next the fireplace, remained firm, and there was the lady seated, safe but motionless, gazing with horror into the yawning chasm opened at her feet. The various members of the company were also safe. From the deep recesses of the different windows, they were gazing anxiously upon that favorite tree, as it rocked to and fro under the fury of the tempest; and little did they conceive that the Great Preserver of men was at that very moment, by their fear for its loss, redeeming their own lives from destruction.

Hast thou, Reader, ever experienced any such deliverance?

Hast it ever been said to thee, "One foot further, one moment longer, and you must inevitably have been lost?" Who thus directed thy movements with such timely precision? Who snatched thee from the danger thou then sawest? Thy ever-watchful Lord—thy ever-wakeful friend. Be thankful: be very thankful. Acknowledge gladly, and gratefully, thy preservations from all dangers seen and felt. Forget not also to bless God for mercy vouchsafed in all the unseen and unknown dangers from which he has redeemed thee. Eternity alone will reveal how many, and how wonderful, through this mortal life, have been our deliverances unawares, from destruction by the ever-watchful care of our heavenly Father.

Review thy various deliverances. In the dark night, how many have they been, and in the bright day, how varied? Thy walks abroad for health—thy toil and labor for the daily bread—thy movements to and fro, on land and sea, are all dependent upon God. Fire might seize thy dwelling—or the midnight robber disturb thy slumbers—an unnoticed descent might cause thy fall, or a rough elevation trip thy foot, or the smooth ice occasion thy stumbling—the ever-watchful providence of God, in each or all of these, it may be, has redeemed thy life from destruction.

Perhaps, however, Reader, not one of all these evils has ever once come nigh to thee? It may be, therefore, that thou hast never thought of any deliverance, or offered to thy God any thanksgiving. Take shame to thyself. Thou hast been enjoying continual deliverance; and because it has been unbroken, thou hast not noticed it. Shouldst not thou rather, therefore, have been the more observant, and have given the greater praise? Alas! that we should need the occasional approach of danger to remind us of our general safety! O how we prize our blessings when we have feared to lose them. Because we have no trials, we look upon our uninterrupted security as a matter of course. Mercies are rained about us, daily, as the manna from heaven, till we cease to regard them as blessings direct from God, or indeed as blessings at all. How many like Hezekiah "render not again according to the benefit done unto them." 2 Chron. xxxii. 25. An almost miraculous deliverance may have rescued a sinner from destruction, and yet not a spark of gratitude be elicited from his adamantine heart. Vows are uttered, and prayers are offered, in the prospect of danger; but no sooner is that danger passed, than the vows are forgotten, and the prayers are discontinued. Strive, Christian, to retain a thankful spirit. Pray for a heart ever sensible of thy Saviour's goodness. Abhor ingratitude. Cultivate a lively remembrance of mercies received. It is a grievous thing after awhile to forget a benefactor. To begin to give our affections to the world and to turn them away from Him who has redeemed our life by the sacrifice of His own, is altogether unpardonable.

God is nearer to thee, O believer, than the nearest danger. If it be His will to redeem thee, nothing can possibly destroy thee. The enemy may be close in pursuit behind—the mountains may encompass thee on either side—and the impassable sea may lie before thee. Destruction may seem inevitable, and deliverance altogether impossible. But all things are possible with God. At His command, the sea opens a path before His people, and returns with overwhelming vengeance upon their enemies.

God is nearer to thee, O believer, than the nearest danger. The wisest councillors may be called together by our bitterest enemy. Their experience and their subtlety may be equalled only by their malevolent determination to destroy us. God can frustrate their counsels, and turn all their wisdom into foolishness. Bloodthirsty enemies may have banded together against us. They may have sworn with an oath that they will not eat nor drink till they have removed us from the earth. The whole train of their iniquity may be laid in secret, and carried out to its completion. The very day may have arrived, which is to crown its execution with the desired success. The Lord, however, is still nearer to His people than the nearest dangers. Deliverance shall break forth suddenly, like the sun from behind a threatening cloud. The enemies of the Lord shall be discomfited, and all their wicked devices shall be recompensed upon their own heads.

God is nearer to thee, O believer, than the nearest danger. Satan may assault, man may rage, and dangers may threaten. God can overrule them all. Be still. Rely upon Jehovah. Leave thyself to His disposal. Fear none of the things that thou mayest suffer. The very hairs of thy head are all numbered, and not one of them can fall without thy Father's knowledge. The very hands of murderers may be upon thee, still God is with thee. They shall not effect their purpose, if it be His purpose to deliver thee. God was near to

Joseph when his brothers seized him. Contrary to their own purpose of immediate death, they cast him into a pit, to perish. God was near to Joseph still, and overruled their malice by their covetousness: "What profit is it if we slay our brother? Come and let us sell him to the Ishmaelites," Gen. xxxvii. 26. Again, therefore, was their purpose changed. Joseph perished not in the pit, but the Ishmaelites carried him into Egypt. Still, however, we are told that "the Lord was with Joseph." And though a lie cast him into prison, yet a dream brought him out of it, for the Lord was with him, (ch. xxxix. 20, 21.) God's power can bring His people into the greatest tribulations, and lead them out of them again, by the most unlikely means. A dream had been the source of all Joseph's troubles, and a dream was made the source of all his elevation.

The destruction of Mordecai seemed inevitable, and near at hand. Let but a few hours pass, and with the morning light the gallows should be completed, which was even then preparing for his execution. But God was nearer to him than the impending destruction. That morning could not the king sleep, and that day was Mordecai exalted to the highest honors. The humbled Haman led him forth upon the king's horse, crowned with the king's crown, and, in a few hours more, was himself hanged upon the gallows which he had prepared for Mordecai.

Dangers may be near, but the Lord is still nearer to His people. Daniel was cast into the den, but God was nearer to him than the lions. The three children walked in the midst of the burning fiery furnace, but the Lord was nearer to them than its devouring flames. A venomous reptile fastened upon the hand of Paul, but God was nearer to him than its poisonous fangs. The waves were heaving under Peter's feet, but Jesus was nearer to him than were the troubled billows.

"Whatsoever the Lord pleases, that doeth He in heaven and in earth, in the seas and in all deep places." Psa. cxxxv. 6. Nothing can resist His will, either to preserve or to destroy. "There is no king saved by the multitude of an host: a mighty man is not delivered by much strength. An horse is a vain thing for safety: neither shall he deliver any by his great strength. Behold, the eye of the Lord is upon them that fear Him, upon them that hope in His mercy. To deliver their soul from death, and to keep them alive in famine. Our soul waiteth for the Lord: He is our help and our shield." Psa. xxxiii. 16—20. The conquering Israelites got not the land in possession by their own sword, neither did their own arm save them; "but Thy right hand, and Thine arm, and the light of Thy countenance, because Thou hadst a favor unto them." Psa. xliv. 3. Leave thyself, O believer, unto thy God. "He is our refuge and strength, a very present help in trouble." Psa. xlvi. 1. "The angel of the Lord encampeth round about them that fear Him, and delivereth them. O taste then and see that the Lord is good. Blessed is the man that trusteth in Him." Psa. xxxiv. 7, 8. The angels can neither deliver of their own will, nor by their own power, but at the command and by the power of God. These sons of light themselves are never safe but in His protection. Trust, therefore, in the Almighty God continually. "The Lord alone is thy keeper: the Lord is thy shade upon thy right hand. The sun shall not smite thee by day, nor the moon by night. The Lord shall preserve thee from evil: He shall preserve thy soul. The Lord shall preserve thy going out, and thy coming in, from this time forth, and even forevermore." Psa. cxxi. 5—8. Rise, then, on the wings of love and gratitude. Soar ever upward to thy God and Saviour. To His redemption thou owest every present deliverance, every temporal blessing, every spiritual and eternal benefit. Let thy spared life, therefore, become thy living sacrifice. The breath God gives in mercy, give back to Him in praise, and say, "Bless the Lord, O my soul, who redeemeth thy life from destruction."

V.

Crowned with Loving-Kindness and Tender Mercy.

Who crowneth thee with loving-kindness and tender mercies. —Verse 4.

HAVING enumerated three special mercies, the soul of the Psalmist rises with the strongest emotions of gratitude. His whole life appears in the review, so far as God was concerned, to be a rich accumulation of blessings. And so bright, so varied, and so multiplied, are the benefits which crowd upon his remembrance, that he now stays not to particularize one of them more than another. He beholds them all glittering together like jewels clustered in a golden diadem, and by a most appropriate, elegant, and expressive metaphor, he rouses his spirit to the highest gratitude and praise, saying, " Bless the Lord, O my soul, who crowneth thee with loving-kindness and tender mercies."

To " crown" may denote the conferring either of the highest honor, or of the utmost perfection. A king is crowned, and thereby raised to the most exalted position. A building is said to be crowned when the top stone is laid upon it. That crowning stone is the finish and perfection of the building—there is nothing more to be added to it. A king may be arrayed with robes of state, and he may be adorned with chains of gold—these also his nobles wear; but it is not till the crown is placed upon his head that he stands forth before the eye, in all the honor, and the glory, the fulness, and the perfection of majesty. So, figuratively, many of the common blessings of this life may be enjoyed by the believer; he may possess health, and wealth, and friends; he may experience providential deliverances—these likewise unbelievers share; but it is not till the loving-kindness and the tender mercy of God in their bestowment, is discerned as a spiritual crown upon these otherwise common mercies, that they stand out in all their beauty, and their honor, their fulness, and their perfection.

The love of God in Christ Jesus, is as a crown of gold upon the head of every true believer. The Giver is greater than the gift. The love that prompts is more precious than the boon it bestows. The believer, therefore, in receiving any, and every, gift from God, should feel and acknowledge that his life is thereby crowned with loving-kindness, and with tender mercies. This it was which gladdened David, and inspired his liveliest gratitude. This was the spiritual crown which he prized more highly than the diadem of pure gold that was set upon his head. He could truly say, "Because thy loving-kindness is better than life, my lips shall praise thee." Psa. lxiii. 3.

Man, taught by nature, has but one mode of valuing everything—its own worth. Man, instructed by the Divine Spirit, has a two-fold mode of valuation for all the things of time, first, as they are in themselves, and, secondly and specially, as they are the gifts of his heavenly Friend. When we receive health, and food, and friends, and raiment, with all the other wide-spread mercies of providence, as daily, customary, and to-be-expected benefits, they become common in themselves, and excite no gratitude in our hearts; but when we receive them as tokens of the love of our Father in heaven, the King of kings, immediately they become to us no longer common, but royal blessings; and just as a courtier prizes very highly any gift conferred by his earthly sovereign, however small its value, so the believer prizes very highly the smallest, even the most common benefits which he enjoys on earth, because they are gifts and tokens of the loving-kindness, and the tender mercy of his heavenly Sovereign. The unbeliever may indeed see and partake of all these gifts, but he understands not their token, he discerns not the love of God in these earthly things, and therefore treats them as common matters, and neither receives nor acknowledges them as they deserve. The monarch, without his crown, passes unnoticed as a common man amid the crowd of human beings; and so, likewise, every temporal mercy, beheld without the love of God in Christ upon it, passes unheeded in the crowd of common blessings. The heathen, the untutored child, and the merely nominal Christian, may fix their eyes with admiration upon the bow of promise, circling resplendent upon the threatening cloud; but they see it not as a sign—they regard it not as a token of the love and the faithfulness of Jehovah. The eye of the true believer, however, no sooner rests upon that common sight, than he recognizes God in covenant, faithful to his promise for a thousand generations; it ceases immediately, therefore, to be a common, and becomes to him a royal rainbow, for its radiant span appears to his eye crowned with the loving-kindness and the tender mercy of the King of heaven.

This is the true spiritual alchymy that turns all things to gold. This is the sure elixir of life. This is the pure joy. This is the one grand transforming and transporting thought, to see the love of our redeeming God in everything, and to behold all that we possess crowned with His loving-kindness and His tender mercies. Oh, thrice happy human spirit, that can thus search, and see, and meet with God.

"In every smiling happy hour
Be this our sweet employ:
This thought refines our earthly bliss
And doubles all our joy."

Behold the crown of the believer! It surpasses in lustre every earthly diadem. The materials of which that crown is composed, are as pure as they are imperishable. What are the gold and the jewels of the monarch, compared with this crown of the believing soul? Is it not wrought with the pure gold of Divine love? Is it not studded with the heavenly jewels of kindness and mercy, of tenderness and truth?

O believer, let the loving-kindness of your God, be the crown of your existence, your boast and your glory, your honor and your joy. Whilst partaking of the varied blessings and benefits with which this world is stored. let your heart regard them as tokens of redeeming love, and then every earthly joy will be crowned to you with heavenly mercy.

The Scripture calls upon us to thank God unfeignedly "for our creation, for our preservation, and for all the blessings of this life," but if we see neither love nor goodness in all these, how can we praise Him for them? If we conceive that we are created with no benevolent design,—or that we are preserved only till some affliction or destruction overtakes us,—or that the mercies we enjoy in the life that now is, are given merely to aggravate by contrast the miseries of that life that is to come, how can we regard our creation, our preservation, and our benefits, as real blessings, as substantial causes for thanksgiving? But when we learn this precious scriptural doctrine, and are taught to view all these as visible proofs and arguments of the invisible love and mercy of God in Christ, then indeed we begin to rejoice in them with a holy joy, and to receive them all as royal blessings, as crowned and perfected benefits. Instead of saying with the melancholy worldling, "I wish that I had never been born," we will, on the contrary, laud and magnify our great Creator, because He called us out of nothing that we might become the joyful recipients of His temporal mercies, and of his everlasting loving-kindnesses. Oh! it is joy, it is bliss, it is life eternal to the soul of man "to know God, and Jesus Christ whom He hath sent." John xvii. 3. "Thus saith the Lord, Let not the wise man glory in his wisdom, neither let the mighty man glory in his might, let not the rich man glory in his riches: But let him that glorieth glory in this, that he understandeth and knoweth Me, that I am the Lord which exercise loving-kindness, judgment, and righteousness in the earth: for in these things I delight, saith the Lord." Jer. ix. 23, 24.

This, O Believer, is the true secret how to use this world as not abusing it, to realize that we live and move, and have our being in God. Let everything, therefore, remind you of the love that God bears toward you. Let everything inspire you with gratitude to your Redeemer, who bought you with His blood. Then will everything be used by you to His glory, and to your own benefit. The very trials of life will cause you to praise Him who sustains you under them, and who has promised that He will either deliver you from their power, or cause them to work together for your good. Thus, also, the prosperities of life will cause you more abundantly to bless that God who bestows them upon you in such rich profusion, when you are altogether unworthy of the least.

Thus amid all the changing scenes of time, and the endless diversity of worldly circumstances, whether you experience the "wonderful goodness" of God when wandering in the wilderness, or captive in the dungeon, when pining under sickness, or tossed upon the stormy deep; or, on the other hand, when multiplied greatly in fields and flocks, and blessed with health and all manner of prosperity; whatever may be your lot, and how many soever may be its changes; —"whoso is wise and will observe these things, even he shall understand the loving kindness of the Lord." Psa. cvii. 43.

Precious and appropriate are the terms which the Psalmist here employs,—"Loving kindness and tender mercy!" Compound terms these are of a most comprehensive and consolatory import. It is not only love, nor only kindness, which the Psalmist here celebrates. It is love and kindness in beautiful and harmonious combination. Love may exist in the heart, and yet not have been exhibited towards us in any outward act. And again, a kind action may be performed to help us in our distress, and yet it may be pity, and not love, which exists within the breast of Him who relieves us. But here, in this Psalm, David exults both in the love that prompts, and in the kindness that performs. He recognizes and acknowledges with joy that there is love in the heart, and kindness in the hand, of God towards him. Again, it was not only mercy which gladdened the Psalmist's soul, it was "tender mercy." The mercy of the Lord is mild and gentle, and gracious in its operation; it is exquisitely tender, and most considerately adapts itself to our situation, and our feelings, to our fears, and our necessities. "The Lord is *very* pitiful, and of *tender* mercy," says St. James, v. 11. David gratefully acknowledges, in another Psalm, that "the tender mercies of the Lord are over all his works." Psa. cxlv. 9. And, again, "Great," he says, "are thy tender mercies, O Lord." Psa. cxix. 156. Therefore he thus prays for them continually, "Let Thy tender mercies come unto me that I may live." Psa. cxix. 77. "O remember not against us former iniquities, let Thy tender mercies speedily prevent us." Psa. lxxix. 8.

The "loving-kindness," also, of the Lord has formed the

favorite topic of all His believing children throughout their generations. This has been their song in the house of their pilgrimage all the days of their life. Hear how Isaiah expatiates upon this theme in the fulness of his heart: "I will mention the loving-kindnesses of the Lord, and the praises of the Lord, according to all that the Lord hath bestowed on us, and the great goodness toward the house of Israel, which he hath bestowed on them according to his mercies, and according to the multitude of his loving-kindnesses." Isa. lxiii. 7. David exclaims, "How excellent is thy loving-kindness, O God! therefore the children of men put their trust under the shadow of thy wings." Psa. xxxvi. 7. Again, speaking in the name of his fellow-worshippers, as well as in his own, he says, "We have thought of thy loving-kindness, O God, in the midst of Thy temple." Psa. xlviii. 9.

The loving-kindness of God formed a most fruitful theme to David. It was his first subject of thanksgiving on awaking from the slumbers of the night. "It is a good thing to give thanks unto the Lord, and to sing praises unto thy name, O Most High. To show forth Thy loving-kindness in the morning." Psa. xcii. 1, 2. It formed the rallying point, the strength and consolation of his soul when cast down and disquieted within him. "Yet the Lord will command His loving-kindness in the daytime, and in the night His song shall be with me, and my prayer unto the God of my life." Psa. xlii. 8. It constituted the frequent topic of his converse and discourses with his fellow-men. "I have not concealed Thy loving-kindness and Thy truth from the great congregation." Psa. xl. 10.

The loving-kindness and the tender mercies of his God formed conjointly the plea and argument of David's supplications in very many Psalms. "Remember, O Lord, Thy tender mercies and Thy loving-kindnesses; for they have been ever of old." Psa. xxv. 6. "Have mercy upon me, O God, according to Thy loving-kindness, according unto the multitude of Thy tender mercies, blot out my transgressions." Psa. li. 1. God himself also makes these the topics of His own most gracious and soul-reviving declarations. "Nevertheless, My loving-kindness will I not utterly take from him, nor suffer my faithfulness to fail." Psa. lxxxix. 33. "I have loved thee with an everlasting love, therefore with loving-kindness have I drawn thee." Jer. xxxi. 3. "I will betroth thee unto Me forever: yea, I will betroth thee unto Me in righteousness, and in judgment, and in loving-kindness, and in mercies." Hosea ii. 19.

Well, therefore, may David call it a "marvellous loving-kindness." Psa. xvii. 7. Marvellous in its origin, marvellous in its excellency, marvellous in its method of communication, marvellous in its immediate effects, and marvellous in its everlasting duration.

Is your life, Reader, thus crowned with the loving-kindness, and the tender mercies of your God and Saviour? Is every earthly benefit, a common, or a royal, blessing, in your estimation? Do you know, and feel, and continually remember, that you deserve nothing—literally nothing, at the hand of God? And, therefore, does even the smallest mercy appear to you in its right light, as a bounty—as a bestowment—as a thing which tells of love, and generosity, and beneficence from above? And is that love which every gift bespeaks, more precious to your soul than the gift itself? And does that love, shining upon every earthly thing, constitute in your eyes its beauty and its honor, its fulness and its perfection? Then surely it will be both your duty and your delight to join heart and soul with David, and daily say, "Bless the Lord, O my soul, who crowneth thee with loving-kindness and tender mercies."

VI.

The Mouth satisfied with Good, and the Strength Renewed.

Who satisfieth thy mouth with good things; so that thy youth is renewed like the eagle's.—Verse 5.

David had experienced more than most other men the vicissitudes of life. He knew both plenty and penury in their varied forms. When scarcity and famine overspread the land, or when circumstances, as in war and wanderings, deprived him for a time of the enjoyment of abundance, he had felt the saddening effects in corporeal weakness and exhaustion. The continuance of want for any lengthened period, produces a wasted and haggard appearance. Premature old age comes on. The bloom of youth gives way to the wrinkles of care, and to the furrows of anxiety. There is neither satisfaction in the mind, nor energy in the frame. The spirit broods discontented within the wasted body, and looks forth with a scowling eye upon the barren fields around. When, also, in addition to all this, the ravages of disease break forth with power, how miserable is the spectacle which famished, sullen, sickened man presents!

But when it pleases God to reverse the scene, how delightful is the contrast. When at His command the clouds drop water, and the sun smiles with blessing upon the land: when the fields produce their grain, the trees their fruit, and the flocks multiply in the fold: when peace returns after war, health after sickness, and plenty after famine, how changed is both the spirit and the aspect of the inhabitants. Anxieties begin to lessen, and hopes to rise within each breast. Fears and listlessness give place to cheerfulness and activity. Mourning and discontent are heard no longer. God has bestowed his "good things." The stricken recipient partakes thereof abundantly. His desires become satisfied. His disease abates. His strength returns. His eye brightens, and his face beams again with renewed health. David had experienced this outward and inward renovation. He reminds his soul of the painful story of the past, by rehearsing to it this pleasant story of the present. He rouses it to gratitude for the Lord's gracious bestowments, saying, "who satisfieth thy mouth with good things, so that thy youth is renewed like the eagle's."

Birds after their moulting season appear to have renewed their youth. Heavy and drooping for a time, losing their strength and their feathers together, they have, as it were, suddenly grown old. But after awhile, their note becomes more cheerful, and their actions livelier; fresh feathers cover, and fresh strength re-animates, them; they appear to have suddenly grown young again. The eagle presents a remarkable instance of this change, which must have been familiar to the mind of David from his childhood. That noble bird, though attaining to a great age, appears after every moulting season, to have renewed its youth; acquiring with fresh plumage, a fresh energy and strength. Thus it affords a suitable and appropriate emblem of man, when renewed in his spiritual and bodily powers by the blessing of his God.

When our great Creator and Preserver vouchsafes abundant sustenance, crowning the year with His goodness, opening His hand liberally, and plentifully satisfying the want of every living thing; when He gives us food, and an appetite to enjoy it; and imparts a contented and a thankful spirit, so that instead of continually craving after more, we feel "satisfied" with the good things already bestowed; when, especially, He blesses these good things to the renewal of our strength after disease, and gladdens our soul within us by the visitations of His holy Spirit, then, indeed, we may be compared to the eagle after its moulting season is over, joyous in its renewed condition, and vigorous in all its resuscitated powers. Who would not say with David in such a case, "Bless the Lord, O my soul, and all that is within me, bless His holy name. Bless the Lord, O my soul, and forget not all His benefits, who satisfieth thy mouth with good things, so that thy youth is renewed like the eagle's"?

Millions upon millions of beings depend upon their Creator, and none of them depend in vain. His resources are infinite beyond their wants. He satisfies the young lions when they cry, and feeds each little raven in its nest. It is "good" and not "evil" which the Lord bestows. To man he is not only a Creator, but likewise a Redeemer; and both in nature and in grace, He has made a full provision of "good things," to "satisfy" the wants both of body and of soul. St. Peter declares that "according to His divine power, He hath given unto us all things that pertain unto life and godliness," 2 Peter i. 3; and St. Paul exclaims, "Blessed be the God and Father of our Lord Jesus Christ, who hath blessed us with all spiritual blessings in heavenly places in Christ." Eph. i. 3. Through the knowledge and participation of these "good things," we obtain deliverance from spiritual weakness and disease, we "escape the corruption that is in the world." In a special sense, also, we may be said thereby to "renew our youth," that is to become again "partakers of the Divine nature." In the infancy of his creation, man possessed the image of his Maker, and enjoyed God's strength in his soul. When we are "new-born" of the Lord the Spirit, we are, as it were, re-stamped with that original image, and are renewed with the spiritual power and energy of our primeval youth. "They that wait upon the Lord shall renew their strength; they shall mount up with wings as eagles; they shall run, and not be weary; and they shall walk, and not faint." Isa. xl. 31.

Great is the "satisfaction" of those who partake of the provision of grace. They eat, and never hunger; they drink, and never thirst. The soul that trusts in Jesus shall never want. All fulness dwells in Him; and of His fulness have all we received, and grace for grace. "In Him are hid all the treasures of wisdom and knowledge:" and "He is of God made unto us wisdom, and righteousness, sanctification, and redemption." 1 Cor. i. 30. United to Christ, we are "complete:" He is our Head, and from Him all the body, having nourishment ministered, increaseth with the increase of God. Col. ii. 3, 9, 19. He is the Vine, and from Him, not only the nearest, but also the remotest, members; the smallest tendrils, equally with the largest branches, receive their nourishment and their fruitfulness. Christ is the Fountain overflowing with blessings; we have but to "open our mouth wide," and He will "fill it" with "good things," to our immediate, constant, and everlasting "satisfaction."

The "good things" of this life, are the gifts of God. Our fields and gardens are rendered fruitful only by His blessing. It is the living God who "giveth us richly all things to enjoy." 1 Tim. vi. 17. In the blindness of our minds, we lose sight of the Giver amid the abundance of His gifts. Without the continual upholding of our God, all things would soon cease to exist. Why does the same field, cultivated by the same hand, and enriched by the same supplies, ever vary in the return it yields? Why is its produce in one year scanty, and in another plentiful? The Scriptures furnishes us with the solution. The hand of the Lord dispenses according to his own good pleasure. The believer, therefore, while enjoying those "good things," which the industry of man procures, recognizes them as all provided by the goodness of his God. Improvements in agriculture, and in every useful science, he contemplates with much thankfulness. He regards these as means, by which the God of heaven increases the fertility of the earth. He looks, however, beyond the framework, and the movements, of the visible machinery, and he fixes the eye of his mind upon the unseen and ever-moving power—the Great First Cause. (See Isa. xxviii. 23—29.) Whatever, therefore, may be the intermediate sources from whence he derives his comfort or his sustenance, the believer looks ever upward, because he knows that "every good and every perfect gift is from above, and cometh down from the Father of Lights." James i. 17.

Real contentment is only to be derived from a knowledge of God in Christ, and of all things centred in Him, issuing from Him, and distributed by Him. It is because the beliver thus looks to the dispensing hand of his God and Saviour, that he is "satisfied" with all his circumstances in life. Confidence in the paternal government of his heavenly Father, and a firm conviction that all things here below are ordained in the hands of the Mediator, his elder Brother, enable him to say, "I have learned in whatsoever state I am, therewith to be content. I know both how to be abased, and I know how to abound: everywhere, and in all things, I am instructed, both to be full and to be hungry, both to abound and to suffer need. I can do all things through Christ which strengtheneth me." Phil. iv. 11—13.

To rest satisfied with that portion which God has allotted, is the incumbent duty of every man. Alas! few are really contented, really "satisfied." They set their hearts on something above and beyond that which they at present enjoy, and consequently the mercies which they actually possess, cease to afford their former gratification. So chequered is the present life, that there is no man without a trial of some kind or another in his earthly lot. If he look only and continually to that trial, comparing his condition with what he supposes it might have been, or contrasting his position with others above him, he may indeed fret himself to death over his real and his imaginary troubles. The more he indulges this temper, the stronger will it become, till, as his besetting sin wilfully encouraged, it will gain the mastery over him, and drive him further and further in estrangement of heart from God. The condemnation of Scripture against murmurers and complainers, is as emphatic as it is universal and deserved.

We must resist, continually resist, the very first risings of discontent. Instead of indulging them, we must oppose them in every possible way. Like Paul, we must "learn" to be contented. He was not naturally more disposed to be so than other men. It was not till he entered the school of Christ, that he acquired that lesson. And after he had been trained there, he gave not the credit to his own patience and endurance, saying, "I can make myself contented anywhere," but wholly to his Teacher, saying, "I am instructed both to be full and to be hungry." Apply thy mind to this lesson, O believer. Strive continually to practice it, or no success can ever be attained. It is emphatically a practical lesson, only to be learned by exercising it. *Try* to feel "satisfied," with your lot. *Try* to be thankful in your every thought, and to show that you are so, by all your words and deeds. *Try* to view things always in their right light. *Try* to look at the bright side of everything. *Pray* for a contented and an unrepining spirit. *Strive* against a peevish fretful disposition. Beware of finding fault with God's arrangements.

Remember that you deserve nothing, that you have forfeited everything, and that all you have belongs to Christ, and comes from Him to you, and still belongs to Him equally as before. Thank Him, therefore, for everything. Cultivate the habit of thankfulness. Give way to grateful feelings. Give no way to murmuring thoughts. Be ashamed of yourself when an envious, or a covetous, or a discontented feeling rises within. Check yourselves whenever a hasty word of complaint is about to escape your lips. Make haste to rectify and recall it, before your fellow-men, if already uttered, and to confess and bewail it before God! Never did a single murmur issue from the lips of Jesus, or rise within His breast. "He had not where to lay His head," yet he never murmured. And dost thou murmur, thou comfortably-lodged disciple? It is an odious thing to hear a Christian groaning as he goes, and ever and anon speaking as if he bore his Master's cross. You pity him, and draw near to help, when lo, you discover that the cross he carries, is of his own making. The cross which Christ gives, imparts vigor to its bearer. Crosses of man's fabrication, are dead logs indeed, and heavy burdens, too heavy to be borne. Christ will not strengthen thee under such a cross. Cast it quickly away, or it will crush thee to the earth. Strive, then, to be thankful. Make it a rule every day to thank God, as well as to pray to Him. Seek out to-day, some blessing that escaped thy grateful notice yesterday; and to-morrow, give special praise for those mercies for which thou hast omitted to bless God to-day. When new objects occur not to your mind, recapitulate old ones, as

David does in this Psalm. Praise God that thou art no longer a fretful murmurer. Be thankful that thou art made thankful. Bless God that he has given thee a contented spirit. Consider how much worse thy case *might* have been —how much worse it *ought* to have been. Consider how much longer thou mightest have been left in pain, or in poverty, or in perplexity. Consider the multitudes of thy fellow-creatures, who are placed in circumstances far more trying than thine. Most men, under trials, are tempted to think each that his own case is the worst, and that his own hardships are the greatest; but it is very wrong, very ungrateful, to give way to that temptation. Satan, doubtless, will often insinuate such thoughts into thy mind. Remember there is no sin in the mere fact that thou art tempted. Our blessed Saviour himself was led up of the Spirit, to be tempted by the devil. Matt. iv. 1. The sin lies in giving way to the temptation. Jesus continually resisted the tempter. He invariably answered, "It is written." Imitate, then, thy Saviour, keep close to Scripture, and thou shalt be safe. It is written, "Be content with such things as ye have: for He hath said, I will never leave thee, I will never forsake thee." Heb. xiii. 5. To every insinuation of the tempter, instantly reply, "It is written, Be content with such things as ye have." Settle it well in thy mind, that the things thou hast, be they less or more than those of thy neighbors, are measured out to thee by thy God and Saviour. Let this, then, be an indisputable argument for thy contentment, under all possible circumstances of thy earthly lot. Satisfied *with* trials and sorrows, *with* sickness and poverty, thou canst never be. Thy Lord does not expect thee to be so. But when thou hast "learned" to regard them as dispensed by a wise, and loving, heavenly Friend, then thou canst be contented *under* them. This is the contentment which God demands of thee. Be satisfied, like the Prophet, with God Himself as your all-sufficient portion, and then, like him, thou wilt be contented under all His dispensations: "Although the fig-tree shall not blossom, neither shall fruit be in the vines; the labor of the olive shall fail, and the fields shall yield no meat; the flock shall be cut off from the fold, and there shall be no herd in the stalls: yet I will rejoice in the Lord, I will joy in the God of my salvation." Hab. iii. 17, 18.

The tide of gratitude increases as it flows. It rises higher and higher both before and around us, and extends itself widely on every side. When we render thanksgivings to our God and Saviour for one mercy, a second presents itself to view, then a third, then a fourth, then others successively arise, and roll in upon our remembrance. The goodness and the mercy of the Lord are, like the mighty deep, unfathomable. His acts of love are, as the ocean waves, innumerable; and innumerable, therefore, should be our acts of thanksgiving:

My soul, in pleasing wonder lost,
  Thy various love surveys:
Where shall my grateful lips begin?
  Or where conclude Thy praise?

Gratitude increases as we offer thanks, and mercies multiply as we contemplate them. A poor woman had fallen into a melancholy and murmuring frame of mind. She made no effort to check the temptation, but considered that she "did well to be angry" and to complain. Her minister tried every argument in his power, but all to no purpose. He spoke to her of temporal and of spiritual mercies, but no response of gratitude was awakened. She said that *she* had "nothing in body or soul to be thankful for." Lifting up his heart in prayer to God for wisdom, he inquired, "Does not your neighbor's husband drink when he is out, and beat her when he comes home?" "Yes," was the only reply. "Does *your* husband do so to you?" "No," was the reluctant answer. "Well then, should not you thank God that you have a kind husband?" No reply was returned. The inquiry was several times repeated, till an assent was obtained. The minister said he would not leave, till she promised to thank God for this mercy, night and morning, upon her bended knees. Having, at last, obtained her promise, he said to her at parting, "I have now shown you one thing which you have to be thankful for, and you must keep your promise till I see you again." Intentionally delaying his return, several days elapsed before he revisited her dwelling. But what a different woman met him now. "Oh," she exclaimed, "I have longed to see you, I have wished to thank you. For a morning or two, I did as I promised, but I did not rightly feel what I said. Then, one day, when I was thanking God that I had a kind husband, I thought I should thank Him that I had healthy children; and when I was thanking him for that, I thought I should thank Him that I had bread to put into their mouths; and when I was thanking the Lord for that, I thought that I should thank Him that I had clothes to put on their backs and a house to cover their heads; and so, Sir, when I was thanking God for one thing, another came into my head, and another still, and now I know not where to stop, or how to thank Him enough; and I feel so happy."

Thus gratitude increases with use. The more thankful we are, the more thankful we shall become, and the more we shall have to be thankful for. The truly humbled, spiritual, mind, will learn the lesson of thankfulness from the most common things, yea even from the most revolting. "Remarkable is the story of the poor old man, whom a bishop found most bitterly weeping over an ugly toad. Being asked the reason of his tears; his answer was, 'I weep, because, that whereas God might have made me as ugly and filthy a creature as the toad, and hath not, I have yet never, in all my life, been thankful to Him for it.'"—*Lightfoot*, vol. 4, p. 63.

Grievous is it when we reflect how insensible we are to our smallest mercies, and how ungrateful for our highest blessings. A visitor to an asylum, was solemnly and suddenly reminded of his great sin in the latter respect. As he passed among the poor lunatics, one of them walked directly toward him and abruptly said, "Have you ever thanked God for your *reason?*" He uttered not another word, but darted off without waiting for a reply, leaving his question to sink deep, as well it might, into the mind of the visitor.

All the gifts of God "are good:" and therefore they afford a solid and lasting satisfaction. It is not after this manner "that the world gives." John xiv. 27. Pleasures, honors, and possessions, either pall, or perish in the using. The immortal soul within us, can never be satisfied with such things as these. There is a felt void and weariness in every enjoyment apart from God. His love transforms all things to gold. The world's love transforms them all to dross. We must have other treasure than this earth can furnish, before the heart can be truly "satisfied." The soul, spiritual and immortal, must have a treasure pure, spiritual, and everlasting. And God has given us such a treasure: He has given us Himself in Christ Jesus. And where our treasure is, there should our hearts be also. Matt. vi. 21. Happy is the man who can truly say—

God is the treasure of my soul,
The source of lasting joy;
A joy which want shall not impair,
Nor death itself destroy.

Oh what a renovation of heart and strength does the blessing of God ensure! He satisfies the mouth with temporal, and the heart with spiritual, "good things," and he blesses each of these so effectually, that they invigorate the entire man, both in soul and body. "His blessing maketh rich, and He addeth no sorrow with it." We may see wealth flow suddenly upon an individual, but ere long we observe also sorrows following in its train. While the world gazes with admiration on the so-called fortunate possessor of the first, he perhaps is feeble and careworn under the secret pressure of the last. But God's blessing adds no sorrow with the good things which He bestows. It yields a full and permanent satisfaction—a satisfaction without a single drawback. The spirit is in peace, and the body is in health. God has satisfied the one, and He has renovated the other. A calm and placid contentment relieves and sustains both the mind and the frame of him, whom Jesus heals by His Spirit and by His power, "renewing youth" or health in each.

How delightful is the period of convalescence. After a long interval of sickness, the play of health again begins to be sensibly felt within our frame. We have been chastened with pain upon our bed, and the multitude of our bones with strong pain: "so that our life abhorred bread, and our soul dainty meat." But now the Lord has become gracious unto us. At the voice of our cry, He has sent deliverance and restoration. "By His blessing our flesh has become fresher than a child's:—We have returned to the days of our youth." Job xxxiii. 25. The long-closed casement is at last thrown open, and the languid patient inhales with delight the fresh air of heaven. It is joy to breathe. We look upon the movements, and the activities, of our fellow men, with wonder and delight. We marvel at the ease with which the laborer plies his work, and at the agility which the children exhibit in their various sports.

When our strength is sufficiently advanced, we issue forth from the chamber of sickness with glad and grateful hearts. We look around upon old scenes with new feelings, and with fresh impressions. Everything seems invested with new charms. It is joy to walk, to gaze, to listen, to stand and inhale the refreshing breeze. The enamelled sky again rivets our attention. Its blue expanse appears more clear and deep. The sun shines to our eye more brilliantly than before. The clouds appear more soft and silvery. The motions of the birds, how swift, how light, how graceful, do they seem. The sea also attracts our admiration. Immense, profound, it inspires us with awe, and its ever-varying surface glancing in the sunbeam, fills us with delight. Every sense we possess brings an addition to our pleasure. How invigorating is the air to the enfeebled frame. How fair seem the fields to the long-imprisoned eye. How sweet once more to the ear is the humming of the bee, and the warbling of the birds. How fragrant are the flowers. How sweet are the fruits. It is very joy to live.

We are conducted to the garden, we are placed upon the lawn, or a seat is provided for us beside the refreshing stream. The water runs swift and clear, and its gentle voice seems to be ever praising the God who bade it flow. The ear listens with delight to its unceasing music, and the eye watches with interest the various motions of its sportive inhabitants. Some we observe glide slowly from side to side; others lie still and motionless in the current; some are floating downward with the stream, while others are forcing their way vigorously against it—and suddenly hosts of young ones shoot rapidly into view, as if contending in a race—here they are hiding under the stones, there they are leaping into the air. How pleasant and joyous is the sight. All nature rejoices. The sun seems to bestow a smile upon the scene, and the sparkling waters to return it. The heart of the invalid is gladdened within him, and his strength is renewed by its gush of joy.

But purer, and higher, and more holy, is the joy of the Christian convalescent, when, from these sweet scenes of nature, he returns again to his chamber. His soul is "satisfied" with goodness,—it is overflowing with spiritual emotion. He goes with all his happiness to his God, and thanks Him for it. He falls upon his bended knees, and pours forth his heart in prayer and praise, "O Thou Preserver of my life, Thou Restorer of my strength, O Christ, Thou good Physician of my soul and body, I bless Thee for this day in which again I have walked abroad. I thank Thee for the light and for the sun, for the balmy air and for the fragrant flowers, for the winged insects and for the warbling birds, for the flowing streams and for their finny tribes. I bless Thee for the garden and its produce, for the trees, and for their varied fruits. I bless Thee for my kind friends, and for my many comforts—this room, this house, this bed, this couch, my fire, my food, my medicine. I thank Thee for my spared life, and for my renewed ability to walk, to see, to hear, to think, to speak. Above all, I thank Thee for this sacred volume; for Thy throne of grace; for Thy instructing Spirit; for a rational mind; and for a heart that seeks its happiness in Thee. Oh help me to prize my many mercies, and to be increasingly thankful for them all. Give me grace to use them as I ought, and to devote them to Thy glory. I dedicate myself anew to Thee. The first fruits of my preserved life, and of my renewed health, I consecrate to Thy service. From this day, let me become more wholly Thine. Thou art my gracious Master. Thou hast bought me with Thy precious blood. Thee only will I serve throughout the whole remainder of my existence. I confess my utter unworthiness before Thee, my multiplied sins and provocations; and that in very faithfulness Thou hast afflicted me. O pardon my many shortcomings, my great ingratitude. Forgive the waywardness, the fickleness, the selfishness of my heart. Renew my soul with spiritual youth. Bring me back to my first love. Keep me ever growing in grace, in humility, in meekness, in thankfulness, in purity of heart, in entire devotedness to Thy service. Dwell in me by Thy Spirit. Restore me to Thine image. Prepare me for Thy glory. And 'when Thou comest in Thy kingdom, Lord, remember me,' so that Thy poor unworthy servant may be found, with Thy redeemed, ascribing to Thy most blessed name, with the Father and the Holy Ghost, one God, all glory and power, all thanksgiving and praise, forever, and forevermore. Amen."

VII.

The Lord executing Judgment for the Oppressed.

The Lord executeth righteousness and judgment for all that are oppressed.—Verse 6.

Among the benefits for which the believer should give thanks unto his God, this is not the least that he has an Almighty Friend to "take his part." Psa. cxviii. 7. Satan is the great adversary of all who love the Lord. The world and the flesh are utterly hostile to His holy and self-denying service. David found this to be the case in the church of old, and we find it to be still the same in the church now.

The Lord God Almighty has condescended to call Himself the "Friend" of His people. He proves Himself to be so in two capacities; for, first, He is not only their faithful Defender, but, secondly, He is also their sure Avenger. Whether Satan or men oppress "the little flock" that believe in Him, He will, sooner or later, certainly execute righteous judgment on their behalf. The present chequered scene is not to continue forever. The last of the Old Testament prophets complained that in his day they called "the proud happy, yea, they that work wickedness," he says,

" are set up : yea, they that tempt God are even delivered." But immediately the Lord the Spirit taught him to add this solemn truth, " Behold the day cometh, that shall burn as an oven : and all the proud, yea, and all that do wickedly, shall be as stubble ; and the day that cometh shall burn them up saith the Lord of Hosts." Then shall it come to pass that we shall " return" from the dust, and shall fully and finally " discern" between the righteous and the wicked : " between him that serveth God, and him that serveth Him not." Mal. iii. and iv.

Retribution is positive. Its hour is appointed, but not yet arrived. Meantime, however, even in this present life, God exercises a providential judgment. Righteousness is the Lord's delight. He hateth wickedness and oppression. The poor, the widow, and the fatherless, have an unseen Defender, who will " come near to judgment," and will be a " swift witness" against " all oppressors." Mal. iii. 5. The Lord will never suffer His people to be trampled on with impunity. Solemn and emphatic are the words by which He appropriates retribution exclusively to Himself: " Vengeance is mine, I will repay, saith the Lord." Rom. xii. 19. Fearful, therefore, is the condition of those who make the Almighty God their foe, by oppressing and casting down His people. He is a just God ; and it were better for such persons that they had never been born, or that they had been drowned in the depths of the sea before they incurred His righteous vengeance ; for as certainly as the wicked executes violence against the just, so assuredly " the Lord executeth righteousness and judgment for all that are oppressed.

How consolatory and sustaining to the persecuted believer is this truth, that God is his Protector. No wonder that the Son of Jesse places this upon his list of benefits received, and acknowledges it with a devout heart, and with fervent thanksgivings. Indeed, David, at this part of the Psalm, passes from personal to general benefits. The goodness of God enlarges his view of the Divine benevolence, and of the minuteness and the universality of His providence. No longer, therefore, does he speak only in his own name, but in that, also, of all the family of God. He selects general terms, and employs the plural number onward from this verse. As if he had said "Here I have enumerated blessings vouchsafed to myself, which others, also, may have enjoyed: now will I record benefits common to all believers, and some even to unbelievers, of which my gracious Lord has made me also a happy partaker."

The Psalmist knew more than most men, that "God is a righteous Judge." Psa. vii. 11. (Margin.) He rejoiced to believe that the "just Lord," and Governor of the Universe, was interested in all that might befall him, and that He would stand up for this defence at the right time and in the right way. This doctrine was the root of his confidence, and the foundation of his strength: "The Lord is on my side;" he exclaims, "I will not fear: what can man do unto me? The Lord taketh my part with them that help me." Psa. cxviii. 6, 7. In three successive Psalms, the contempt, the opposition, and the oppression, of the unrighteous, are appealed against to the Lord, His aid is implored, and His assistance is celebrated: "Have mercy upon us, O Lord, have mercy upon us: for we are exceedingly filled with contempt. Our soul is exceedingly filled with the scorning of those that are at ease, and with the contempt of the proud." Psa. cxxiii. 3, 4. "If it had not been the Lord who was on our side, now may Israel say; If it had not been the Lord who was on our side, when men rose up against us: then they had swallowed us up quick, when their wrath was kindled against us." Psa. cxxiv. 1—3. "As the mountains are round about Jerusalem, so the Lord is round about his people from henceforth even forever. For the rod (or oppression) of the wicked shall not rest (not remain long) upon the lot of the righteous." Psa. cxxv. 2, 3.

Every human being, who is not walking in the narrow way that leadeth unto life, presents an obstacle to the entrance of others upon that way. He is a moral hinderance to all with whom he happens to meet. In the social and domestic intercourses of life, we are helping each other onward to heaven, or onward to hell. Our looks, our words, our casual acts, and our accustomed habits, have a powerful influence on all with whom we associate. In this sense, "no man liveth to himself." His example tells with effect upon his fellows. One man may be marked amongst his neighbors as a firebrand, casting sparks on every side of him, irritating the minds of others, exciting jealousy, suspicion, and heart-burnings amongst the members of a whole community, so that the first principles of religion, the love of God and of our neighbor, may be for a time well nigh obliterated. Another man may be unnoticed for any positive evil, and yet, by his destitution of religion, he may be as a moral icicle amongst his fellow-men, communicating a chill to the spiritual atmosphere around him, cooling the religion of others, and producing a blight on the souls of all with whom he comes in contact. Cold and heat, fire and water, are not more repulsive of each other, than are light and darkness, truth and error. The tendency of every man "born after the flesh" is to persecute him that is "born after the Spirit." The quiet man is, in his own way, as truly opposed to vital godliness as is the violent man. There may be no outward persecution or ostensible oppression, but there will be the estranged affection, the averted countenance, or the contemptuous glance; there will be marked indifference, or cool and settled opposition, to every one who speaks to him earnestly, though it may be kindly, for his everlasting welfare. Let him walk quietly on in his own way to ruin, and he will let you walk quietly on in your own chosen path to heaven. But entreat him, with some portion of that urgency which the case demands, to forsake his way and his thoughts, and to turn unto the Lord with all his heart, immediately he regards you as a troubler, and counts you for an enemy. He will address you, it may be, with constrained outward civility, but it will be with inward contempt, and determination against you. His heart is set upon his own way, and he will oppose and oppress you with silent disdain, or with open ridicule. Thus, in one form or another, the scriptural axiom is painfully verified in the experience of God's children, that all who "will live godly in Christ Jesus shall suffer persecution." 2 Tim. iii. 12.

Under the pressure of personal, social, or domestic trials of an oppressive character, the believer may be tempted to forget God, as Asa did in his national affliction. "The king of Israel," we read, "encompassed his land, so that none might go out or come in to Asa king of Judah." But instead of placing his whole confidence in God, Asa made a league with the king of Syria, an enemy to the true faith. By this unholy compact, he gained, indeed, a temporary deliverance, but he lost the favor of his God, and he brought upon himself innumerable troubles. The Prophet was sent to him with this solemn message, "Because thou hast relied on the king of Syria, and not relied on the Lord thy God, therefore is the host of the king of Syria escaped out of thine hand. Were not the Ethiopians and the Lubims a huge host, with very many chariots and horsemen? Yet, because thou disdt rely on the Lord, he delivered them into thine hand. For the eyes of the Lord run to and fro throughout the whole earth, to show Himself strong in the behalf of them whose heart is perfect toward Him. Herein thou hast done foolishly: therefore from henceforth thou shalt have wars." 2 Chron. xvi. 7—10.

Remember this truth, O believer, under every trial, that "the eyes of the Lord" are upon thee. He will show Himself strong on behalf of all those that trust in Him. Act not hastily and "foolishly," in thine own strength. The very scheme thou formest for thy deliverance, may prove to be the source of thy greatest trials. Some injudicious word, some rash self-confident act, may plunge thee into still deeper waters. To thee also it may be said, "From henceforth thou shalt have wars." The remainder of thy days may be embittered by feuds and strife, by jealousies and misunderstandings. Thy escape from one present pressing trial, may be purchased at the enormous price of continually-increasing troubles, which shall terminate only with thy life. Remember that "a soft answer turneth away wrath," Prov. xv. 1; and that in quietness and confidence shall be your rest. Meekness and gentleness bring their own reward. Imitate thy Saviour. Did He resent any indignity? Was He quick to repel every attack? Did He take pains to answer every varied aspersion? Is not this the true description of the Master, and ought it not also to be that of every disciple? "Who, when He was reviled, reviled not again; when he suffered, He threatened not; but committed Himself to Him that judgeth righteously." 1. Pet. ii. 23. "He was oppressed, and He was afflicted, yet He opened not His mouth; He was brought as a lamb to the slaughter, and as a sheep before her shearers is dumb, so He opened not His mouth." Isa. liii. 7.

The forms of oppression, through which the children of God are called to pass, are indeed various: they are all, however, measured, apportioned, and appointed by God. That particular form of trial which is sent to each, is assuredly the best for each: yet, alas! we often think that a trial in any other form, would be more suitable to our own individual case, and be less hard to bear. The wounding of the flesh will prove beneficial to some; the wounding of the spirit must be the medicine for others. Examine closely the state of thy soul. See if the root of bitterness be not in this, that "thy heart hath departed from the Lord." Jer. xvii. 5. To cure thy backsliding soul, there may not only be sicknesses and bereavements, and losses of property, administered, there may be sent also a sharp thorn, that shall touch thy spirit to the quick. Misunderstandings with your nearest and dearest relatives may arise; family tempers and estrangements may well-nigh overwhelm your spirit. You may be oppressed by a master, by an employer, by a husband, by a parent, and every advice you offer for their eternal good may be scornfully rejected, and yourself denounced as a hypocrite, and commanded to be silent. In this form of trouble, you may, perhaps, not discern the hand of the Lord, as clearly as in your other trials. You may not, therefore, experience as sensibly, His support under it, as at other times; and you may often be brought to your wit's end, with wave after wave of perplexity. Poor tempest-tossed soul, what wilt thou do? Hasten with it to the throne of grace. Speak more to God concerning it, than to thy fellow-men. Bear it all meekly, and thy Fellow-Sufferer will strengthen thee. In patience possess thou thy soul. The eye of God is upon thee in pity, more than in anger. He awaits to be gracious unto thee. At the voice of thy cry, when He shall hear it, He will answer thee. "And though the Lord give you the bread of adversity, and the water of oppression (margin); yet thine ears shall hear a word behind thee, saying, This is the way, walk ye in it, when ye turn to the right hand, and when ye turn to the left," Isa. xxx. 21. Wait thou upon Him. Be meek, be gentle, be patient. Return kindness for coldness, love for hatred, prayers for reproaches. Be not eager to take thy own part, and God will be more ready to take it for thee. Fret not at this, or at that, particular form of trial: it is the lot appointed for thee by unerring wisdom, and by paternal love. What God does, thou knowest not now, but thou shalt know hereafter. Soon thy Lord will show Himself strong on thy behalf. The Lord is a refuge for the oppressed, a refuge in times of trouble: and they that know His name, will put their trust in Him. Psa. ix. 9. "For thy Lord, the Jehovah, and thy God, pleadeth the cause of His people." Isa. li. 22. "For the oppression of the poor, for the sighing of the needy, now will I arise, saith the Lord: I will set him in safety from him that puffeth at him." Psa. xii. 5. Cleave thou, therefore, only to Him. Leave thyself implicitly in His hand. The Lord will appear on thy behalf. Hasten not forward in thine own strength: "Stand still and see the salvation of God."

"If the Lord be for us, who can be against us?" is the triumphant language of St. Paul, Rom. viii. 31. Let this truth be deeply settled in our minds, under every form of oppression, and it will make us more than conquerors over all the power of the enemy. St. Peter likewise, thus encourages our hearts: "If ye be reproached for the name of Christ, happy are ye." 1 Peter, iv. 14. And St. James adds this testimony and exhortation: "Count it all joy when ye fall into divers temptations" or trials. James i. 2. Our blessed Saviour Himself also, thus encourages and consoles His disciples: "Blessed are ye, when men shall revile you, and persecute you, and shall say all manner of evil against you falsely, for My sake. Rejoice, and be exceeding glad: for great is your reward in heaven: for so persecuted they the prophets which were before you." St. Matt. v. 11, 12.

Instead, however, of animating their hearts by the sustaining and exalting view, which these and other Scriptures present, and which our Saviour and His Apostles enjoin, many oppressed believers lose sight of the honor of the cross. They feel their trials in too personal a manner, and too easily therefore become disheartened and cast down. Let them remember that, as it is for Christ's sake they suffer, so it is for Christ's sake that they are to bear, and by His grace to bear patiently. "What glory is it, if when ye be buffeted for your faults, ye take it patiently? but if, when ye do well, and suffer for it, ye take it patiently, this is acceptable with God." 1 Pet. ii. 20. "If any man suffer as a Christian, let him not be ashamed: but let him glorify God on this behalf." 1 Pet. iv. 16.

The Christian is apt to say, "If the charge were true, I could bear it; but to be accused so wrongfully, and to be oppressed without cause, is hard to bear!" Under this trial, the believer is tempted to forget that Jesus his blessed Master, was always accused wrongfully; he becomes also too eager to defend himself, instead of being the more earnest to commit his case to God. An attempt to set himself right amongst worldly men, is not always accompanied with success, and is often attended by further irritation and wounding of the feelings. There are cases where vindication is necessary and becoming; but in a vast number of instances the Scriptural rule is at once the safest, and the easiest, "Let them that suffer according to the will of God, commit the keeping of their souls to Him in well-doing, as unto a faithful Creator." 1 Pet. iv. 19. Live down reproach. Be more diligent than ever in well-doing. Act like Daniel, that no enemy may have any fault to find, save concerning the law of your God, Dan. vi. 5; and soon your once-oppressed Lord will execute righteousness and judgment for your oppressed heart. If, however, you distrust your God, if you doubt whether He will appear on your behalf, that unbelief will lead you to take measures hastily for your own deliverance, and to pursue them eagerly to your own great damage, unless God, in mercy, prevent. Therefore, let us "take heed, lest there be in any of us an evil heart of unbelief, in departing from the living God." Heb. iii. 12. When the Lord brings us into trial, we must pray for grace patiently to abide therein, till He Himself bring us out. "Wait on the Lord; be of good courage, and He shall strengthen thine heart: wait, I say, on the Lord." Psa. xxvii. 14.

By this peculiar form of trial, the Refiner is purifying thy soul. He is assimilating thee to the likeness of thy Lord. We must be made like to Jesus. Of Him, it was emphatically written, "He was oppressed." Isa. liii. 7. This He suffered for thy sake; and to thee, as to the Philippian Christians of old, this double honor is "given in the behalf of Christ, not only to believe on Him, but also to suffer for His sake." Phil. i. 29. Oh seek, therefore, earnestly seek that the complete will of the Divine Purifier may be fulfilled in thy soul. Seek with St. Paul, "to know the fellowship of Christ's sufferings," and to be "made conformable," if it were necessary, even "unto His death." Phil. iii. 10. The bruising of the perfume brings out its richest odor. Be thou a willing sufferer of the bruise that heals—a thankful and a pleased bearer of the pressure of The Bruised Hand; then, no longer fretting against this peculiar form of trial, thou wilt bless the All-wise God, thy all-loving Lord, who has appointed it for thy eternal benefit, as well as bless Him also, like David, because He "executeth righteousness and judgment for all that are oppressed."

VIII.

The Lord making known His ways to Men.

He made known His ways unto Moses, His acts unto the children of Israel.—Verse 7.

THE Lord is not only the faithful Avenger of His people's wrongs, but He is also the gracious Instructor of His people's souls. The Psalmist celebrates His goodness in Revelation, as one of the covenanted mercies which he had received. He here specifies it as a delightful subject of his heartfelt thanksgivings: "He hath made known His ways unto Moses, His acts unto the children of Israel."

Deeply are we indebted to the Lord, for the Revelation which He has been pleased to make of Himself, of His character, and of His ways. We might have been left to our own unaided imaginations, to our own fancied discoveries. Whither these would have conducted us, experience has amply shown. Man destitute of revelation sinks into the grossness of idolatry, and becomes a blinded worshipper of the host of heaven, of the meanest reptiles, yea, and of the stocks and the stones of the earth. Without the direct teaching of the "Only Wise God," men grope in spiritual darkness. They "seek the Lord, if haply they may feel after

Him, and find Him, though He be not far from every one of us." Acts xvii. 27. It is, therefore, a most gracious instance of the mercy of the Lord towards us, that He condescends to meet the blindness of His creatures, and to manifest Himself to them by the immediate inspiration of His own Spirit. "Bless the Lord," then, O our souls, and all that is within us bless His holy name. "Bless the Lord, O my soul, and forget not all His benefits; for He hath made known His ways unto Moses, His acts unto the children of Israel."

Among the many peculiar tokens of the Divine favor toward the Hebrew race, this is not the least, that He who dwelleth in the thick darkness revealed Himself to their forefathers, "You only have I known of all the families of the earth." Amos iii. 2. Indeed, next to the high honor that "of them as concerning the flesh Christ came," Rom. ix. 5; this is to be regarded as the pride and glory of their nation, "chiefly, because that unto them were committed the oracles of God." Rom. iii. 2. "He sheweth His word unto Jacob, His statutes and His judgments unto Israel. He hath not dealt so with any nation: and as for His judgments, they have not known them. Praise ye the Lord." Psa. cxlvii. 19, 20.

The Lord brought the children of Israel to His footstool. He gave His good Spirit to instruct them, and He set them to be the teachers of the Gentiles. But even amongst these, the Lord hath not wholly left Himself without witness. From the beginning of the world Jehovah had made Himself known in various ways to men. Our first parents heard the voice of the Lord God in the garden of Eden. Even Cain, the murderer of his only brother, was privileged to hear the tones of that Voice which had called creation into being. To Noah, also, and doubtless to others of the antediluvian Patriarchs, did the Eternal God make known His purposes and declare His mighty acts.

But whatever measure of light, by revelation, existed before and after the deluge, the fact is certain, that the nations sinned against light and knowledge. They did not like to retain the true God in their remembrance. His holiness was a continual bar to the indulgence of their sinful propensities. They desired to have gods congenial to their own wicked inclinations. They became vain in their imagination; their foolish heart was darkened; and God gave them up to their own heart's lusts. Rom. i. 21. The nations became willing and debased idolaters; and had not God of His mercy interposed, they would all, without exception, have remained idolaters still to this very day. It was entirely of His own free and undeserved goodness that the Lord God called Abram out of Ur of the Chaldees. He who was to become the Father of the faithful, was himself the child of an idolater, and a youthful worshipper of things which are no gods, but the work of men's hands. It was the good pleasure of Jehovah to make Himself known to this blinded Chaldean, and to choose his descendants in whom to continue and to complete the line of revelation. How, therefore, shall we sufficiently extol the condescension of Him who "talked with Abram," Gen. xvii. 3;—who revealed to him both His present thoughts and His future purposes; who took him into covenant with Himself, bestowed on him the name of Abraham, and honored him with the title of the Friend of God? What shall we say to this? —Shall we not, "as grateful Gentiles," join the worshipping company of Israelites, and "stand up to bless the Lord our God for ever and ever; and say, Blessed be Thy glorious name, which is exalted above all blessing and praise. Thou, even Thou, art Lord alone: Thou hast made heaven, the heaven of heavens, with all their host, the earth, and all things that are therein, the seas, and all that is therein, and Thou preservest them all; and the host of heaven worshippeth Thee. Thou art the Lord the God, who didst choose Abram, and broughtest him forth out of Ur of the Chaldees, and gavest him the name of Abraham; and foundest his heart faithful before Thee, and madest a covenant with him to give the land of the Canaanites, * * * to his seed, and hast performed Thy words; for Thou art righteous: Thou camest down also upon Mount Sinai, and spakest with them from heaven, and gavest them right judgments, and true laws, good statutes and commandments: and madest known unto them Thy holy Sabbath, and commandedst them precepts, statutes, and laws, by the hand of Moses, Thy servant: and gavest them bread from heaven for their hunger, and broughtest forth water for them out of the rock for their thirst, and promisedst them that they should go in to possess the land which Thou hadst sworn to give them. Thou gavest also Thy good Spirit to instruct them, and withheldest not Thy manna from their mouth, and gavest them water for their thirst." Neh. ix. 5—8; 13—15; 20.

Of all preceding believers, it was to "the son of Pharaoh's daughter," that, in the most clear and abundant manner, the Lord "made Himself known;" as Nehemiah rehearses in this history, and as David testifies in this Psalm. A burning bush in the wilderness was not more surely exhibited to the eye of Moses, than the voice of the Lord God was vouchsafed to his ear, and the purposes of the great "I Am" were communicated to his mind. In Egypt also, then amid the solemn judgments at the Red Sea, and on the Mount of Sinai, did the High and Lofty One that inhabiteth eternity, "make known His ways to Moses, and His acts unto the children of Israel." Forty days and forty nights, on two several occasions, was Moses honored to remain in sacred communication with the Most High God. In the tabernacle also of the congregation, the Lord revealed Himself to His chosen servant, and "spake unto Moses face to face as a man speaketh unto his friend." Exod. xxxiii. 11.

Some, however, may be tempted to ask,—"What have we to do with Moses?" We answer, "Much, every way." The manifestation of God to him, and to the Israelites, has proved a fruitful source of instruction to succeeding generations: "The things that were written aforetime, were written for our learning, that we, through patience and comfort of the Scriptures, might have hope." Rom. xv. 4. We must not peruse the pages of the Old Testament, as mere records of history, in which we have no concern. The Old Testament and the New, make one Bible. The believers under both, make "one body." The Law and the Gospel emanate from "one God." They both point to the "one

Mediator." The object of the one is equally the object of the other,—to bring man home as a prodigal to his Father's house, and to engage him to fight against sin, and Satan, and the world, unto his life's end. The faithful are all enlisted under the same banner. The entire line of an army is affected by everything that befals the soldier in advance. We have a common cause with Moses, a common suffering, and a common triumph. Christians of "to-day" are fellow-soldiers with the faithful Israelites of "yesterday;" and both are "one in Him, who is the same yesterday, and to-day, and for ever." Heb. xiii. 8. The warfare is one. The Captain of their salvation is one. The glory of the victory shall be undivided.

Whatever happened to the ancient believers was for "ensample" to their successors; and it is written, "for our admonition, upon whom the ends of the world are come." 1 Cor. x. 11. We, who are living in this late day, enjoy the benefit of all former revelations. Let us therefore not be insensible to our mercies. They have been greatly increased since David's time, yet see how gratefully he speaks. Imitate his thankfulness; yea, endeavor to surpass it. Thy benefit, Oh Christian, greatly exceeds that of the Psalmist, so likewise should thy gratitude. What Historians have recorded, what Psalmists have celebrated, and Prophets have foretold, what Evangelists have narrated, and Apostles have testified, should call forth our ardent praise to Him, who condescended to reveal Himself to their minds, and to speak to us by their mouths. When God spake to Moses, His infinite mind designed also our benefit, and spake to us. When He gave the Law from Mount Sinai, He looked forward to every, even the latest, member of His Church. Let us give thanks therefore, for this benefit, and let us realize our oneness with the whole body of the faithful. Moses received the Law in the hands of the Mediator; so likewise do we. The acts of God toward the children of Israel were all performed in Christ; and in Christ we share the benefit. We are all one body in Christ; we all eat the same spiritual meat; we all drink the same spiritual drink: "for they drank of that spiritual Rock that followed them, and that Rock was Christ. Therefore let us not tempt Christ, as some of them also tempted, and were destroyed of serpents." 1 Cor. x. 4, 9.

The Revelation from the Most High is like Himself,—holy, and just, and good. The most apparently opposite declarations therein, are not really opposite; for that one Spirit who inspired them, can never contradict Himself. The Omniscient God sees no imperfection in the Volume of His own inspiration; and all things it contains will soon be made clear likewise to us: "What we know not now, we shall know hereafter." Meantime, it is the province of faith to anticipate that knowledge, and to enable us now to receive "with the spirit," what we shall then receive with "the understanding also." Faith sees everything in God's light, and therefore beholds no imperfection, and acknowledges no contradictions, in His word of truth. The language of faith is that of the inspired Psalmist, "The law of the Lord is perfect, converting the soul: the testimony of the Lord is sure, making wise the simple. The statutes of the Lord are right, rejoicing the heart: the commandment of the Lord is pure, enlightening the eyes. The fear of the Lord is clean, enduring for ever: the judgments of the Lord are true and righteous altogether. More to be desired are they than gold, yea, than much fine gold; sweeter also than the honey and the honeycomb. Moreover, by them is thy servant warned; and in keeping of them there is great reward." Psa. xix. 7—11.

Reader, do you value the sacred Scriptures as King David did? Are they sweeter than "honey" to your taste? Are they more desirable than "gold" in your estimation? Have they converted your soul, and imparted wisdom to your mind? Have they rejoiced your heart, and enlightened your eyes? Then you will readily declare for yourself "that the law of the Lord is perfect, and His testimony sure—that His statutes are right, and His commandments pure"—yea, you will joyfully add that His judgments "are true and righteous altogether."

The Bible is the Book of God, and the Book of His Church. It is the Book of inspiration and of truth; of history and of prophecy; of instruction and of consolation. The Bible is the Book of promises and of warnings; of faith and of hope; of purity and of power. It is the Book of peace and of pleasantness; of light and of life. The Bible is the book of spiritual conversion, and of never-ending salvation. The Bible is the best Book for Time, and the only Book for Eternity.

The Word of God is the instrument of our regeneration. James i. 18; 1 Pet. i. 23. It is the means of the sanctification of our souls. John xv. 3. It is the sword of the Spirit, by which we overcome our spiritual foes. Eph. vi. 17. It makes us wise unto salvation, through faith, which is in Christ Jesus. 2 Tim. iii. 15. In it we have eternal life, because it testifies of Him. John v. 39.

Oh what a comforter in sorrows is the Book of God—what a guide in perplexity—what a light in darkness—what life in death! How many of the sons and daughters of affliction, when worn with languor and disease, have been heard to testify regarding the Book of the Lord, "This is my comfort in my affliction: for Thy word hath quickened me." Psa. cxix. 50. Mark the testimony of a young naval officer on his dying bed, when but twenty-four years of age: "There is nothing like the Bible. I never tire of that. I never feel lonely or weary when reading it:" and again he said, "I love to have this blessed Book open before me; for I can only sleep a few minutes at a time; and when I open my eyes, it is so pleasant to light upon some sweet passage."—*Memoirs of the Hon. R. M.*

Lady Jane Grey to her sister Lady Catharine, gave her dying testimony to the value of the Bible, by writing thus, on the blank leaf of her Greek Testament, the night before she suffered: "I have here sent you a book, which, although it be not outwardly rimmed with gold, yet inwardly it is more worth than precious stones. It is the book, dear sister, of the laws of the Lord: it is his testament and last will * * * * and shall lead you to the path of eternal joy; and if you with a good mind read it, and with an earnest desire to follow it, shall bring you to an immortal and everlasting life. It will teach you to live, and learn you to die: * * * if you apply diligently to this book, trying to direct your life after it, you shall be an inheritor of such riches, as neither the covetous shall withdraw from you, neither thief shall steal, neither yet the moth corrupt."

It is our happy privilege to belong to a Kingdom, which, in the most public manner, and on the most solemn occasion, honors the Word of God above all earthly things. It is not the Sword of state, nor the golden Orb of dominion; it is not the Sceptre of authority, nor even the Crown of gold, which constitutes the last and highest gift, presented by the British Nation, to the Royal Person on the day of Coronation—no, it is the WORD OF GOD! For, after all these things have been presented, "the Archbishop shall bring the Holy Bible, and say: Our Gracious Queen; we present you with THIS BOOK, THE MOST VALUABLE THING THAT THIS WORLD AFFORDS. Here is wisdom; this is the Royal Law; these are the lively oracles of God. Blessed is he that readeth, and they that hear the words of this Book: that keep and do the things contained in it. For these are the words of eternal life, able to make you wise and happy in this world; nay, wise unto salvation, and so happy for evermore, through faith which is in Christ Jesus; to whom be glory for ever. Amen."

Reader, is the Bible to you "the most valuable thing that this world affords"? Is it the book, by the light of which you have determined to guide your life? Is it the book, on the faith of which you have resolved to die? Are you making a good use of your Bible, for the enlightening of your mind, the sanctification of your heart, and the regulation of your conduct? Do you daily draw water with joy out of these wells of salvation? Jesus was a diligent reader of the Bible in the days of His flesh. He treasured up the promises in His heart. He lived by faith upon the written word. He knew what Moses had written regarding Himself. He knew what the Psalmists had sung, and what the Prophets had foretold, of His sufferings as the Redeemer, and of the glory that should follow. 1 Pet. i. 11. Read the Old Testament, because Jesus read it. Prize the Old Testament, because Jesus prized it; and prize the New Testament, which tells you of His life, and of His righteousness; of His blood, and of His death; of His resurrection and ascension; of His present intercession, and of His speedy return in glory. Oh thus look for Jesus, and read of Jesus, in the Book of God, and it will be the Book of Life for ever to your precious soul.

The Holy Bible has been described "as the garden of Eden, and the Book of Psalms as the tree of life in the midst." Reader, have you heard the voice of the Lord God therein? In the cool of the evening, and at other times, do you love to walk with God in this garden of inspiration? Can you say with Jeremiah, "Thy words were found, and I did eat them, and Thy word was unto me the joy and the rejoicing of my heart"? Jer. xv. 16. Do you unfeignedly bless God for the Bible? Is it a matter of heartfelt thankfulness to you that Moses wrote, and that David sang, and that Isaiah and others prophesied? Are the four Gospels on one subject more than enough in your apprehension? or do you count the sayings and doings of your blessed Saviour so precious, that you could have wished that they had been "written every one"? John xxi. 25. Do you receive the Epistles spiritually and practically, as addressed to yourself? And do you faithfully apply their counsels, and warnings, their admonitions and promises, to your own temper, life, and conversation? And, especially, do you peruse the whole volume of inspiration in the light of the Sun of righteousness? Does Jesus shine in every page, and bring the broad day of salvation into your soul? Walk continually in that light. Give thanks for that light. Delight thyself in thy Lord. Delight thyself also in His Word. Read, mark, learn, and inwardly digest the Holy Scriptures. Say like Job, "I have esteemed the words of His mouth more than my necessary food." Job xxiii. 12. Say with David, "O how love I Thy law! it is my meditation all the day." "How sweet are Thy words unto my taste! yea, sweeter than honey to my mouth!" "Thy Word is a lamp unto my feet, and a light unto my path." "Thy testimonies have I taken as an heritage for ever: for they are the rejoicing of my heart." "Therefore I love Thy commandments above gold, yea, above fine gold." Psa. cxix.

Art thou as a "babe" in the faith, and anxious to grow in grace, and in the knowledge of thy Lord and Saviour?—"Desire the sincere milk of the Word, that thou mayest grow thereby." 1 Pet. ii. 2. Art thou as a "young man" in the truth, and longing to be strong in the faith which is in Christ Jesus?—here is "strong meat" in the Word of God; and "if it abide in thee, thou shalt overcome the wicked one." Art thou as a "father," grown old in the service of the Best of Masters?—here is the unerring and consolatory Word wherein thou mayest "know Him that is from the beginning," whom time cannot change, whom age cannot enfeeble, and whose love and wisdom cannot decay. In that Word, He has said, "I will never leave thee, I will never forsake thee." Dear aged pilgrim, take this promise for thy staff. Grasp it firmly with the hand of faith. Go forward resolutely through this wilderness, leaning upon it; and ever and anon, as thou advancest, look upward to Jesus saying, "Remember Thy word unto Thy servant, upon which Thou hast caused me to hope," Psa. cxix. 49; and then through the remaining states of thy pilgrimage, He will enable thee "boldly to say, The Lord is my helper, I will not fear what man shall do unto me." Heb. xiii. 6.

IX.

Manifold Benefits Flowing out of the Character of God.

The Lord is merciful and gracious, slow to anger, and plenteous in mercy. He will not always chide: neither will He keep His anger for ever. He hath not dealt with us after our sins; nor rewarded us according to our iniquities.—Verses 8, 9, 10.

Having separately enumerated seven special benefits which he had received from his God, the Psalmist returns to his most cherished theme, and expatiates with delight on seven-fold excellencies of Jehovah. He appears to feel that he can never speak enough of the goodness of his Redeemer, nor sufficiently extol the freeness, and the fulness, of His forgiving love. The heart of the Psalmist glows with emotion, "and while he is musing the fire burns within him." The mercies of the Lord appear so vast, and His kindnesses so varied and innumerable, that he can no longer stay to specify each individual blessing singly and by itself. Streams of refreshment had continually crossed his path, through all his earthly pilgrimage; and now, when he attempts, in his own thoughts, to trace up each of them to its source, he finds that they all issue out of the same overflowing fountain. He turns, therefore, to drink of that fountain itself, and he finds it to be full, and free, and satisfying to his soul. The unnumbered and varied mercies which he had successively tested, he here finds in their sum and substance, there essence and their perfection. God in Christ is that Fountain. With ravished heart, therefore, he now sets himself to the contemplation of this glorious Being, from whom all mercies flow; and he exclaims, "All my springs are in Thee." Psa. lxxxvii. 7.

It is in the character of God, revealed in Jesus, that our strength and our security, our peace and our happiness, are all centered. From the best gifts, the richest graces, the dearest friends, we must rise upward to God. Therefore, David says, "My soul wait thou only upon God, for my expectation is from Him. He only is my rock and my salvation. He is my defence. I shall not be moved. In God is my salvation and my glory. The rock of my strength, and my refuge, is in God." Psa. lxii. 5—7. The knowledge of God was spiritual life—"eternal life," to the heart of the Psalmist. He knew the Lord not only in His attributes and acts, but also in His character and feelings. "It is not," as if he had said,—"it is not only in what God has done for me, but in what God Himself is to me, that I most exceedingly rejoice!" Therefore, his determined resolution was this: "My soul shall make her boast in the Lord." Psa. xxxiv. 2. See how he exemplifies this resolution in the eighteenth Psalm: "I will love Thee, Oh Lord, my strength. The Lord is my rock, and my fortress, and my deliverer; my God; my strength in whom I will trust: my buckler; and the horn of my salvation, and my high tower." With a similarly joyful and appropriating faith, does the Psalmist pour forth his gratitude in this hundred and third Psalm. In this portion of it, David appears to delight himself exceedingly in the Lord his God. He exults in the twofold persuasion, that whatever is good, or useful, or desirable, is centred in God; and secondly, that whatsoever God thus is, and has, He is to him, and has for him, and that for ever, through Christ Jesus. Blessed persuasion! It is at once the sure foundation, and the crowning topstone, of all true happiness. May this persuasion be ours in life and death! God is the Fountain of all blessedness—a Fountain, the healing virtue of which, to fallen man, freely and fully flows, through the pierced heart of His only Son, and our Elder Brother: "For it pleased the Father that in Him should all fulness dwell." Colos. i. 19. Yea, again, adds the Apostle, "In Him dwelleth all the fulness of the Godhead bodily." Coloss. ii. 9. And all this fulness is made over to us "in Him; whether things present, or things to come; all are yours; and ye are Christ's, and Christ is God's." 1 Cor. iii. 32. St. John, who lay in the bosom of that Fulness, thus invites us all to become partakers of it with himself: "That which we have seen and heard declare we unto you, that ye also may have fellowship with us: and truly our fellowship is with the Father, and with his Son Jesus Christ. And these things write we unto you, that your joy may be full." 1 John i. 3, 4. The "joy" of the Psalmist, as a partaker of this Divine fellowship, was "full" to overflowing with these sevenfold benefits—"The Lord is merciful and gracious, slow to anger, and plenteous in mercy; He will not always chide: neither will He keep His anger for ever. He hath not dealt with us after our sins, nor rewarded us according to our iniquities."

The Lord is most compassionate and "merciful" in His thoughts and feelings towards us, and He is truly "gracious" in His manner of expressing these feelings, and of manifesting that mercy. Instead of being swift to punish, as He might justly be, He is "slow to anger;" and so far from being easily provoked, and soon exhausted in patience by repeated offences, on the very contrary "He is plenteous in mercy." God may occasionally hide His face from His people—but "He doth not always chide." He may take vengeance on their inventions, and punish them with His rod,—but "He doth not keep His anger for ever." No man may doubt or deny these six truths, for this is the proof and evidence of them all—"He hath not dealt with us after our sins, nor rewarded us according to our iniquities?" Is there one of our shortcomings, or our transgressions, which He has visited as it deserves; or as our omissions of duty, and our commissions of offence, are visited by men? How imperatively do these sevenfold blessings demand the immediate gratitude, and the unreserved devotedness, of every human being! Where is the individual to be found, upon the surface of the globe, who can prefer a charge against the holy God, and say, He hath laid upon me more than is just? If, on the contrary, we must all acknowledge that He has laid less than He justly might, how powerful, how constraining, how irresistible, becomes the argument, and the obligation, upon every living man to stir himself up with David, to love and to serve the Lord with most willing obedience, and to say, "Bless the Lord, O my soul: and all that is within me, bless His holy name, who hath not dealt with me after my sins, nor rewarded me according to my iniquities."

The long-suffering of God towards our fallen family, is one of the most marvellous and delightful themes on which the mind can meditate. It would be altogether beyond belief, had not God himself declared it, and did not our own experience, over and over again, convince us of the fact. Nor is this long-suffering the result either of ignorance or of indifference. The Lord fully knows every unholy thought which His creatures entertain, and He discerns every unworthy motive by which they are actuated. He hears every idle word, and "all the hard speeches which ungodly sinners utter against Him." Jude 15. He observes every sinful action they perform, and He marks all the ungodly deeds which they commit. He discerns, He hears, He marks, all this, over the whole circumference of the globe, at every moment of time, both by night and by day, on the sea and on the land; He abhors it all with infinite abhorrence, and yet He breaks not forth in vengeance upon this world of sinners. Look at the nearest town or village, or at any other, with which you are best acquainted. Say, are the great majority of its inhabitants meek and holy, pious and self-denied, humble, charitable, and heavenly-minded? Is it only the minority amongst them who are worldly, covetous, high-minded, and lovers of frivolty and pleasure? The conclusion to which observation causes you to come, in reference to that one town or village, will apply also to every other town and village in these three Kingdoms. Remember that these are professedly Christian kingdoms: and then, if you carry out the same conclusion to all other Christian countries, who shall accuse you as either mistaken or uncharitable? If such be the state of Christendom, what is the condition of the whole heathen world? Put, then, together the innumerable towns and villages of this habitable globe, and say, is there one of them where sin and nature do not predominate above grace and goodness;—where even to human eyes and ears, there is not more cursing than blessing, more profanation than prayer, more open wickedness than professed godliness?—and say then can a holy God look down upon any one of them with pleasure? If not, why does He not sweep the whole world into destruction in a moment? The only answer that can be given is this—Because He is a long-suffering God!

Did the Most High "lay righteousness to the line, and strict justice to the plumbline," there is not a human being that could stand the measurement. We must all have been cut off in the first moment that we sinned: "If Thou, Lord, shouldst mark iniquity, O Lord! who shall stand?" If He should call us to an account for only "one out of every thousand" of our transgressions, we should be consigned to everlasting perdition. "The wages of sin," of all and every sin, "is death." Rom. vi. 23. "Cursed is every one," saith the Scripture, "that continueth not in all things that are written in the book of the law to do them." Gal. iii. 10. If, then, our deserved reward be "death," what have we to say against God, seeing that we are this day alive? Does not our very existence testify to the long-suffering of our God? Yes, every breath we draw, every step we take, every hour's happiness that we enjoy, every friend that gladdens our earthly lot, every new day that opens to us after another, all speak to us of mercy and long-suffering from on high. Well therefore has the prophet Jeremiah, in the very midst of his most pathetic lamentations, thus expostulated with himself and others, "Wherefore doth a living man complain, a man for the punishment of his sins?" Lam. iii. 39. If we are still alive, and not yet cast into the burning lake, we have no cause to complain, but every cause to be thankful.

True it is, that suffering is the consequent of sin. The Psalmist does not declare that God never punishes iniquity. On the contrary, he plainly intimates that He does punish it; for His words refer to the measure of that punishment. The Lord does indeed deal with us *for* our sins, *because* of our sins. He does chastise us *on account* of our transgressions; but never in this life, "*according* to our iniquities," up to the measure of our provocations. That measure is to be meted out to the unbelieving and impenitent in the world to come. Yet even there, in the torments of "the worm that never dies, and of the fire that never shall be quenched," no sinner, through the endless ages of woe, shall be able to arraign the sentence of the Great Judge, and say, My punishment is *greater* than my iniquities deserve! No!—never once shall it be. "The Lord is righteous in all His works, and holy in all His ways." He will not in this life, He will not in the life to come, "lay upon man more than right, that he should enter into judgment with God." Job. xxxiv. 23.

The good news of mercy in Christ Jesus are commanded to be "preached in ALL the world, to every creature." Mark xvi. 15. "The wrath of God is also revealed from heaven against ALL ungodliness and unrighteousness of men." Rom. i. 18. These two truths should run broad and parallel throughout the earth. They demand equal publicity: they should find equal admission into every heart. The MERCY of the Lord is not proclaimed to man that he may continue in sin, but that, on the contrary, he may be turned from it. "God having raised up His Son Jesus, sent Him to bless you," says the Apostle, "in turning away every one of you from his iniquities." Acts iii. 26. The WRATH of God is not declared against a man when turning from his sin, but when remaining in it, or returning to it. Let these two truths be deeply impressed upon our minds. Let them be broad and bright before our eyes,—shining with meridian clearness. He who sits upon the throne of the universe is merciful and gracious, but at the same time justice and judgment are the habitation, or basis, of His throne. Psa. lxxxix. 14. God "commandeth all men everywhere to repent." Acts xvii. 30. He graciously promises mercy and forgiveness to all those that truly turn to Him. But if any man will not turn, He will whet His sword; He hath bent his bow, and made it ready. He hath also prepared for him the instruments of death." Psa. vii. 12. Is, therefore, "God unrighteous who taketh vengeance?—God forbid!" Rom. iii. 5, 6. We are sure, says the Apostle, that "the judgment of God is according to truth." He must be as true to His threatenings, as He is faithful to His promises. Men "despise the riches of His goodness, and forbearance, and long-suffering:" They presume upon that mercy, which is designed to lead them to repentance. In the hardness and impenitency of their hearts, they "treasure up unto themselves wrath against the day of wrath, and revelation of the righteous judgment of God." That day is at hand,—that solemn day; and then God "will render to every man according to his deeds. To them who, by patient continuance in well-doing, seek for glory and honor and immortality, eternal life: but unto them that are contentious, and do not obey the truth, but obey unrighteousness, indignation and wrath. Tribulation and anguish upon every soul of man that doeth evil, of the Jew first, and also of the Gentile: but glory, honor, and peace to every man that worketh good, to the Jew first, and also to the Gentile: for there is no respect of persons with God. For as many as have sinned without law shall also perish without law: and as many as have sinned in the law shall be judged by the law; in the day when God shall judge the secrets of men by Jesus Christ." Rom. ii. 7—12.

"To-day," while it is called "to-day," the voices of the Law and of the Gospel sound commingled in our ears. Soon their voices will have died away,—but the blessing and the curse, which they have respectively proclaimed, will be left behind, as the inheritance of their respective followers. Those who have turned from sin to Christ, will inherit the blessing. Those who have turned from Christ to sin, will inherit the curse. The "children of the blessing" will experience, that though the Lord did chasten them for their backslidings, and punish them for their provocations, yet that it was in very love and mercy to their souls. They will thank Him, therefore, for His chidings, and bless Him for all His corrections; perceiving that "He doth not always chide"—and joyfully acknowledging that "He has not kept His anger for ever." The "children of the curse" will discover, that though the Lord was "merciful and gracious, slow to anger, and plenteous in mercy" toward them, in the days of their earthly life; yet in like manner as they put away His goodness from them, and "would none of His reproof," so Jesus Himself will say, "Those mine enemies, who would not that I should reign over them, bring hither, and slay them before Me." Luke xix. 27. For "then shall the Lord Jesus be revealed from heaven with His mighty angels, in flaming fire taking vengeance on them that know not God, and that obey not the Gospel of our Lord Jesus Christ: who shall be punished with everlasting destruction from the presence of the Lord, and from the glory of His power." 2. Thess. i. 7—9.

God is "merciful" even to His enemies in this life, but it is only to those that love Him, that His mercy will be exhibited in the life to come. This Psalm was written by a believer, and its declarations are applicable only to the faithful. Culpable beyond expression, is he, whosoever would pervert the words of this ninth verse, to uphold his own fabricated system of charity and mercy, falsely so called. The argument that would abate the punishment of the wicked, would terminate also the blessedness of the righteous; for the same Scriptures which reveal "eternal salvation" to the one, Heb. v. 9, have revealed "eternal condemnation" to the other. Mark iii. 29. We tremble, and indeed we ought to tremble, at the awful truth. But let not these tremblings in our flesh, produce any tremblings in our faith: "God is not a man that He should lie; neither the Son of man that He should repent; hath He said, and shall He not do it? or hath He spoken, and shall He not make it good?" Num. xxiii. 19. He, who was love and charity personified,—Jesus, in whose benignant breast there dwelt more mercy, than the collected tendernesses of the whole human race could furnish, has Himself declared, "These shall go away into everlasting punishment, but the righteous into life eternal." Matt. xxv. 46. It is enough, therefore, that the lips of Incarnate Love have pronounced these words. We leave the whole question as He has stated it, assured that the end will prove that "the Lord is upright, and that there is no unrighteousness with Him." Psa. xcii. 15.

With this comforting persuasion of the integrity of the Lord in all the principles of His government, let us proceed to consider their practical application to ourselves. In that eternal world the conscience of the sinner will re-echo the sentence of the Judge. Every lost spirit will then perceive the justice of its condemnation, for thus prophesied the seventh from Adam: "Behold, the Lord cometh with ten thousand of his saints, to execute judgment upon all, and to CONVINCE all that are ungodly among them, of all their ungodly deeds which they have ungodly committed, and of all their hard speeches which ungodly sinners have spoken against Him." Jude 14, 15. Are we, then, let us ask ere it be too late,—are we convinced of the righteousness of the Lord in all our tribulations? Have we been taught by Divine grace to justify the Lord's dealings with ourselves, under losses, sufferings, and bereavements, in this vale of tears? Or do we "kick against the pricks," and rebel against the Hand that smites us? Do we scowl like Cain, and mutter "my punishment is greater than I can bear"? Or can we, and do we, testify from our very hearts, each of us for himself, "The Lord hath not dealt with me after my sins, neither hath He rewarded me according to my iniquities? All men can thus testify: that is, all men with truth and justice have reason, and ought, to bear witness to the Lord's long-suffering towards them. They all live by His sufferance, they all depend upon His bounty, they are all safe by His protection. All men, therefore, can, but alas! all men do not, thus heartily testify of the loving-kindness of their God. Hence arises the necessity for this double question,—Can you, and do you, imitate the example of the Psalmist? Can you set to your seal that God is good? Are you convinced that you have reason to speak favorably of the Lord's dealings with you? And, being so convinced, do you rejoice to speak favorably of His name? Do you take pleasure in celebrating His mercy? Do you watch for opportunities to tell forth His goodness? Do you try to incite others to extol His long-suffering to them and to yourselves, saying, like David, "O magnify the Lord with me, and let us exalt His name together"?

If this be your delight, go on to still higher graces. Pray

like the Apostles, "Lord, increase my faith." Never stagger at the promises of God through unbelief. Be deeply learned in the excellencies of Jesus. "Acquaint thyself with Him, and be at peace, and thereby good shall come unto thee." Grow in the knowledge of thy Lord and Saviour. Meditate on all His revealed offices, characters, and relationships. Ask the Holy Spirit to enable thee to believe with a firm faith that God really is what the Bible describes. At all times, and under all circumstances, trust in Him. Be deeply persuaded that thy Lord is "merciful and gracious, slow to anger, and plenteous in mercy." Hold fast by Christ's love, whatever appearances may say to the contrary. Have anxieties befallen thee? Dost thou toil and labor with little apparent profit or progress? Does a sea of trouble encompass thee? And dost thou sometimes fear that all these indicate thy Saviour's frown? Oh no!—still wait. Even if it be so, He will "not always chide." Soon thou shalt see Him through the gloom. Hearken, and His voice will reach thee above the storm, saying, "It is I, be not afraid." Do not, therefore, Oh do not hastily conclude from earthly trials that God is angry with thee. Satan will tempt thee so to think; but resist him. Say, "It is written"—"If ye be without chastisement, whereof all are partakers, then are ye bastards, and not sons," Heb. xii. 8; and again, "Whom the Lord loveth, He chasteneth, and scourgeth every son whom He receiveth." But if Satan still "thrust sore at thee to make thee fall," Psa. cxviii. 13; and if thine own conscience cry likewise against thee that God has much reason to be angry; still hope in God through

Christ, and answer, "I know that I have greatly grieved my Lord;" but "it is written"—"He will not keep His anger for ever;" and I know that even now "He has not dealt with me after my sins, nor rewarded me according to my iniquities"—"therefore will I praise the name of the Lord with a song, and magnify Him with thanksgiving."

What we all need, by the grace of the Holy Spirit, is to have lively impressions, continually on our hearts, of the truths which we here learn, that we may be stirred up to diligent performance of the duties here inculcated. We must lay them up in the heart. It is not enough to have a mere passing notion of them in the head. It is one thing coldly to say, "I know that God has not dealt with me as I deserve," and quite another to say this with a deep consciousness of the sins that we have committed, and a vivid sense of His long-suffering in forbearing with them. David possessed both of these. In this ninth verse he utters this double truth, with this twofold consciousness. It was no mere simple admission in the mouth of David. He felt it more than a sharp two-edged sword within him: "For the Word of God is quick, and powerful, and sharper than any two-edged sword, piercing even to the dividing asunder of soul and spirit, and of the joints and marrow, and is a discerner of the thoughts and intents of the heart." Heb. iv. 12. In these verses the Psalmist fixes upon our mind both what God has done to us, and what we have done to Him. His words exalt the "merciful" Creator, and abase us the sinful creatures. They exhibit the conduct of the Most High in bright contrast with that of man. He has been "gracious" to us in all His dealings, and we have sinned against Him times and ways without number. We have daily provoked Him to His face, and yet He has not once punished us according to the amount of our transgressions. Again and again therefore let it be repeated, "He has not dealt with us after our sins, nor rewarded us according to our iniquities."

Oh the goodness of God and the unworthiness of man! Thy long-suffering Lord, and my multiplied transgressions, who shall declare! Oh touch and teach my inmost soul. Rouse me from insensibility, and quicken me to life. Pour upon my heart Thy enlightening Spirit; and, bright as the sun, irradiate my mind with these two truths—Thy goodness, and my unworthiness. All revelation teaches me—all Nature certifies me—all experience convinces me—every day, every hour, and every circumstance, cries aloud to me of Thy goodness, and my unworthiness? These, the two grand facts in the history of my past life, are also the two great truths in the recorded Scriptures of my God; these, the first lessons of my infant faith, shall also be the last utterances of my departing breath,—Thy goodness, and my unworthiness!

X.

Immeasurable Benefits.

GOD'S MERCY—ITS HEIGHT—ITS EMBLEM—HEAVEN'S HEIGHT.

For as the heaven is high above the earth, so great is His mercy towards them that fear Him.—Verse 11.

So enlarged does the heart of the Psalmist become with meditating on the long-suffering goodness of his Lord, that language fails any longer to express the emotions which rise within his breast. So vast, so glorious, is the theme, that it overpowers his mind. If, even in reference to earthly things, there are thoughts which lie too deep for utterance—which labor for adequate expression; how much more will this be felt by the believer, when the Omniscient Spirit has led his mind into the deep things of God?

In the renewed soul, there are depths of sorrow, and heights of joy which cannot possibly be described. On the one hand, loathings of self and sin are awakened by the Holy One, which can find vent only in sighs and tears. The Refiner searches into the innermost recesses of the human spirit, the soul becomes agitated to its centre—a living fire from the sanctifying Spirit has entered it, and sins, like snakes before unnoticed issue from their lurking-places, hissing yet retreating, writhing yet resisting in every part. We become wretched and appalled at the spiritual conflict—at the war of elements, within us. Words fail upon the tongue. Even prayer dies away from the lip. But then, even then, blessed be God, His own Spirit condescends to pray from within us, and to make intercessions on our behalf "with groanings that cannot be uttered." Heb. viii. 26. This is indeed a sorrow which the world knoweth not, and with which a stranger cannot intermeddle. On the other hand, there is also a spiritual joy which overpowers expression. When the love of God is shed abroad in the heart by the Holy Ghost, and the Spirit Himself beareth witness with our spirit, that we are the children of God; when the sweet consciousness of God's love to us, and of our love to Him, is imparted to the soul—and when this felt blessedness of holy mutual love, awakens an intense longing for nearer and never-ending communion, Cant. ii. 5—7; then indeed the soul feels lost in that love which passeth knowledge; the language of emotion supersedes the language of expression—the Lord God Almighty is silently "resting in His love," and the enraptured soul is resting therein with Him. Zeph. iii. 17. (Margin.) St. Peter thus appeals to his Christian brethren for the truth of this ineffable and thrilling joy in their adorable Redeemer: "Whom having not seen," he says, "ye love: in whom, though now you see Him not, yet believing, ye rejoice with joy unspeakable and full of glory," 1. Pet. i. 8.

Believers under the Old Testament dispensation were privileged, like believers under the New, to know that love which passeth knowledge. David was a partaker of this unspeakable spiritual joy. In this, and other Psalms, he labors to express emotions which no language can adequately describe. He had enumerated various blessings. He had specially alluded to, and mentioned, several times, the "mercy" of the Lord. But his sense of that long-suffering mercy was far too great to be comprehended within the mere term. He turns therefore from the use of direct statements to employ illustrative comparisons; and in the next verses introduces the most beautiful and appropriate images that can possibly be imagined. He feels himself, also, to be so unworthy of that mercy, that he searches in vain for the cause of it in himself. No sooner, however, does he turn to meditate on the character of God, than the true cause bursts at once upon his view. He joyfully discovers the truth, that the reason why God had not dealt with him according to a limited measure of mercy, was because His mercy is itself immeasurable. The most immeasurable thing, therefore, in the whole visible creation must now become to Him, instead of words, the proper symbol, the appropriate expression, of that mercy. And having said in the verses just before, that the Lord was "merciful and gracious," and that He had "not dealt with him after his sins, nor awarded him according to his iniquities;" he amplifies and illustrates his idea, and exclaims, in the 11th, "For as the heaven is high above the earth, so great is His mercy towards them that fear Him. As if he would say, "This is the reason why the Lord shows such marvellous long-suffering towards me, because His long-suffering is utterly inexhaustible."

Our sins and iniquities are immeasurable in their guilt. How, then, shall our fears be quieted? By remembering that there is something more immeasurable still—the mercy of the Lord! Does the vastness of this declaration cause thy faith to stagger? And dost thou say, "But how shall I believe in a mercy like this, which I can neither see nor prove?" Here is a mode of measurement proposed, which you daily see, and which you can constantly apply. Go forth from thy dwelling-place, and look upward to the heavens. Seest thou the blue sky?—Dost thou doubt its existence?—Canst thou measure its height? That heaven is but one of the letters in God's universal alphabet, by which he carries on, in part, the education of His children. All believers have been instructed in this school. Abraham, the father of the faithful, received here the rudiments of his knowledge; and the Almighty God Himself condescended to instruct him. Ignorant as a child, and unbelieving, this illuminated letter was pointed out to him by the finger of his Divine Teacher,—"Look now toward heaven, and tell the stars, if thou be able to number them; and He said unto them, So shall thy seed be. And he believed in the Lord; and He counted it to him for righteousness." Gen. xv. 5, 6.

David, also, gained heavenly wisdom in the same school. The one looked upward to the heaven, and beheld in its countless host, a picture of his own countless posterity. The other looked up into the same heaven, and beheld in its immeasurable height, an emblem of the immeasurable mercy of his Redeemer. David studied God in His works, and he studied these works in God. The heavens, we know, were the frequent object of his contemplation; equally, we doubt not, when he was a simple shepherd, as when he was a mighty king. The cool of the evening, perhaps, might find him reclining on a verdant bank, while his flock was browsing around him. His favorite harp is in his hand. No human listener is near, while he sings to himself, and to his God, in untutored strains of grateful melody. Emotion kindles with his lays, and soon rises above them. The notes of his harp become gradually faint and silent. His outstretched fingers cease to sweep its strings, for his eyes and his thoughts have become fixed on the heavens, as if he were gazing through them upon its happy inhabitants: and, while his wrapt soul is thus listening to the spiritual music of its own emotions, he fancies for the moment that he hears the strains of the angelic choir. David, when a king, delighted in the frequent contemplation of this great work of the Almighty, and in the grandeur of the view, all lofty thoughts of his own grandeur as a monarch were lowered to the ground. "When I consider Thy heavens," he says, "the work of Thy fingers, the moon and the stars, which Thou hast ordained, what is man, that Thou art mindful of him? and the son of man, that Thou visitest him?" Psa. viii. 3, 4.

Well, indeed may the survey of the magnificent canopy of the heavens abase man in his own estimation. For the same reason, however, it should exalt, unspeakably exalt, the Great God, in the apprehension of every intelligent being. We, who cannot pierce its height, nor scan its breadth, though spread out before us, how insignificant small! He, who made that heaven out of nothing, how immeasurably great! Night tells us of His matchless power. Day showeth forth His surpassing splendor. "The heavens declare the glory of God, and the firmament showeth His handy-work. Day unto day uttereth speech, and night unto night showeth knowledge. There is no speech nor language, where their voice is not heard. Their line is gone out through all the earth, and their words to the end of the world. In them hath he set a tabernacle for the sun." Psa. xix. 1—4.

It is this "voice" of the heavens, which David has here caught in his inmost soul. The lesson which he learned from it, and which he here transcribes for our instruction, is this, "For as the heaven is high above the earth, so great is His mercy toward them that fear Him."

The "fear" here spoken of, is not a slavish dread, but a child-like reverence. The more we love an earthly parent, the more respect do we entertain towards him. "God is greatly to be feared in the assembly of the saints, and to be had in reverence of all them that are about Him." Psa. lxxxix. 7. Such is the sentiment which the Scriptures denote by the term "fear." The love of an inferior to a superior, of a subject to a king, must always be thus accompanied. Those who acknowledge not the greatness and the authority of the Lord, are described as having "no fear of God before their eyes." Rom. iii. 18. But of the righteous it is said, "Happy is the man that feareth alway." Prov. xxviii. 14. True, indeed, the Scripture declares that there is "no fear in love." 1 John iv. 18. We are not afraid of those whom we regard with affection,—we are not apprehensive that they will do us injury—nor alarmed at approaching into their presence. Such would not be the feeling of a child toward a parent, but of a slave toward a tyrant. It is filial and spiritual fear that is here spoken of. Natural fear will cast out love from the heart; but the Apostle declares that "perfect love casteth out fear, because fear hath torment:" and he who gives way to such tormenting apprehensions, will be afraid to draw near unto God as a Father reconciled in Christ Jesus, and "is not made perfect in love." But, on the contrary, that "fear" which characterizes the children of God, is filial,—is based on love towards Him, and cannot exist without it. The holy sentiments of fear and love are mutually productive and mutually strengthening—they act and re-act, with increasing benefit upon each other. The consciousness of having sinned against God, increases the apprehension of His mercy—and the apprehension of His mercy re-acts upon the heart with a double sense of its unworthiness, the more we feel this unworthiness, the more thankful we are to hear of forgiveness; and the more we believe in the pardoning mercy of God, the more we hate ourselves for ever having sinned against Him.

The "fear" of the Lord is absolutely necessary to our due appreciation of His immeasurable mercy. Indeed, without this, we dare not trust ourselves to enlarge upon the delightful theme. There are many men now living in their sins, who speak constantly of God's mercy. They say without hesitation, "We all know that He is a most merciful God!" But what is the effect of this knowledge upon those, in whose hearts this holy "fear" does not dwell? Is it to make them love God the more? Nay, on the contrary, Is it not to make them love sin the more? Their doctrine is, "God is very merciful:" and their conclusion is, "*therefore* He will not be strict against us, and why should we be strict against ourselves?" On the other hand, what is the effect of a knowledge of God's mercy upon the man that fears Him?" Is it not to make him say, "God is merciful, *therefore* I will never willingly offend Him any more?" "The fear of the Lord," therefore, is truly called "the beginning of wisdom." Psa. cxi. 10.

Man, by nature, has no sense of the immeasurable guilt of his sin, and therefore he can have no appreciation of the immeasurable mercy of his God. We neither see, nor feel, sin, as we ought, till we are born again of God's Holy Spirit. The natural "heart is deceitful above all things." Jer. xvii. 9. We are ever ready to take as favorable a view of our own case as we possibly can. We do not wish to believe that we are so very bad, as some passages of the sacred Scriptures appear to declare. Indulging this low view of sin, and not conceiving ourselves to be very great sinners, we must necessarily entertain a very low view of that mercy which forbears with us: and hence, also, we shall be led to argue that God may easily forgive, seeing that we have not committed any great wrong. This is the inward feeling of unregenerate man. He says, "Surely it is easy for God to forgive me?" It is evident, therefore, that he can never be truly sensible of the Lord's kindness, nor really thankful to Him, as he ought to be, so long as he thinks and speaks in this self-righteous manner. Our hearts must be possessed by a deep view of sin, and there is but one only way to obtain it—that is, to learn it at the cross of Christ. Go thither in thought, and behold how much He suffered for your transgressions, and thence learn their magnitude and their malignity.

For the sake of illustration, take a man who entertains a low view of sin, but who nevertheless admits, that he has *some* sin; for the Scripture saith, "if we say that we have no sin, we make God a liar." Begin, then, the argument at the very lowest point, after this manner. Let us suppose that you have committed only one sin, and that you can look back upon your past life, and see it to be free from guilt, save in a single instance. I do not ask what that instance may have been. It is sufficient that you yourself have a conscious remembrance of it. Perhaps you have asked your fellow men; perhaps you have gone to the standard of the world, and their judgment has agreed with that of your own mind, that it was a small sin, and did no great harm to any one. Now come with me to another standard, and ascertain whether it will give a similar judgment. Behold your Saviour on the cross! The Son of the Most High God expires in agony upon the tree. For what? For your sin! And unless he had died, that one sin never can be pardoned. Is it, then, a small sin? Is it a trifle? Has your one sin done no great harm, when it has broken the law of the Most High God, and also crucified His only Son? Learn here, then, at the cross of Christ, that, however small, in your own sight, and in that of your fellow men, every sin is heinous in the sight of God. If there were not another sinner in the whole world but yourself, and if you had only committed that one sin, so offensive is it to a holy God, that Christ Jesus must have undergone all this suffering, and this bitter death, or it would certainly shut you out from heaven, for "therein can enter nothing that defileth."

The progress of the argument from this point, is as easy, as it is self-evident and undeniable. If the smallest sin, if a single sin, be thus hateful to God, what must two sins be? What must great sins be? What must be the sins of a day, of a week, and of a year? What must be the sins of ten, twenty, sixty, and seventy years? If one sin be thus immeasurable in its guilt, as to require immeasurable suffering, how immeasurable is the guilt of a whole life? How infinitely abhorrent to the Lord, must be our oft-repeated and aggravated transgressions?

It is, then, at the cross of Christ that we learn the exceeding greatness of God's mercy, and the exceeding sinfulness of our own sin, and see its awful depth. Let that depth teach us the corresponding depth of God's mercy; and let the vastness of the Lord's continued mercy, and of His multiplied loving-kindnesses, cry out to us of the enormity of our continued provocations, and of our multiplied transgressions. Let us thus travel in thought between God's conduct to us, and our conduct to Him. Let the one send us back to the other, with an increased, and an increasing, apprehension of these two great truths, God's mercy, and our own sinfulness, till we see both the one, and the other, to be indeed immeasurable; and then shall we be truly able to join with the Psalmist and say, "For as high as the heaven is above the earth, so great is His mercy toward them that fear Him."

Reader! dost thou "fear" God? If so, then immeasurable mercy is above and around thee. The Book of Truth teaches thee for thy comfort to say "The Lord has not rewarded me according to my iniquities: for according to the height of the heaven above the earth, so great is His mercy toward them that fear Him:" see marginal reading.

Whatsoever amount of this "fear" you now possess, pray to the Spirit of grace to increase it continually within your breast. The Apostle says, "Let us have grace, whereby we may serve God acceptably with reverence and godly fear." Heb. xii. 28. Cultivate diligently, therefore, the sentiment of holy fear. Watch anxiously against everything that would weaken it within you. For this purpose keep these two truths continually in remembrance, and say often to yourself, Immeasurable guilt—Immeasurable mercy! The former will fill your heart with humility. The latter will fill it with gratitude and joy. You will fear to offend a God who has been so immeasurably merciful to your soul. And you will also inwardly feel that you can never sufficiently love, never sufficiently serve, never sufficiently praise, so merciful a God and Saviour. Again and again say over to yourself, Immeasurable guilt—Immeasurable mercy! Let the one be as an ocean beneath your feet, and the other as the heavens above you, with Jesus near. Look not to the latter only, lest, like Peter, you presume. Look not to the former only, lest, like Peter, you despair. Look at both equally, and you will be safely preserved. Christ will come into your tempest-tossed bark: and then to the vessel of your soul the "love" of God will be as the sail, and the "fear" of God will be as the ballast, and over the immeasurable ocean of this sinful life, you shall have Christ for a Pilot, a steady and a prosperous voyage for your course, and a joyful entrance at last into the haven of rest, the heaven of God's immeasurable mercy.

XI.

Immeasurable Benefits Forgiveness.

THE BREADTH—UNBOUNDED: ITS EMBLEM—EAST FROM WEST.

As far as the east is from the west, so far hath He removed our transgressions from us.—Verse 12.

"God is love." Men have all sinned against Him, and yet a second time it is written "God is love." 1 John iv. 8, 16. That God loved His enemies, we never could have supposed, had He not Himself declared it. And even now that He has revealed that blessed truth in the unerring Word, we feel it difficult to believe that He really does regard us in Christ Jesus, with a love alike unmeasured and immeasurable, as undeserved as it will be by us for ever undeservable. So exceeding great and precious are the declarations of the Divine love contained in the Scriptures, that we feel tempted to regard it as presumptuous to apply them to ourselves. Yet the fact is as indubitable as our transgression. God so loved the world that He gave His only begotten Son to die for it; and a little reflection will convince us that God's love must be worthy of the heart in which it dwells—at once originating in Himself—love's boundless Fountain—and flowing forth in streams as unexhausted now by ages that are past, as inexhaustible hereafter by ages that are yet to come. That the Eternal Father should love His own dear Son, with an ardent, pure, and endless affection, we might readily have supposed; but that He should regard us with a sentiment at all approaching to that love, we never could have imagined. How astonished, therefore, do we feel to hear that dear Son declare, that the love with which His Father regards us, is the very same wherewith He himself is loved. "I have declared unto them Thy name, and will declare it: that the love wherewith Thou hast loved Me, may be in them, and I in them." John xvii. 26. Glorious declaration! It unfolds to us one of the highest honors which we enjoy in union with the second Adam. "Behold what manner of love the Father hath bestowed on us, that we should be called the sons of God." The love which surrounded us in creation is surpassed—most marvellously surpassed—by the love which embraces us in Redemption. All the saints are called to "comprehend," that is, to be for ever going forward more and more to "comprehend what is the breadth, and length, and depth, and height; and to know the love of Christ, which passeth knowledge, that they might be filled with all the fulness of God." Eph. iii. 19.

A love which "passes knowledge," must necessarily also surpass expression; we can only therefore judge of it by its proofs, and by its effects. The great proof of that love was given in delivering up that only begotten Son, who was so intensely loved, to be put to death as our Surety. And one of the blessed results of that love so demonstrated, is the complete forgiveness through Him of our transgressions.

David here thanks God a second time for that forgiveness. And so vast and wonderful does it appear to him, that he feels lost in the contemplation. In the third verse he blessed the Lord for the forgiveness of all his iniquities: and now in this twelfth verse he praises Him for the fulness and the perfection of that forgiveness. Marvellous truth—ALL MY INIQUITIES COMPLETELY PARDONED! The Psalmist knows not how to express the overpowering thought. His laboring mind seizes upon a most appropriate metaphor, and makes two most opposite points in nature unite to illustrate the wondrous theme. Nothing in creation presents a more complete idea of distance to the mind, than the rising, compared with the setting, of the sun. That glorious luminary was seen in one direction in the morning; it is seen in the very opposite direction in the evening. How vast is the space which it seems to have traversed. No power can bring it back to its former apparent position, or make the two opposite points to meet! Such is the illustration. Now turn to the East, and travel in thought to the remotest point. Were God of His mercy to take away your sins and place them there, how great would be the distance between your sins and you! Yet this is but half of the declaration of the Psalmist. Turn now to the West, and extend your thoughts again before you to the remotest point; then imagine your soul to be carried to that point in the arms of a sin-pardoning God, and that all your transgressions are left in the far East, how vast, how amazing, how incalculable, would now be the distance between your soul and them! Such is the declaration of the Psalmist regarding the freeness, the fulness, and the completeness, of God's forgiveness. "My sins," as if he had said, "were lying upon me as a weighty burden ;—they pressed upon my guilty conscience as utterly unpardonable: but God hath pardoned them. He hath taken them completely away. No power can bring them back against me, or make my sins and me to meet together again for condemnation. Bless the Lord, O my soul, and all that is within me bless His holy name, for as far as the east is from the west, so far hath He removed my transgressions from me."

Forgiveness, on the part of God, is neither partial nor temporary, like that of man. God pardons with a full heart. Man is ever ready to cast up afresh the old transgression. He forgives, but he does not forget. There is a painedness in his mind, and a peculiarity in his look and manner, even while he declares that he forgives, which impress us with a conviction that he does not admit us to the same place in his regard which we enjoyed before. The act of forgiveness necessarily places him in a superior, and ourselves in an inferior position, in reference to each other; and the consciousness of this inferiority produces a painedness also in our minds, and a peculiarity in our look and manner, which, even while we acknowledge our offence, repels him from advancing further to thorough reconciliation. So imperfect are all the best virtues in men, and so prone are we to misunderstand, and to misinterpret, the good we witness in each other. There is also, sometimes, an extraordinary movement in the human breast, of dislike arising toward those whom we have offended. Why? Because we fancy that they must dislike us! This feeling, wherever it obtains, must tend to still further estrangement. And thus, while forgiveness may have been pronounced and accepted, with sincerity on both sides, there is still a little poison left in the wound, so that it cannot become perfectly healed.

Forgiveness and entire reconciliation do not, therefore, always accompany each other between man and man. They invariably, however, accompany each other between God and man. They both originate in, and are consummated by, the rich and sovereign grace of God in Christ Jesus.

Pardon is vested in the hands of the God-Man, to be dispensed as He pleases. Matt. ix. 6. And a question here rises, On whom does Christ bestow this blessing? We reply, On those who draw near to Him as their only Surety and Sacrifice. Christ says, "Him that cometh to me I will in no wise cast out." John vi. 37. The poor sinner receives a full and free remission, whenever, under the drawings of the Divine Spirit, he comes to Jesus confessing his transgressions. Every sin, also, that he subsequently commits, he must confess, in like manner, over that sacrifice, and Christ will pardon it. This was typified under the Law. There was no pardon without confession—and no confession but over the blood of a sacrificial victim: and every time that an Israelite, who had sinned, brought his trespass-offering, and confessed over it his iniquity, he was to return from the altar with peace of conscience, and with thankfulness of heart, believing that he was a pardoned man. In like manner, the Christian is to come to Christ every time that he has sinned, and is to confess his transgression over Him, as his only trespass-offering; and he is to return from the throne of grace with peace of conscience, and with thankfulness of heart, believing that he is a pardoned man. None but those who believe in Jesus, and who turn from all their sins to His sacrifice, have any part or lot in this forgiveness. All others live in their sins, and die in their sins. Awful condition! involving this more awful conclusion, that they shall rise again in their sins, and stand before His judgment seat in their iniquities.

All those, however, who turn from sin to Jesus, are warranted, nay, commanded, to believe that they receive in Him, and from Him, an immediate, cordial, and complete forgiveness: as says the Apostle, "By Him all that believe are justified from ALL THINGS, from which ye could not be justified by the law of Moses." Acts xiii. 39. The language of Scripture is most explicit on this point. Its declarations are as comprehensive and varied, as they are truly consolatory and delightful. Simile after simile is employed to denote the fulness of the Divine forgiveness. Statements, arguments, assurances, promises, are multiplied to put our doubts to shame, and to banish all weakness and wavering from our faith.

When, for instance, the Lord Jehovah revealed His name and character to Moses, He proclaimed Himself to be "The Lord, the Lord God, merciful and gracious, long-suffering, and abundant in goodness and truth, forgiving iniquity, and transgression, and sin." Exod. xxxvi. 6, 7. Three terms are here employed, as it were to show that every possible *form* of guilt comes within the compass of the Lord's forgiveness :—and, that there is also no *degree* of it beyond the reach of pardon, He thus graciously assures us, "Come now and let us reason together, saith the Lord; though your sins be as scarlet, they shall be as white as snow; though they be red like crimson, they shall be as wool." Isa. i. 18. And yet, again, to prove that even *multiplied offences* shall not cut off the true penitent from the enjoyment of this blessing, the Lord thus instructs His Prophet to declare: "Let the wicked forsake his way, and the unrighteous man his thoughts: and let him return unto the Lord, and He will have mercy upon him; and to our God, for he will abundantly pardon" (margin, multiply to pardon). "For My thoughts are not your thoughts, neither are your ways My ways, saith the Lord." Isa. lv. 7, 8.

Thus we learn the truth of our blessed Saviour's declaration, that "all manner of sin and blasphemy shall be forgiven unto men." Even a word spoken against Himself shall be forgiven. The one only sin which He declares to be unpardonable, is the speaking evil of, or against, the Holy Ghost. Matt. xii. 31, 32.

What words, therefore, shall express the unlimited efficacy of the blood of Jesus, that blood which was expressly shed "for the remission of sins"? Matt. xxvi. 28. "Behold the Lamb of God, which taketh away the sin of the world." John i. 29. "It behoved Christ to suffer, and to rise from the dead the third day: and that repentance and remission of sins should be preached in His name among all nations, beginning at Jerusalem." Luke xxiv. 46, 47. Therefore the Apostles went everywhere preaching the glad tidings, and saying, "Be it known unto you therefore, men and brethren, that through this Man is preached unto you the forgiveness of sins." Acts xiii. 38. "For Him hath God exalted with His right hand, to be a Prince and a Saviour, for to give repentance to Israel, and forgiveness of sins." Acts v. 31. "To Him give all the prophets witness, that through His name, whosoever believeth in Him, shall receive remission of sins." Acts x. 43. "Repent ye therefore, and be converted, that your sins may be blotted out, when the times of refreshing shall come from the presence of the Lord." Acts iii. 19.

This full proclamation of forgiveness in the name of Jesus, is based on the ground of the New Covenant, ratified in His blood. That covenant is as large, as gracious, and as free, as heart can desire. If we had framed its terms ourselves, we could not have made them more favorable to our own case than God Himself has written them; for the Eternal Jeho vah most graciously promises therein, not only to forgive, but also to forget, the transgressions of His people! "I will make a new covenant with the house of Israel, and with the house of Judah. I will put my laws into their hearts, and in their minds will I write them: for I will forgive their iniquity and remember their sin no more." Jer. xxxi. 31—34, compared with Heb. x. 17, 18. What more, then, can be wanted after this? And yet, alas! we are slow to believe, and quick to doubt, the forgiveness of our God! And because we cannot find any goodness or worthiness in ourselves, on which to ground our plea for pardon, we are soon apt to give way to despondency and apprehension. Even this state of mind the Lord condescends to meet, by graciously revealing to us another argument of forgiveness, and saying, " I, even I, am He that blotted out thy transgressions FOR MINE OWN SAKE, and will not remember thy sins." Isa. xliii. 25. And again, in order to dispel every lingering suspicion of the reality and the fulness of His mercy, He declares in the very next chapter, " I have blotted out as a thick cloud thy transgressions, and as a cloud thy sins; return unto Me, for I have redeemed thee." Isa. xliv. 22. No wonder that Isaiah immediately exclaims, " Sing, O ye heavens, for the Lord hath done it. Shout, ye lower parts of the earth: break forth into singing, ye mountains, O forest and every tree therein; for the Lord hath redeemed Jacob, and glorified Himself in Israel." Oh, most gracious Lord, " There is forgiveness with Thee, that Thou mayest be feared, and with Thee is mercy and plenteous redemption." Psa. cxxx. 4—7. " Who is a God like unto Thee, that pardoneth iniquity, and passeth by the transgression of the remnant of His heritage? He retaineth not His anger for ever, because He delighteth in mercy. He will turn again, He will have compassion upon us; He will subdue our iniquities; and Thou wilt cast all their sins into the depths of the sea." Micah vii. 18, 19.

How immeasurable, therefore, do we learn, is the nature of that benefit, which the Psalmist has here celebrated. Every form of sin (with but one exception), every degree of sin, even oft-recurring sins, we are here instructed may obtain forgiveness. The readiness, the freeness, and the completeness, of that forgiveness, are put beyond all possibility of contradiction, for our loving Redeemer promises to "forgive," and to "forget" our iniquities—and to "blot out" the records of them from His book, "for His own sake." Yea, though they were like a "thick cloud" between us and the sun, He promises to erase them from the face of the heaven, and cause us to bask in the sunshine of the Divine favor;—and though they pressed upon us as an armed host in close pursuit for our destruction, yet would the Lord cast them into the very "depths of the sea:" and, though they came as an array of accusing witnesses, eager to give in their testimony to our discredit, yet would the Lord "remove" them from us, "as far as the east is from the west," and leave not a single transgression to appear against us within the whole visible horizon!

For this marvellous and immeasurable forgiveness, we are for ever indebted to the gracious Mediator. God gave that Mediator to us in His love; and have we with love accepted Him? The consent of all the parties, concerned in any transaction, is necessary to give it effect each in his own behalf. Reader, you are one of the parties concerned in this transaction, for you committed the sin. Your consent is therefore necessary to give it effect for your salvation: for no man is to be saved against his own will. All God's people are made "willing" to consent to this mode of salvation in the day of the Spirit's power. Psa. cx. 3. The transaction between God the Father, and His Son, the appointed Mediator, you can never annul. "If you believe not, yet He abideth faithful." That work of the Mediator is to stand, and to be admired through all eternity, whether you approve of it or not. To you as a natural man, the great truth of which we here speak, will, alas, appear only as foolishness; for in your own wisdom you will neither understand nor believe it. Therefore you will never be willing of yourself, to append to it the seal of your approbation and adherence. But, oh, let me beseech you, for your own sake, to cry earnestly to the Lord God to "work in you to will and to do" by his good Spirit. Cry to that Spirit to enlighten your mind to know "the things that are freely given you of God." 1 Cor. ii. 12. Intreat of Him to produce in you true repentance and a lively faith, that you may be enabled to confess your sins over the blood of this Mediator, and to believe that God is faithful and just toward Him to forgive your sins for His sake, and to cleanse you from all unrighteousness. 1 John i. 9.

Better were it for you never to have heard of Christ, than to hear and not to accept of Him. Better far will it be for the poor heathen in the day of judgment than for you. They have never heard of that Saviour whom you reject. But if you reply, that you do not reject Him, and that all that can be charged against you is, that you do not give as much time or attention to his religion as perhaps you might, then the Bible asks, "How shall we escape if we *neglect* so great salvation?" Heb. ii. 3. The neglecting of the salvation, is the rejecting of the Saviour. There is no neutral ground. You must adopt one or other of the two alternatives. If the work of Christ were yet to be undertaken, and if God consulted you whether this Mediator should be appointed or not; there would be room for you to consider the proposal, and either to accept, or to decline it, and propose another. But now that the work has been already accomplished, no room remains but only to accept or to reject the Saviour.

Oh, consider your position! Realize the solemn, but blessed, circumstances, in which the death of Christ has placed you. God, the Great Creditor, has accepted the Surety's payment of your debts; and He has therefore given you into the hands of the God-Man, who has bought you with His blood. This gracious Surety is waiting, and calling, upon you to acknowledge and to embrace Him as your Redeemer. Jesus is stretching out His hand of mercy toward you. He weeps over you, and says, "Oh that thou wouldst know, even thou at least in this thy day, the things that belong unto thy peace, before they be for ever hid from thine eyes." "To-day," then, "while it is called to-day, harden not your heart." God has appointed Christ, and do you refuse Him? God has accepted Christ, and will you reject Him? God laid your iniquities upon His head, and will you not be thankful for such an act of unparalleled mercy? Ungrateful man! the very least sin would sink you to perdition. O, that you were wise. Take warning ere it be too late. "Behold, now is the accepted time; behold, now is the day of salvation." An Almighty Saviour with His great salvation is standing at your door. Every blessing it contains, He bids you take, without money and without price. Listen to His gracious word: "Behold, I stand at the door, and knock: if any man hear my voice, and open the door, I will come in to him, and will sup with him, and he with Me." Rev. iii. 20. But have you barred the door of your heart against Him? Undo these bars, I entreat you. Put aside every doubt, cast off the chain of unbelief. Open wide the door of your heart to Christ. "As though God did beseech you by us, we pray you in Christ's stead, Be ye reconciled to God." 2 Cor. v. 20.

The blessedness of pardon, and of reconciliation, who can describe? To be made friends again with the King of Heaven; to have our sins pardoned—our persons accepted—and our love returned; to be freed from every fear, liberated from every debt, and gladdened in every feeling; to have no more differences, no more estrangement, and no further separation from the Father of our spirits: this is indeed joy unspeakable.

The blessedness of pardon, and of reconciliation, who can describe? The prodigal returns home to his Father's house, and his sins are not once mentioned unto him, Ezek. xviii. 22,—his Father casts them all behind His back, Isa. xxxviii. 17,—his debts are blotted out of His book, Isa. xliii. 25,—they are remembered no more, Heb. x. 18. Happy prodigal, but prodigal no longer! Thy Elder Brother neither frowns at thee for thy return, nor chides at others for thy reception. All that the Father hath is His, and all that He has He gives to thee. The "sandals" put upon thy feet, are His "preparation of the Gospel of peace." Eph. vi. 15. The "ring" placed on thy finger, He has obtained for thee as a token and pledge of higher honors. And the "best robe" now brought forth to array thee, is the best in heaven—it is the robe of righteousness which Jesus has wrought out. Happy prodigal, but prodigal no longer! Does this unexpected joy and gladness at thy return, fill thee with remorse at thy long estrangement? Dost thou not look upon a reconciled Father, and upon an Elder Brother whom thou hast pierced, and art thou in such bitterness at times that thou canst not forgive thyself, or believe that They can forgive thee? And do thy past sins not unfrequently rise up, like a thick cloud, to darken the sunshine of thy soul? Hear that Father and that Brother saying with one voice, "I have blotted out as a thick cloud thy transgressions, and as a cloud thy sins." Isa. xliv. 22.

In the progress of thy course through life, do infirmities encompass thee, and besetting sins sometimes obtain the advantage? Do their present pressure, and their past remembrance, weaken thy faith, straiten thy prayers, and mar thy intercourse with God? Take courage: hold on thy way, contending against all sin. Plead with Him His own promise. Cry to Him in the all-prevailing name of Jesus, and He will cast all thy transgressions, not into the waves to be again thrown up, but into the very "depths" of the sea, never more to appear against thee.

Or art thou drawing near to the close of thy earthly day? Is thy sun sinking in the far west of life? Say, hadst thou a stormy morning, and a chequered day of clouds and sunshine? And didst thou often fear that gloom and darkness would envelope thy departure? Behold, at evening time it shall be light (Zech. xiv. 7), if thou dost hold fast the beginning of thy confidence steadfast unto the end. Heb. iii. 14. "The sun shall be no more thy light by day; neither for brightness shall the moon give light unto thee: but the Lord shall be unto thee an everlasting light, and thy God thy glory. Thy sun shall no more go down; neither shall thy moon withdraw itself: for the Lord shall be thine everlasting light, and the days of thy mourning shall be ended." Isa. lx. 19, 20. Made one with Christ, the Sun of Righteousness, thy setting shall be bright and radiant with His glory. Fear not; Jesus is with thee; and, behold, at His word, how serene are the heavens around thee. The winds are hushed. The sea is calm. The sky is clear. Its vault is glowing with His golden beams. Where now are the storms that alarmed thee in the morning? Where now are the clouds that darkened thine onward path? They are scattered and gone; if sought for, they cannot be found. Jer. l. 20. Calm, then, on the bosom of thy God, sink thou to rest: and as thou goest down, even thy lips shall be heard, by grace, to say, Bless the Lord, O my soul, for "as far as the east is from the west, so far hath He removed my transgressions from me."

XII.

Immeasurable Benefits—Pity.

ITS DEPTH—UNFATHOMABLE: ITS EMBLEM—A FATHER'S.

Like as a father pitieth his children, so the Lord pitieth them that fear Him. For He knoweth our frame, He remembereth that we are dust.—Verses 13, 14.

THESE verses present to us the third metaphor, by which the Psalmist attempts to measure, and to magnify, the goodness of his Lord. He had just before extolled the greatness of His mercy, and expatiated on the completeness of His forgiveness. The height of the heaven above the earth, and the distance of the east from the west, were made to lend their aid in illustration of these truths. Yet, striking as these comparisons are, they do not satisfy the mind of the Psalmist—they do not adequately unfold the character and the excellency of His Lord. David, therefore, employs another illustration, as touching as it is appropriate; and follows it up by an explanatory argument, as simple as it is conclusive. He selects the most revered name which the human vocabulary can furnish: he instances a relationship in which love and authority, wisdom and grace, tenderness and compassion, are exhibited in rich and harmonious combination; and by a single word he presents to us a picture, which every human being can recognize, appreciate, and admire.

Who that has experienced the love, and the pity, of a parent, or that has felt the yearnings of a father towards his child within his own breast, can read these words without understanding or emotion? We comprehend their meaning at a glance. We feel their power as we listen to their sound. The pity of a parent is the purest, the tenderest, the highest, which this world can furnish; and such, we understand, is the pity of the Lord. The paternal character and relationship on earth, are the types of a paternal character and relationship in heaven. A father's tender feeling towards his children, presents the best possible illustration of the feelings of the Great God in Christ Jesus towards them that fear him.

David felt in himself that he was altogether unworthy of the mercies which he had acknowledged in the previous verses—unworthy even of the very least of them. Like believers in all ages, doubtless the Psalmist was often tempted to question whether he was indeed a child of God. But now, the more minutely that he gave his attention to these mercies, the more that his mind became impressed, and his gratitude awakened, by the contemplation of them, the more do their marvellous origin open to his view. His mind had been occupied with the enumeration of the benefits which he had received, and now it becomes joyfully absorbed by the discovery of this living truth—this gracious secret—which they disclose,—that in the very heart of God there exists a paternal pity towards him! This enables him at once to perceive that there is only one way in which these bestowments can be correctly accounted for on the part of God—one only way in which they can either be rightly accepted, duly acknowledged, or properly employed on the part of man. He had ascended from mercy to mercy, and now he has reached the climax of his blessedness in the heart of God as his Father, and, therefore, he pours forth his highest notes of praise upon this highest string of all earthly relationships, and says, "Like as a father pitieth his children, so the Lord pitieth them that fear Him. For He knoweth our frame, He remembereth that we are dust."

The right contemplation of our blessings, leads us directly into the heart of their Bestower. "Every good gift and every perfect gift is from above, and cometh down from the Father of lights, with whom is no variableness neither shadow of turning." James i. 17. The Psalmist rises above and beyond the mercy displayed in works of beneficence, and the forgiveness exhibited in acts of pardon. These are outward—these are expressions—these are results—these are streams. David now passes from the outward to the inward,—from the expression to the feeling,—from the results to the cause,—from the stream to the fountain. He searches into the inner workings and recesses of the Divine benevolence, and rejoices to behold immeasurable compassions treasured there,—the heart of God abounding with paternal pity. Oh, rich and inexhaustible mine in the Divine bosom! Blind and ignorant creature that I am, I valued it not at all. I sought my pleasures and my profits, on the mere surface of things. I knew not this hidden wealth; but He that knew it from all eternity, the only begotten Son, hath come forth out of that bosom, to declare its treasures to my soul, to lead me into that mine, and to make it all my own!

Glorious is the discovery which a poor sinner thus makes, under the guidance of the good Spirit. Trials, difficulties, and disappointments, may have attended all his previous searchings. Now, by that unerring Spirit, he is led away from things seen and outward, and he is taken down, as it were, underground, by a deep and dark descent. He is led along through the various workings of sin and self, where the cross-shafts of Satan, and the world, and the flesh, meet him at every turn. Tremblings, it may be, seize his limbs, cold damps stand upon his forehead, and temptations to go back, and hesitations to go forward, rise thick and fast upon his heart. Aided, however, by divine grace, he grasps more firmly the safety lamp of the Word, as it brightly burns with the oil of the Spirit. Re-established in confidence, he presses courageously forward, and reaches the spot where the rich vein shows itself. Entranced, he gazes with admiration upon its sparkling brightness, and scans in vain its breadth and length, its depth and height; these, he is informed, are all immeasurable: and astonished is his soul, with a great astonishment, when he is next informed, "All this is yours in Christ."

What a discovery for thee, poor sinner, that thou hast a treasure in the heart of God! Where now are thy regrets, after the surface-world thou hast left? Where are the fears that oppressed thee in the dark and terrible passages of thy descent? Where are thy temptations to return? Are they not all fled at this joyful discovery? Welcome, wilt thou now say, welcome is the darkness of the pit, welcome are the damps of self-abhorrence, and welcome are the difficult and narrow passages of the world, since I have found this treasure at the end of them. Oh, it is good for me that I have been afflicted. The bitterest weanings from things seen and superficial, have been to me most blessed. Gladly do I give up whatsoever the world holds dear. For very joy, I will now sell all that I have, and buy this priceless field. Hither will I repair by night, by day, that I may count my spiritual wealth. Descending to my hidden treasure, standing within this spiritual mine, above and beneath me, on the right hand and on the left, are the rich ores of grace. I am surrounded still with God. His heart abounds with thoughts, desires, and purposes of love and pity towards me. Oh, it is good for me to be here—to be hid in God through Jesus Christ. "How precious are Thy thoughts unto me, O God, how great is the sum of them! If I should count them, they are more in number than the sand. When I awake, I am still with Thee." Psa. cxxxix. 17, 18.

Of all the names by which Jehovah has revealed His character, there is none more endearing than the title of Father. Man by nature knows not God in this near relationship. One great object of the Saviour's mission into our world was to manifest the Father. "I have declared unto them Thy name, and will declare it, that the love wherewith Thou hast loved Me, may be in them and I in them." John xvii. 26. Teaching his disciples how to address their Great

Creator, the blessed Redeemer said, "When ye pray, say Our Father."

The God we have offended, presents Himself before us in the relation of a Father, and invites us to occupy toward Him the position of children. This is the relation from which sin had cast us out, and to which Christ has come to restore us. He condescended to occupy the place of an earthly child, that we might obtain the privilege of heavenly adoption. That adoption not more surely implies mutual obligations, than by grace it certainly ensures their mutual performance. "But I said, how shall I put thee among the children, and give thee a pleasant land, a goodly heritage of the hosts of nations? and I said, thou shall call me, My Father; and shalt not turn away from Me." Jer. iii. 19.

The title of Father, applied to God, implies that He is able and willing to bestow all the kindness and the benefits which a child may require. To call ourselves His adopted children, implies that we are bound and desirous to render to Him all the obedience and affection which a parent can demand.

Really to know God as a Father in Christ Jesus, will both effectually convince our heart of His paternal "pity," and inspire it with filial "fear." Without this knowledge we can neither appreciate the former sentiment on His part, nor exhibit the latter on our own. Indeed, we never scripturally and spiritually know the great God, till we have learned to regard Him in Christ Jesus as our Father. We may know a great deal about the Maker of heaven and earth: we may believe that He is, and that He possesses wisdom and power unrivalled, and holiness and goodness unsurpassed. We may be able to describe the whole circle of His glorious attributes; but a collection of attributes, however glorious, is not God. The Jews, His covenanted people, their scribes, their priests, and learned doctors of the law, knew a great deal about the Almighty; they conceived that they had learned all that was necessary to be known of Him; and they could even in words declare that He was their Father. But Jesus, His true Son, told them that they knew Him not. John viii. 21, 54, 55.

Till the heart of man, as a child, is brought to know and to love God as a Father in Christ Jesus, all other knowledge of Him is ineffectual to salvation. It is the felt and sanctifying apprehension of this nearest and most important of all relationships which unites us to our Great Creator in the closest bond, and produces within us the purest love, the deepest reverence. Suppose a child to have been early separated from its parents, by one or other of the many vicissitudes of life, and to have grown up to manhood without any personal knowledge of its father. It may have been in a dark night, amid the perils of the deep, when a gallant vessel struck upon a rock, and went to pieces before the morning dawn. Some of the passengers and crew may have found a watery grave, while "some on boards and some on broken pieces of the ship, may have escaped to land." A young emigrant-merchant may have sought, amongst the rescued remnant on the strand, for his wife and child, but he may have sought in vain; and then, disconsolate and miserable, he may have gathered the wreck of his fortunes together, and wandered whithersoever a way presented itself. Reluctant to return to his native country, he may have travelled from place to place, and at last settled as a merchant in a busy city, but with his thoughts continually reverting to the objects of his bereaved affections, now sunk together, as he supposes, in their last sleep. But perhaps it may be that the mother alone was laid beneath the billow. The buoyant clothing of the child may have floated its light burden on the surface, and the same surging timber which struck down the one, may have borne off the other in safety. Drifted away to sea, a passing vessel may have picked up the weeping child, and carried it to a land of strangers. Suppose that child to advance in years, ignorant of its native country, and speaking a language which its parents had never known; and suppose, that, with energies developed and advantages supplied, he goes forth into the world to push his fortunes on land and sea; and that in the pursuit of business, he is brought into acquaintance with foreign nations and with various merchants. We may conceive that in his intercourse with these, he meets, in a far-distant city, with a merchant whose intelligence delights him, whose kindness wins upon his regard, and whose probity and honor render safe all his transactions. Would not self-interest bind him to that merchant, and make him anxious to secure his favor, while respect and admiration would be increased at every successive interview. That youth might, after a time, conceive that he knew that merchant, and that he had become well acquainted with his character. So indeed he might in many important respects, and for the general requirements of business; but, if we suppose that this merchant is his father, how obvious is it that he does not yet know him in the one only relationship which is to bind his heart to him for ever, and which is to constrain him to give up with joy his own separate interests, and to regard those of his merchant friend as paramount in importance to his own, and as actually including and promoting them.

Suppose, then, that in the progress of their acquaintanceship, some circumstance occurs that incites inquiry on the part of the elder merchant. Suppose, that, in the process of that inquiry, one fact transpires after another which produces certainty in his mind, and that he seeks an opportunity to make himself known to him as his father; how great would be the inward change in the younger? How deepened now would be that respect which he had before entertained? How inflamed into love would be that admiration which had been before kindled? And how overjoyed would he be to find that he had a place in the home and the heart of that hitherto merchant stranger, but now newly-discovered father? That youth would feel that now he began to know him in the fullest sense. Now would he cease from the pursuit of his own business and of his own interests; now would he regard them as all merged in the business and the interests of his father—now former connexions and relation ships would be held subservient to this one grand, all comprehensive, relationship; and now no longer wandering and restless, he would dwell at home, and find his truest happiness in union and communion with his father.

Reader, you are this shipwrecked child. In a dark night

of sin you were separated from your Father. Your life has been spared, and your energies have been developed in the course of years. Various objects in life have solicited and engaged your attention; and, amid the variety of your other pursuits, you may have entered upon the business of religion. All its transactions you may have discharged with punctuality and attention, so as to have profited above many your equals. Gal. i. 14. In the interchanges of that business-religion, you may have had dealings with a Great Being whom you called God, and you may have formed the highest respect and admiration for His sacred character. All your intercourses with Him may have been seduously prosecuted in the way of business, in the path of duty, in the pursuit of your own interests. Diligent and exact in the performance of your different obligations, you may yet have felt no real pleasure in their performance—and, like other men after duty was over, you may have thought that when you had read your portion of Scripture, and said your prayers ("performed your devotions," as it is called), you were all right, and that therefore you could now enjoy yourself, and indulge in everything agreeable, either to your circumstances or your inclination. A conviction, too, might have inwardly possessed your mind that this Great Being had His interests to promote, and that you also had yours; and that were these united, you could depend on His support; but that were these separated, you must each seek after your own. You might have conceived that you knew this God, and that you were well acquainted with His character and his attributes, and you might have flattered yourself that you were rising in His favor, and that, ere long, you might hope to regard Him as your friend. All this time the true God was to you only as a stranger. But suppose that in the course of your formal services, God revealed Himself to you as your long lost Father, and that by the blessed inward persuasion of the Spirit of His Son, you were enabled to cry "Abba, Father," how great would be the change? How blessed would now become all your intercourses with Him under this transporting knowledge? How joyful would become all your performances of religious service? The irksome sense of duty would give way to the feeling of delight, the spirit of bondage would be cast out by the spirit of adoption. Now would you begin to know God; now would your own personal interests become merged in those of your newly-discovered Father; now all former connexions and relationships would be held subservient to this one paramount relationship; and now no longer seeking and hoping to purchase His favor by your religious performances, you would rejoice in His favor already bestowed in Jesus, and serve Him from love already felt. All the admiration and respect which the knowledge of God's attributes had awakened, would now be deepened a hundred fold, and made immediately and for ever effectual, shedding abroad over your heart, at one and the same moment, a filial love and a filial fear.

By this verse the Psalmist bids you carry these sentiments with you to the close of life—to cheer each difficult step as you advance, to gladden each solitary hour, to lighten every oppressive burden, and to remove every shadow of anxiety: for this is the gracious assurance which it contains, "Like as a father pitieth his children, so the Lord pitieth them that fear Him."

The "pity" here spoken of is one of the deepest and purest emotions in the human breast. It is not the mere pity of a superior to an inferior, of a master to a servant, of a judge to a criminal. It is not the cold pity of a stranger to a beggar, when he gives an alms. It is not the pity of a rich merchant, when he drops some expressions of commiseration over a poor bankrupt that has lost his all. Nor is it that better feeling, with which one kind neighbor visits another in his sickness, and administers to his wants; nor yet is it that deeper emotion, with which the pious parents of a happy family deplore the helpless condition of the children of a departed friend, now left orphans and desolate. No, it is none of these which the Psalmist here means. It is the pity with which these parents regard their own children that he here describes—a yearning emotion, deep and full, which none but parents feel. In parental pity there is no scorn—no implied superiority on their part, no insinuated inferiority on ours. It is not a pity which mortifies and lowers while it relieves, but, on the contrary, which gladdens and elevates the soul. It is the tender yearnings of a compassion which watches over a much-loved child—which sympathizes with its every pain, enters into its varied feelings, supplies its numerous wants, and anticipates its unuttered desires. It is a pity which begins at birth, lasts through life, and terminates only with death. It is a pity which listens to the cries of infancy, bears with the waywardness of youth, and patiently and perseveringly administers to soul and body. It is a pity which grows with a child's growth, and strengthens with its strength—which compassionates its youthful ignorance, its fretful tempers, its impatient moods—a pity which is long-suffering through successive years: which distinguishes between the offence and the offender, punishing the one, and yet loving the other—a pity which fastens on the least, and it may be the last, glimmering of penitence in the back-sliding child, which hates to cast him away, and longs for his return to reconciliation and affection. In a single word, the word of the Psalmist, it is parental pity—the parental pity of God our Father—a pity which is entertained only by parents towards their children, and which God, as a Parent, entertains towards His—a pity which leads the earthly and the heavenly Parent, tenderly to consider all the feelings and the desires, all the circumstances and the necessities, of each individual member of the family, and to provide for all alike with readiness and faithfulness, with fulness and delight.

The difference between the pity of the Lord and the pity of man, may be illustrated by the difference between the pity which a parent, and a stranger, exhibit towards the same object. You gaze, perhaps, on the wan and wasted countenance of a child, whom you had seen before in the bloom and the brightness of health. You observe its drooping, pining state, and you feel within you an emotion of pity. But, however full and sincere that feeling may be within your own breast, how far short does it come of that deep and constant, that self-denying and all-absorbing pity, which flows in full tide from the heart of the parent to that sickly child! Such is the illustration which God Himself employs to unfold the fulness, the constancy, the tenderness, the intensity of His own pity towards His people: "As one whom his mother comforteth, so will I comfort you." Isa. lxvi. 13.

Instantaneous and irrepressible are the feelings of a parent at the discovery of suffering in a child. Words cannot utter them. The trembling hand; the agitated frame; the gushing tear; the prompt and energetic efforts to relieve, proclaim the presence and the power of parental pity. Nor is this displayed only toward the gentle and the good; even the unthankful and the forward are included in the tender commiserations of parental pity. Who pities the prodigal?—the Parent! Who thinks most frequently of the absent youth?—the Parent! Who embraces, yea, runs to meet him at his return?—the Parent! Who pities, it may be, even the rebel, and strives to save his life?—his intended victim, the Parent! Who, of all the human race, weeps inconsolably at his death, and exclaims, Would God I had died for thee?—that one only man who could add as a Parent "My son, my son."

Unfathomable as is the depth of parental pity in the breast of man, how deep and inexhaustible must be the pity which resides in the heart of God! And as the Saviour, when adducing the goodness of parents to their children, rises infinitely above it in His argument, and concludes, "How much more will your heavenly Father give good things," even the Holy Spirit, "to them that ask Him!"

compare Matt. vii. 11, with Luke xi. 13, so ought we to rise infinitely above the height to which this beautiful comparison, this appropriate illustration, of the Psalmist has raised us, and argue thus, "If an earthly father pitieth his children, how much more doth our heavenly Father pity them that fear Him."

The pity of the Lord is infinite, like all His other attributes. Unlike that of some earthly parents, it is not a weak, or a fitful,—not a promiscuous, or a temporary pity. It is not a mere sentiment that lies at one time idly in the breast, and then at another flows forth with indiscriminate profusion. The pity of the Lord is not an evanescent feeling, not a fitful compassion; but a calm, constant, and everlasting principle. It is founded on the holiness, regulated by the wisdom, poured forth by the love, made fruitful by the power, and rendered permanent by the unchangeableness, of Jehovah. The pity of the Lord is altogether pure and perfect, entirely free and full; alike boundless, inexhaustible, and everlasting.

As earthly parents have their pity deepened, and called forth into lively exercise by the knowledge of their children's helplessness; and, even after they have grown up to years, retain in full remembrance the weak and tiny form in which these children once lay within their arms, "SO the Lord pitieth them that fear Him. For He knoweth our frame, He remembereth that we are dust!" This is the explanatory argument added by the Psalmist. Man carries about with him the frame-work of mortality. He sees it daily, and makes it subservient to all his wants and wishes. Yet he knows it not. In the ignorance of his uninstructed mind, he understands not the original construction of his own frame —the marvellous mechanism of his various parts—the different functions of its individual members—or the unity and the mutual dependence of the whole. All these are beyond the reach of common observation. They stand out only before the eye of careful study, and of minute and long-continued investigation; and even then, only in part. The vast majority of mankind pass away out of the world, without knowing, or seeking to know, the nature of their own mortal frame. But the Great Creator "knoweth our frame." Every part of it is open to His eye. All its excellencies and its defects, are conspicuous to His gaze. His hand formed it at the first; and all the reasons for the peculiar formation of its various parts were maturely weighed by Him. It was no mere physical power which caused the human being to stand erect upon the earth—it was the deliberate act, the considerate purpose, of the Most High. God had said, "Let there be light," and there was light. God had said, "Let the earth bring forth," and the earth brought forth. He spake, and it was done. But when man was about to be created, the Triune Jehovah spake as it were in counsel: "Let us make man after OUR image." It was a deliberate act of creation—an act in which forethought, wisdom, love and power, were all harmoniously exerted. Not that these were wanting in the creation of the whole material world, but that in the creation of man they were conspicuously and pre-eminently exhibited. The Lord, then, "knoweth our frame," because He is the Creator of it. He also "knows" it, because He is its continual Preserver. We live, we move, we have our being in God. All would go wrong in the multiform and complex machinery of our bodily frame, did not the Lord continually watch over its various movements. His perfect knowledge of every part, enables Him at once to give to each that special care which it requires. The forethought and the love, the wisdom and the power, so conspicuously displayed in the original creation of our frame, are all exhibited in its daily and hourly preservation. Again the Lord "knows" it, because He never ceases to bear a continual "remembrance" of its original composition. This is here assigned by the Psalmist as one great moving cause of His paternal pity. When the Lord beholds the sins and the short-comings, the sufferings and the death of those that fear Him, He pities them as a father pitieth his children; "for He remembers that they are dust." Man himself forgets this fact. Our self-love would hide it from our sight, and our pride would banish it from our recollection. But the Lord ever remembers it. The day, the hour, the very moment, of man's creation, are all fresh before the Eternal Mind. Upon the selected spot of earth the Omniscient Eye was fixed,—upon its particles of dust the Almighty Hand was laid, and instantly the perfect form of the first man lay moulded on its mother earth. Thus the Lord God formed man out of the dust of the ground. And never has He forgotten that moment, or that work. He saw the uncreated Adam in his original dust. And He beholds all His created children also in their native nothingness. When he sees man vaunting himself in pomp and power, He regards him as a piece of animated dust. And to keep his children ever humble, He bids them look upon the rock whence they were hewn, and to the hole of the pit whence they were digged. Isa. li. 1.

To those who fear the Lord, and who strive to please Him, this "remembrance," on the part of their heavenly Father, is most soothing and consolatory. They feel assured thereby, that He who thus intimately "knows their frame," and has so "long remembered" whereof they were made, will pity, will comfort and sustain them, in all the difficulties and dangerous paths of their earthly pilgrimage. A parent ever looks upon his child with the knowledge and the remembrance of its once infant helplessness. The child carries not this knowledge about with him; but the parent never can divest himself of the remembrance, nor cease to be actuated by the pity, which that recollection awakens. The pity of the Lord is based on the same ground: "He knoweth our frame, He remembereth that we are dust:" and therefore He will neither exact, nor expect, more from us than we are able to perform. Had we constructed a living being out of the ground, who, when he came to act for himself, should prove disobedient and ungrateful, we should be disposed to call his origin to remembrance, and say, What could we expect from a pillar of dust! And such is man to the Most High God—a pillar of dust! The Lord remembers this. In dealing with all the children of Adam, He does not forget their feeble origin. Even when He chastises us for our sins, His heart pities us under every stroke; "for He knoweth our frame, He remembereth that we are dust." It is written, "The Lord doeth not afflict willingly, nor grieve the children of men." We read that "His soul was grieved for the misery of Israel," when they cried to Him in the soreness of their strait, and in the bitterness of their repentance. Judges x. 16. "In all their afflictions," we rejoice to be informed that "He was afflicted:" and the angel of His presence saved them: in His love and in His pity He redeemed them, and He bare them and carried them all the days of old. Isa. lxiii. 9. The heavenly Parent never forgot that they were dust.

Earthly parents may not at all times act with unvarying consideration. They may at one time exact too much, and at another expect too little, from their children. They may not make adequate allowance for their different dispositions, or their peculiar infirmities. The sensitive feelings of one child they may not understand; and the individual circumstances of another they may altogether overlook, or not sufficiently remember. But it is not so with our heavenly Father. "He knoweth our frame." He possesses a thorough understanding of our whole nature—its failings and its feelings—its wants and its dispositions—its tendencies and its propensities—its strength and its weakness. In calling us to the performance of duty, in exhorting us to follow after good, and in warning us against approaches to evil, throughout our whole pilgrimage from earth to heaven, "He remembereth that we are dust." His ancient people were comforted and encouraged by this humbling, yet remarkable topic: "Fear not, thou worm Jacob." Isa. xli. 14. "But now thus saith the Lord that created thee, oh Jacob, and He that formed thee, oh Israel, fear not." Isa. xliii. 1. God was mindful of their original nothingness.

Many are the proofs and instances recorded in Scripture that the "Lord is very pitiful, and of tender mercy." James v. 11. When Jesus was come near and beheld the city of Jerusalem, "he wept over it" at the thought of its destruction. Luke xix. 41. So full of pity was His tender heart, that it was ever alive to human suffering, and continually touched with a feeling for our infirmities. Again we read that, when Jesus saw Mary "weeping, and the Jews also weeping which came with her, He groaned in the spirit and was troubled, and said, Where have ye laid him? They said unto Him, Lord, come and see. Jesus wept. Then said the Jews, behold how He loved Him." John xi. 36.

When our blessed Lord was passing through His bitter agony in Gethsemane, His pity was not absorbed by His own sufferings. He "knew the frame" of His slumbering disciples. He remembered that they were "dust:" and from that remembrance His pity made for them that only apology which could at all extenuate their conduct: "The spirit is willing, but the flesh is weak." Matt. xxvi. 41.

Let us fervently thank God through Christ Jesus for His paternal pity. Let us praise Him for His continual remembrance of our lowly origin. Let us ever bear that origin in remembrance ourselves to keep us truly humble; and let a sense of our nothingness before Him, cause us constantly to draw closer to the Lord. The exhibition of His pity as that of a Father, teaches us at once our duty and our privilege. It is our duty to fear Him as children, and it is our privilege to love Him as a father. It is our duty never to distrust His pity, and it is our privilege to believe that His pity is inexhaustible. It is our duty to glorify His pity by imitating it in our conduct towards our fellow men, and it is our privilege to rejoice in that pity as embracing all who fear Him, equally with ourselves, and ourselves equally with them.

Blessed is the life of the believer—joyful is his duty—and glorious is his privilege! He is called to live with God as a child with a father. He is commanded to cast all his care upon that Father's wisdom, and all his sins upon His pardoning love. And he is privileged to know assuredly that God as his Father in Christ Jesus, pitieth and careth for him. 1 Pet. v. 7. Is this, dear Reader, the blessed life you are now leading? Is this the joyful duty you are daily discharging? Is this the glorious privilege you are hourly enjoying? In Christ Jesus you are welcome to enter on them all with thanksgiving at this very moment. "The Spirit and the bride say, come. And let him that heareth say, come. And let him that is athirst come. And whosoever will, let him take the water of life freely." Rev. xxii. 17.

XIII.

Everlasting Benefits.

EXHIBITING THE LENGTH OF GOD'S LOVE, IN CONTRAST WITH THE BREVITY OF HUMAN EXISTENCE.

As for man, his days are as grass: as a flower of the field, so he flourisheth. For the wind passeth over it, and it is gone; and the place thereof shall know it no more. But the mercy of the Lord is from everlasting to everlasting upon them that fear Him, and His righteousness unto children's children; to such as keep His covenant, and to those that remember His commandments to do them.—Verses 15—18.

Amid the many changes of the world, and the passing away of its generations, how desirable, how necessary, how delightful, is it to possess enduring realities, and to look forward to the enjoyment of everlasting happiness! Such is the substantial possession, and the gladdening prospect, of the true believer. He, alone, of all the children of men, can afford both to hold the world at its real value, and to let it go as of no value. He alone can calmly and joyfully contemplate the rapid flight of time and the nearness of eternity. He alone can "take joyfully the spoiling of his goods" by oppressors; the spoiling of his health by sickness; the spoiling of his strength by age; the despoiling of his life by death; knowing, in himself, that he has in heaven, and in God, "a better and an enduring substance." The man of the world labors, through fear of the discovery, to conceal the inscription which is written on all things here below: the true believer, on the contrary, labors to decipher its various letters, and courageously gives utterance to the universal maxim which they contain, Vanity of vanities—all is vanity!

The Psalmist possessed this spiritual courage, because he possessed the true spiritual wealth. He felt that he could afford to lose everything on earth, even life itself, because he could lay his hand on a counter-balancing, and a far higher, gain. When, therefore, he had made the admission that man is but "dust," he does not suddenly turn from the melancholy subject, and recoil from its further contemplation. On the contrary, he proceeds immediately to enlarge upon the theme; and is led to place, in juxtaposition with it, another theme so glorious in character, that it strips the former of its horror, and lightens its dark shade. Indeed, it is only as the necessary shading to his picture, that the Psalmist introduces this sad topic. The subject which he had proposed for his pencil was the goodness of the Lord. It was not his object and intention to speak of human nothingness in this Psalm. But mark how incidentally the doctrine is introduced, or rather introduces itself. He had been ruminating on the marvellous pity of the Lord, and rejoicing to regard it as that of a tender-hearted Father; and finding no way to account for the existence of that pity, he was naturally, and, as it were, necessarily led to add, "for He knoweth our frame, He remembereth that we are dust." The greatness of God's pity leads him to assign his own insignificance as its cause. The prominency of that bright object in the fore-ground, casts this deep shadow behind it; and, as he proceeds to impart breadth and depth to that shadow, by disposing his colors in relief, behold another object stands out to view, with vividness and reality, as occupying the largest space upon his canvas—the "mercy of the Lord." Contrast gives the fairest estimate, and sets forth the fullest beauty. The Psalmist, therefore, having grouped together Special benefits, Manifold benefits, and Immeasurable benefits, having illustrated the height of God's mercy, the breadth of His forgiveness, and the depth of His pity, proceeds to depict the length of His love, in Everlasting benefits. And preparatory to introducing this bright, unfailing, and glorious subject, he strikingly displays its contrast with the nothingness of man, and the brevity of human existence, and says: "As for man, his days are as grass: as a flower of the field so he flourisheth. For the wind passeth over it, and it is gone; and the place thereof shall know it no more. But the mercy of the Lord is from everlasting to everlasting upon them that fear Him, and his righteousness unto children's children; to such as keep His covenant, and to those that remember His commandments to do them."

The two great topics of these verses, the everlasting "mercy" and "righteousness" of the Lord, are alike designed to be illustrated by this comparison with human weakness and vanity; they were each written for the immediate consolation of those who then feared God; and they also belonged equally as blessings to all who preceded them in existence, as they do to every generation of their successors. Each of these important topics presents more matter to our thoughts than a single chapter can contain: and to the consideration, therefore, of the former, we will at present direct our attention.

The "everlasting mercy" of the Lord is only to be described as one of the "unsearchable riches of Christ." We derive, however, some aid in our contemplation of it, by the consideration of our own mortality, our own brevity of existence. Having stated in the previous verse what man himself is—"dust" the Psalmist next proceeds to describe what man's life is,—"As for man, his days are as grass: as a flower of the field so he flourisheth: for the wind passeth over it, and it is gone, and the place thereof shall know it no more."

There are here two comparisons; first "grass;" and secondly, "a flower of the field." In every climate under heaven man beholds his own frail and perishing emblems. The grass is universal;—and its decay is universal. It breaks forth in the spring, and it is cut down, or withers, in the autumn. And man himself is like the grass on which he treads. He is formed out of the same dust; he passes through the same changes; and he returns into the same dust again. Should any one, however, demand for himself a more flattering emblem than the grass, the Psalmist here presents him with another in "the flower of the field." And since the Saviour has declared that "even Solomon in all his glory was not arrayed like one of these;" this comparison instituted by the Psalmist, may well be regarded as favorable in the highest degree. But yet, though we take man thus represented at his best estate—though we contemplate him as adorned with all that wealth, and grandeur, and royalty, can supply, what is he, even then, but as a " flower of the field" ? He is elevated indeed above the blades of grass in the common field of humanity ; and it may be also that he is more useful, and more remarkable, in some peculiar properties, than the great majority around him ; but yet is he not with them equally evanescent ? "Man" in his highest earthly glory, is as a " flower" in its full bloom ; yet beautiful indeed are they both in their brief season. What an attractive object on the plain, even at a distance, is a flower enamelled by the verdant grass ! Tall and fair, its beauty of color, its elegance of form, draw forth our admiration. The eye rests with satisfaction on its progressive beauties. It is lovely in the unfolding bud ; it is lovelier still in full-blown perfection. The sun discloses its loveliness, and the soft air diffuses its fragrance. We survey it with delight, and we return, from time to time, to gaze upon its rich and varied hues. But ere long, a wind, which we had scarcely observed, has blighted its beauty. The drooping head betrays its decay, and anon, a few withered leaves testify that it is gone. How great is our disappointment ! We now look around in vain. The wind has passed away. The sun shines forth again with enlivening beams. The air is balmy and delightful as before. Shall we see our fair flower again ? Ah, no. It is gone, and the place thereof knows it no more. And such is man ! He may be strong and vigorous as the grass, or he may be fair and flourishing as the flower of the field. The elegance of his manner, or the valor of his arm; the wisdom of his mind, or the sweetness of his disposition; the beauty of his example, or the fragrance of his benevolence; the integrity of his principles, or the elevation of his rank; may have made him as a "flower" among his fellows. The place of his birth, or of his residence, may have been recorded by the historian, and the grandeur of his achievements emblazoned by the heralds of fame. "When the ear heard him, it may have blessed him; and when the eye saw him, it may have given witness to him." But a wind, a breath, an unseen, an unnoticed influence, passes over him, and he is gone; and the post in the camp, or the senate, which he filled; the position in society which he adorned; the place in the family, where he was loved, knows him no more, for ever! "All flesh is grass, and all the glory thereof as the flower of grass. The grass withereth, and the flower thereof fadeth away."

This is a dismal consideration—a dark and uninviting picture. To those who know not God in Christ Jesus, it is dismal without relief—a dark picture without light. In this world, we behold children bereft of parents by the remorseless hand of death; we behold friend snatched away from the embrace of friend; and, suddenly, or slowly, we witness one after another sink into the tomb; their pity and their love are buried with them: in that very day their thoughts of kindness towards us, their purposes of benevolence, all perish. The long promised preferment, the anxiously expected elevation, was just about to be realized, and lo! the warm-hearted friend, or the generous patron, by whom it was all to be secured, sinks in death; and we behold the place of profit, or the post of honor, conferred upon a stranger! But more bitter still is that living death, where mercy expires in a patron's heart, and pity grows cold in the bosom of a friend; when promises are forgotten, professions are falsified, and expectations are crushed. These are some of the mortifications of this passing world, where life and death weave busily the chequered winding-sheet of human hopes. These, alas! are painful facts. They present themselves to the observation of every man; but because they are unpleasant, they are not welcomed by the natural heart; and all mention of death, and of the grave, is studiously avoided. This is perfectly natural to fallen men. Few persons possess the courage, in all cases, to seek to know the worst. It is always the safest course to ascertain the real state of a case; and it is just because religion seeks to make us safe, that it declares the case to us in its true nature. Men, however, are often too impatient to listen to all that religion unfolds. They turn from its opening statements, saying, "We cannot bear to hear all this: it makes us melancholy. The Bible is constantly speaking of death and the grave, the brevity of life, and the nearness of eternity." Men thus allow their minds to become impressed with their own hasty and erroneous conceptions. They imagine that the business of the Scriptures, and the object of God's ministers, is to speak only of these sad and melancholy things. But in this they are greatly mistaken. It is not the end and object of God's Word to make known these painful truths. They are all known already. They are existing facts—universally existing facts. The Bible does not make them, but relates them. It is as a means to a high and glorious end, that they are adduced. The proper business and object of the religion of truth, is not to proclaim death, but to publish life;—not to announce the grave, but to disclose the resurrection;—not to make them melancholy and dispirited, but to bid them "rejoice in the Lord alway." This is the grand and immediate end which religion has in view. The faithful ministers of Christ likewise, do not seek to darken the picture of human life—it is dark enough already. Their object, rather, is to introduce the lights of heaven amongst the dark shadows of earth, that they may exhibit to man the whole portraiture of his position. Those who look upon the completed picture, receive very different impressions from the man who has seen it only in its unfinished state. Indeed, of such a person, we truly remark: "He has not seen the picture!" So, in like manner, we say: "Till you know life and immortality brought to light by the Gospel, and brought to your own soul, you do not know the Gospel—you do not understand the Bible." Judge not of the whole by a part. Conclude not that David speaks in this joyous Psalm only of melancholy and dispiriting subjects, because he has here alluded to them in this single portion of it. His object is the same with the entire word of God—to recall our attention to existing facts, that we may more gladly welcome the counterbalancing truths. See how he rejoices immediately to announce them. With what an emphasis does that word "but" fall upon our ear—"As for man his days are as grass.

BUT the mercy of the Lord is from everlasting to everlasting upon them that fear Him."

What a glorious doctrine, "everlasting mercy!" What marvellous contrast do these two truths present—"our momentary life!"—"God's everlasting mercy." Who need hesitate, or fear, to contemplate the one, that can fix his eye upon the other? David does not hesitate. On the contrary, the consideration of the brevity of his life, gives zest and relish to his soul for this immortal food, this all-sustaining truth, that "the mercy of the Lord endureth forever;" and the more he ruminates on that mercy, the more unsatisfactory and fleeting does his earthly existence appear. The one doctrine sends him back to the other, with more vivid impressions of their respective reality and power. It is as if he had said, "Every day I live, I feel more certainly that my life is but a passing shadow. Yesterday I was not—to-day I am—to-morrow I may not be. But the mercy of my Lord is the same yesterday, and to-day, and for ever. It did not commence with my existence; and, blessed be His name, it shall not terminate with it, for His mercy is from everlasting to everlasting."

Mark, in this declaration of the Psalmist, how he invests the mercy of the Lord with an eternal character. Of Jehovah, it is said: "Even from everlasting to everlasting Thou art God." Psa. xc. 2. And of His mercy, it is here declared, that it also is "from everlasting to everlasting." An eternal Being must have corresponding attributes. Mercy is not a mere passing sentiment, but an everlasting principle in the Divine bosom. Feeling, apart from principle, has no existence in God. Every emotion has an adequate, a reasonable, and an eternal basis. Mercy was not first excited in the Great Creator when Adam began to breathe, or when he ceased to be obedient; mercy preceded man in his innocence, and led to his creation: it is "from everlasting." Mercy followed man in his sin, and led to his redemption: it is "to everlasting." There never was a time when God was not merciful; there never shall be a time when God shall not be merciful to them that fear Him. It assuredly is so, for God has said it. It necessarily must be so, for it is God's nature. He cannot deny Himself—he will not alter His principles.

His name is JEHOVAH { I WAS WHAT I WAS.
I AM WHAT I AM.
I WILL BE WHAT I WILL BE.

He can only declare His Being and attributes. "I lift up my hand to Heaven, and say, I LIVE FOR EVER." Deut. xxxii. 40. "I am Alpha and Omega, the beginning and the ending, saith the Lord, which is, and which was, and which is to come, the Almighty." Rev. i. 8. This glorious truth has been the joy of angels; when revealed, it became the joy of saints. All the inhabitants of heaven unite to "worship Him that liveth for ever and ever." To the Triune Jehovah, angels and archangels, cherubim, and seraphim, continually do cry, "Holy, holy, holy, Lord God Almighty, which was, and is, and is to come." All the saints and patriarchs from the beginning found this blessed doctrine to be the solace of their souls. Abraham called upon the name of the Lord, THE EVERLASTING GOD. Gen. xxi. 33. Moses also declared to all Israel, for their encouragement, "THE ETERNAL GOD is thy refuge, and underneath are THE EVERLASTING ARMS." Deut. xxxxiii. 27. The Psalmist thus comforts himself under the pressure of disease and the expectation of dissolution: "My days are like a shadow that declineth; and I am withered like grass: but thou, O Lord, shalt endure for ever; and Thy remembrance unto all generations. Of old hast Thou laid the foundation of the earth; and the heavens are the work of Thy hands. They shall perish, but Thou shalt endure; yea, all of them shall wax old like a garment; as a vesture shalt Thou change them, and they shall be changed: but Thou art the same, and Thy years shall have no end." Psa. cii. 11, 12, 25—27. Isaiah gladdened the Church by declaring that this should be a special name and title of the Redeemer: the Everlasting Father, or Father of the everlasting age. Isa. ix. 6. By the same argument he calls upon all believers to repose with continual confidence upon God, saying, "Trust ye in the Lord for ever: for in the Lord Jehovah is everlasting strength:" xxvi. 4. And, again, by it He both chides and comforts God's murmuring people: "Why sayest thou, O Jacob, and speakest, O Israel, my way is hid from the Lord, and my judgment is passed over from my God? Hast thou not known? hast thou not heard, that the EVERLASTING GOD, the Lord, the Creator of the ends of the earth, fainteth not, neither is weary? there is no searching of His understanding." xl. 27, 28. He adduces this doctrine for the encouragement of the Israelites, and twice over assures them that God shall be their "everlasting light." lx. 19. 20. He represents also

Gentile believers deriving hope from the same unfailing source: "Doubtless Thou art our Father, though Abraham be ignorant of us, and Israel acknowledge us not: Thou, O Lord, art our Father, our Redeemer; Thy name is from EVERLASTING." lxiii. 16. God himself makes this the ground of a most gracious declaration to all that fear Him: "For thus saith the high and lofty One that inhabiteth ETERNITY, whose name is Holy; I dwell in the high and holy place, with him also that is of a contrite and humble spirit, to revive the spirit of the humble and to revive the heart of the contrite ones." Isa. lvii. 15. Jeremiah rejoiced to testify that Jehovah is the true God, the living God, and an EVERLASTING KING. x. 10. Micah exulted in prophetic vision, and declared, "But thou, Bethlehem Ephratah, though thou be little among the thousands of Judah, yet out of thee shall HE come forth unto ME that is to be Ruler in Israel; whose goings forth have been from of old, from EVERLASTING." v. 2. Habakkuk also desired to soothe his troubled spirit by this consolatory truth: "Art Thou not from everlasting, O Lord my God, mine holy One? we shall not die." i. 12. St. Paul teaches us that all creation manifests the "eternal power and Godhead" of Jehovah. Rom. i. 20; and he declares that the Gospel is to be made known to all nations according to the commandment of the "everlasting God." Rom. xvi. 26. To this effect, also, God the Father and God the Son give their united testimony: "Thus saith the Lord, the King of Israel, and his Redeemer the Lord of hosts; I am the first, and I am the last, and beside ME there is no God." Isa. xliv. 6. And St. Paul declares that it was through the ETERNAL SPIRIT, that the Redeemer offered Himself without spot to God. Heb. ix. 14. Shall we not then pour forth our gratitude and praise to the triune and glorious Jehovah, saying, "Now unto the KING ETERNAL, immortal, invisible, the only wise God, be honor and glory for ever and ever, Amen." 1 Tim. i. 17.

This everlasting God not only thus possesses everlasting attributes, but He also bestows everlasting blessings. He sends the "everlasting Gospel" to be preached "unto all them that dwell on the earth." Rev. xiv. 6. Therein He freely promises "everlasting life" to all them that believe. John iii. 16. And therein also He administers "everlasting consolation" to their souls under all their troubles. 2 Thess. ii. 16. He informs them that He has laid an "everlasting foundation" in Christ Jesus, Prov. x. 25; that He has erected, and prepared thereon "everlasting habitations." Luke xvi. 9. And that to these He has graciously opened an "everlasting way." Psa. cxxxix. 24. And how great soever may be their difficulties, or numerous their foes, yet the Lord delivers His people by an "eternal redemption," Heb. ix. 12; bequeaths to them an "eternal inheritance," Heb. ix. 15; and makes them an "eternal excellency." Isa. lx. 15. The everlasting Redeemer becomes "the Author of ETERNAL SALVATION to all them that obey Him." Heb. v. 9. And causes all things to work out for them "a far more exceeding, even an ETERNAL WEIGHT OF GLORY." 2 Cor. iv. 17.

"Every good gift and every perfect gift is from above, and cometh down from the Father of lights, with whom is no variableness, neither shadow of turning." James i. 17.

God's plans and purposes are not short-sighted and vacillating, like those of men; they are "eternal purposes." Eph. iii. 11. The covenant which He has ratified in the blood of Jesus is "an everlasting covenant." Heb. xiii. 20. It is "ordered in all things and sure." 2 Sam. xxiii. 5. The fountain of God's love is eternal, and therefore the streams that issue from it are everlasting: "The Lord hath appeared of old unto me, saying, Yea, I have loved thee with an everlasting love: therefore with loving-kindness have I drawn thee." Jer. xxxi. 3. There is nothing in us by nature that can attract the mercy of the Lord. If it originate not in His own bosom, if it flow not forth spontaneously from its own fulness, it never can exist at all: "And herein God commendeth His love towards us, in that while we were yet sinners Christ died for us." Rom. v. 8. We deserved His wrath; but God, says the Apostle, is "rich in mercy, for the great love wherewith He loved us, even when we were dead in sins." Eph. ii. 4. His mercy, therefore, is "from everlasting,"—and, blessed be His name, it is also "to everlasting." "God is not a man that He should lie, nor the son of man that He should repent." Thy God, O believer, is an unchanged, an unchanging, and an unchangeable Friend. A mother may forget her only child, yet will not the Lord forget them that fear Him. The mercy of the Lord, promised in His word, is "from everlasting to everlasting" towards you. It is an over-abounding, and an ever-abounding mercy. It passes understanding; having length without termination, depth without bottom, height without summit, and breadth without bound. Go back into ages past, you cannot reach its beginning. Go forward into ages to come, you cannot reach its end. It is immeasurable, unfathomable, insurmountable, incomprehensible. And why is it thus four-fold in perfection? Because it is "from everlasting to everlasting."

To whom does the Lord show this amazing mercy? To them that "fear" Him. "Surely I know," said the wisest of men, "that it shall be well with them that fear God, which fear before Him." Eccles. viii. 12. This is the third time that David in this Psalm has mentioned this special charac-acteristic of God's people. And why should "fear" form one of their grand distinctive qualities? Because it was one of the characteristic marks of their Divine Head. It was foretold of Jesus, in most remarkable language, "The Spirit of knowledge and of the fear of the Lord," shall rest upon Him, "and make Him of quick understanding in the fear of the Lord." Isa. xi. 2. The same Spirit in measure rests upon all the family of God. This constitutes their most prominent feature, their universal family likeness. Among the children of the Lord there are not a few timid and desponding souls. They cannot satisfy themselves that they love God, or that they glorify their Saviour, or that they are born again of His Spirit. Many anxious questionings on these points rise often within their breasts. But here is a point on which there can, and must, be no doubt. Every child of God ought to be able to declare, at least thus much regarding himself, that he "fears" God, that he would tremble to offend Him, that he would hesitate, and refuse, to do that which he knew to be contrary to His holy will. None but the most hardened of rebels would venture to utter an opposite sentiment, and say, "I am not afraid to offend God." It is not, however, by the profession of the lips, but by the direction of the life, that we are to judge whether this true fear of God is implanted in our hearts. Many say that they fear God. The wicked are afraid of God, yet they do not "fear" Him. The devils tremble at His presence, yet they do not "fear" Him. Multitudes of professing Christians show by their daily conduct, that they are not afraid to offend Him. They appear to live for themselves—fulfilling the desires of the flesh and of the mind. They do not seem to make this a subject of earnest questioning and self-examination.—"Is the thing I am now about to do pleasing, or displeasing, to God? Is it agreeable or contrary to His word?" Such inquiries, it is to be apprehended, are as unfrequent to their minds, as they are unwelcome to their hearts. To the man, however, who fears God, this is neither a strange nor a disagreeable question. He sincerely desires to please and to glorify his Redeemer in all things, and therefore he fears to displease Him in thought, or word, or deed. Nor can it be too often repeated, that this fear is not a slavish dread, but a filial affection. Every right-hearted child is afraid to offend his parents, and yet he is not afraid of his parents. The two sentiments are quite distinct. We may not in the least be afraid of a father, and yet be all the more afraid to grieve him.

This distinction ought carefully to be borne in mind in the perusal of the sacred Scriptures. There the word "fear" is employed in the two opposite senses of slavish dread and of filial reverence: The Apostles desire to exclude the former kind of fear from the hearts of all God's children: "We have not received," says St. Paul, "the spirit of bondage again to fear; but we have received the Spirit of adoption, whereby we cry Abba, Father." Rom. viii. 15. And St. John testifies, "There is no fear in love; but perfect love casteth out fear: because fear hath torment. He that feareth is not made perfect in love." 1 John iv. 18. It is this tormenting fear—it is this servile dread, which the Apostles so strongly condemn.

The "fear of the Lord," on the other hand, of which the Psalmist here speaks, is his treasure. Isa. xxxiii. 6. It is the beginning of wisdom, Prov. ix. 10; it is a fountain of life, Prov. xiv. 27; it imparts strong confidence, Prov. xiv. 26. "The Lord taketh pleasure in them that fear Him." Psa. cxlvii. 11. He will bless them. Psa. cxv. 13. He will fulfil their desires. Psa. cxlv. 19. "His mercy is on them that fear Him from generation to generation." Luke i. 50. Well, therefore, might the Psalmist say, "Oh fear the Lord, ye His saints, for there is no want to them that fear Him." Psa. xxxiv. 9.

The "mercy" of the Lord to His children is "everlasting" in its duration, and we rejoice to learn that their filial "fear" toward Him is "everlasting" also: "They shall be my people, saith the Lord, and I will be their God: and I will give them one heart, and one way, that they may FEAR ME FOR EVER, for the good of them, and of their children after them: and I will make an everlasting covenant with them, that I will not turn away from them, to do them good; but I will put MY FEAR IN THEIR HEARTS, THAT THEY SHALL NOT DEPART FROM ME." Jer. xxxii. 38—40. Blessed covenant! Who would not wish to be included in its provisions? Who will refuse to join in earnest supplication for himself and others, "O Lord, who never failest to help and govern them whom Thou dost bring up in Thy steadfast fear and love; keep us, we beseech Thee, under the protection of Thy good providence, and make us to have a perpetual fear and love of Thy holy name; through Jesus Christ our Lord. Amen."

But art thou often sad, O Fearer of the Lord, by reason of thy unworthiness? Canst thou scarcely realize that this everlasting mercy is thy everlasting portion? Do tormenting fears beset thy spirit? And instead of the light of God's countenance, do clouds and darkness appear to surround His throne, so that thy prayers do not pierce through to Him, nor His favor shine forth to thee? Has thy soul been desolate, and in widowhood of feeling, as if bereft for ever of consolation? And art thou tempted to question in despondency, like Asaph, "Will the Lord cast off for ever? and will He be favorable no more? Is His mercy clean gone for ever? doth His promise fail for evermore? Hath God forgotten to be gracious? hath He in anger shut up His tender mercies?" Psa. lxxvii. 7—9. Check thyself immediately as he did, and acknowledge, "This is my infirmity; but I will remember the years of the right hand of the Most High." Yes, thou afflicted, tossed with tempest, and not comforted, remember thy Redeemer. In the days of His flesh He offered up prayers and supplications, with strong crying and tears, unto Him that was able to save Him from death, and He was heard in that He feared. Heb..v. 7. Thou also fearest God, thou also shalt be heard. Thank God that thou fearest Him at all, and thou shalt fear Him yet more. Yea, thou shalt love Him and praise Him. Therefore "fear not; for thou shalt not be ashamed: neither be thou confounded; for thou shalt not be put to shame: for thou shalt forget the shame of thy youth, and shalt not remember the reproach of thy widowhood any more. For thy Maker is thine Husband, the Lord of hosts is His name; and thy Redeemer the Holy One of Israel; the God of the whole earth shall He be called. * * * For a small moment have I forsaken thee; but with great mercies will I gather thee. In a little wrath, I hid my face from thee for a moment; but with everlasting kindness will I have mercy on thee, saith the Lord thy Redeemer. * * * For the mountains shall depart, and the hills be removed; but my kindness shall not depart from thee, neither shall the covenant of my peace be removed, saith the Lord that hath mercy on thee." Isa. liv. 4—10.

O what a blessed, what a comprehensive word is "mercy!" Clemency and bounty, grace and compassion; every kind, and tender, and interested, feeling in the heart of God; and every manner of blessing and benefit flowing in consequence from His hand,—All this is mercy:—Mercy from God—Mercy to a sinner—to an enemy—to a rebel! Who can rightly speak of mercy?—who, then, can rightly speak or think of everlasting mercy? The poor sinner pitied, pardoned, blessed, all his life-long unceasingly in time, and all his life long unceasingly through eternity,—this is EVER-

LASTING MERCY. Who can ever sufficiently thank and praise and bless our covenant God for EVERLASTING MERCY?

Wondrous subject for eternal praises—the everlasting kindness of the Triune Jehovah! Amazing covenant of endless mercy? Time cannot terminate it. Death cannot dissolve it. Satan cannot destroy it. The unchanging and unchangeable covenant of love is established by the oath of the Father, is ratified by the blood of the Son, and is secured by the seal of the Eternal Spirit. Oh, this is joy above joys. It is unspeakable and full of glory. It is an ecstasy of gladness to my soul. It furnishes me with a new song,—an everlasting song of gratitude and praise. The "Lord of Hosts," the "God of the whole earth," covenants that He will have "everlasting mercy" upon His people, and that they "shall fear Him for ever!"—The Lord Jesus, my "Maker," my "Redeemer," the "Husband" of my soul, doth covenant that I shall "not depart" from Him, and that He will "never turn away" from me! "Bless the Lord, O my soul, and all that is within me bless His holy name. Bless the Lord, O my soul, and forget not all His benefits; —For the mercy of the Lord is from everlasting to everlasting upon them that fear Him." Therefore "Blessed be the Lord God of Israel from everlasting, and to everlasting. Amen, and Amen." Psa. xli. 13. "O give thanks unto the Lord, for He is good; for His mercy endureth for ever. O give thanks unto the God of gods: for His mercy endureth for ever. O give thanks to the Lord of lords: for His mercy endureth for ever. WHO REMEMBERED US IN OUR

LOW ESTATE: FOR HIS MERCY ENDURETH FOR EVER. AND HATH REDEEMED US FROM OUR ENEMIES: FOR HIS MERCY ENDURETH FOR EVER. O GIVE THANKS UNTO THE GOD OF HEAVEN: FOR HIS MERCY ENDURETH FOR EVER. Psa. cxxxvi. 1—4, 23—26.

XIV.

Everlasting Benefits—Righteousness.

The mercy of the Lord is from everlasting to everlasting upon them that fear Him, and His righteousness unto children's children; to such as keep His covenant, and to those that remember His commandments to do them.—Verses 17, 18.

THE term "righteousness" is applied to the Most High in Holy Scripture, in various senses; but principally to God the Father in His invariable rectitude as a Ruler, and to God the Son in His perfect obedience as a surety. The former is eternal—"from everlasting to everlasting." The latter, being accomplished in the time of Christ's earthly life, is strictly "to everlasting"—as the Psalmist here expresses it, "unto children's children." The effects of that righteousness, however, are equally applicable to all who lived before, as to all who lived, or shall live, after it was finished. That righteousness is as absolutely necessary for the salvation of the former, as of the latter; and we may justly consider the Psalmist to speak here of "righteousness" equally with the "mercy" of the Lord, as "from everlasting to everlasting upon them that fear Him," as well as unto their "children's children;" for the Scripture testifies of the Lord Jesus, that He is "the Lamb slain from the foundation of the world." Rev. xiii. 8.

The rectitude of Jehovah's government stands as a fundamental doctrine to the whole volume of inspiration. The Law, the Histories, the Psalms, the Proverbs, the Prophecies, the Gospels, the Epistles, and the book of Revelation, all maintain the wisdom, the integrity, and the benevolence of the King, who ruleth in the armies of heaven, and among the inhabitants of the earth. Dan. iv. 35. It is the province of faith to maintain this doctrine in the face of all appearances to the contrary, and in opposition to all the cavillings of men. If we yield to these, we possess no true faith in God. The question of Abraham, "Shall not the Judge of all the earth do right?" Gen. xviii. 25, lies at the foundation of all our present peace, and of all our future hopes. If it once be even conceived in thought that the High and Holy One, in any, the slightest, particular, ever deviated from the path of strictest rectitude, immediately our religion is overthrown, our confidence is shaken, our misery is commenced, the sun is fallen from the moral heavens, and gross darkness envelopes us on every side. But God forbid the thought. The very supposition is abhorrent to the mind. "Let God be true, and every man a liar." There is no unrighteousness with Him. The day is coming when each man's apparently tangled web of life, shall appear to have been wound up rightly to its minutest thread. The loom of time, with all its perplexing machinery, is working out one grand design, to be displayed through all eternity; and angels, with archangles, and the Lord's redeemed, will gaze thereon with holy admiration; and the harpers of heaven, when they behold it, will sing this song of Moses and the

Lamb: "Great and marvellous are Thy works, Lord God Almighty; just and true are Thy ways, thou King of saints." Rev. xv. 3.

If ever, Reader, when trials beset, and perplexities surround thee, when disappointments befall, and expectations are thwarted, thou feelest tempted to question the allotments of Providence, and to be envious at the prosperity of others, remember that danger is very near thy soul. Thou standest on slippery and forbidden ground. Asaph confesses that when he ventured to tread thereon, his "feet were almost gone, his steps had well-nigh slipped." But he hastily retreated. He turned away his eyes from the further contemplation of the chequered scenes of earth. He went into the sanctuary to gain fresh instruction, and the result was, that he became thoroughly ashamed of his murmuring thoughts. His conscience smote him, and he felt self-condemned. He grieved that he should have given way, even for a moment, to entertain the slightest doubt of the rectitude of God's dispensations. And, therefore, at the very commencement of his seventy-third Psalm, he gives this emphatic testimony against all gainsayers: "Truly God is good to Israel, even to such as are of a clean heart." Bear thou similar testimony to thy own tempted spirit, and against all the questionings of others. Begin every argument by saying with Asaph: "Truly God is good;" and shut up every argument by saying again with him: "It is good for me to hold me fast by God, to put my trust in the Lord God."—*Last verse, Prayer-book version.*

"The Lord reigneth, let the earth rejoice." Clouds and

darkness may be round about Him, but "righteousness and judgment are the basis of His throne." Psa. xcvii. 1. Hold fast, therefore, by God. Retain to thy dying hour this all-important truth of the righteousness of thy heavenly Father. Never let it go; for "this is the victory that overcometh the world, even our faith" in God. "Though thy fig-tree do not blossom, nor fruit be in thy vines; though thy olives should fail, and thy fields yield no meat; though the flock be cut off from thy folds, and there be no herd in thy stalls;" yea, and though every one of these should prosper abundantly with thy neighbor, yet hold fast this truth, "the Lord is righteous in all His ways, and holy in all His works;" and then, with the tried, but triumphant Prophet, thou also shalt be enabled to add: "Yet I will rejoice in the Lord; I will joy in the God of my salvation." Hab. iii. 17, 18.

The second meaning of this term, "righteousness," may be considered as that which the Psalmist has here more especially in view—the perfected obedience of the Lord Jesus as a Surety, thus foretold by the prophet Daniel: "He shall bring in everlasting righteousness." Dan. ix. 24. The words are remarkable. To "bring in," implies that it was new—that no such thing had been seen on earth before as an "everlasting righteousness." The goodness, or innocence, of our first parents in the garden of Eden, soon gave way before temptation—it was not everlasting. The goodness of all the children of men is but as the morning cloud, and as the early dew it passeth away. There is no everlasting righteousness but that of the Lord Jesus Christ. He voluntarily condescended to be born under the Law, and to render to all its requirements a complete and perfect obedience. The first Adam dishonored the Law of God, and Jesus, the second Adam, "magnified the Law, and made it honorable." As a Divine Person in human form rendering it obedience, He exalted that Law immeasurably, so that "the Lord is well pleased for His righteousness' sake." Isa. xlii. 21. He was perfectly holy in His own nature, and needed no righteous acts whatsoever for His own benefit. But it was for our benefit, and for the glory of the Lawgiver, that He fulfilled each iota and tittle of that Law. Every thought of His heart was in full accordance with its holiness. Every word of His lips was in perfect harmony with its justice. Every action of His life was in complete fulfilment of its benevolence. And thus He demonstrated to the universe, that the Law which the devil had impugned, and which man had broken, was "holy, and just, and good." Rom. vii. 12. A perfect man had never appeared on earth after Adam fell; and therefore a perfect righteousness had never been presented to the Divine Lawgiver by any in human form. But at length Christ, the perfect man, appeared on earth, and presented a complete and perfect righteousness unto God. He rendered an undeviating obedience to His Law, and so "brought in" an everlasting righteousness into the world. And since He ascended into heaven, there has not been found another born of woman, fulfilling, like Him, the whole law of righteousness. "All have sinned," as before, so after, Christ, "and come short of the glory of God"; and "Christ is the end," the grand and only end, "of the law, for righteousness to every one that believeth." Rom. iii. 23, and x. 4.

The righteousness of the Lord Jesus is declared by the inspired pen both of Daniel and of David, to be "everlasting:" and that it must be so, in its very nature, is abundantly evident. Was it not wrought out by a Divine Person?—Was it not perfected according to an everlasting standard?—And is it not laid by God as the only ground of human salvation, from the beginning to the end of time? The efficacy of the obedience of the Lord Jesus endures throughout all ages. The world shall perish, but the righteousness of Christ perisheth not. Time shall terminate, but the righteousness of the Redeemer shall see no end. Its fragrance will continue for ever. Its leaf will be green, and its fruit will be sweet throughout all eternity. This glorious truth, the inspired Prophet most emphatically declares, "The work of righteousness shall be peace, and the effect of righteousness quietness and assurance for ever." Isa. xxxii. 17. Clothed in this righteousness, the saints of God will appear before His throne without a single spot or stain. Immaculate in this righteousness, they can never again be sullied, but they will be without fault for ever and for evermore. Realizing this blessed condition as his present privilege, the Prophet Isaiah thus gives utterance to the full ecstasy of joy which it had awakened in his heart: "I will greatly rejoice in the Lord, my soul shall be joyful in my God; for He hath clothed me with the garments of salvation, He hath covered me with the robe of righteousness, as a bridegroom decketh himself with ornaments, and as a bride adorneth herself with her jewels." Isa. lxi. 10. David also joyfully declares, "My mouth shall show forth Thy righteousness and Thy salvation all the day; for I know not the numbers thereof. I will go in the strength of the Lord God: I will make mention of Thy righteousness, even of Thine only." Psa. lxxi. 15, 16. And St. Paul exclaims, "What things were gain to me, those I counted loss for Christ. Yea, doubtless, and I count all things but loss for the excellency of the knowledge of Christ Jesus my Lord: for whom I have suffered the loss of all things, and do count them but dung, that I may win Christ, and be found in Him, not having mine own righteousness, which is of the law, but that which is through the faith of Christ, the righteousness which is of God by faith." Phil. iii. 7—9.

To renounce our own fancied righteousness, and to accept the everlasting righteousness of Christ, is one of the hardest lessons of the Gospel. Man tenaciously clings to the idea of his own merits. He cannot conceive why, or how, he is to be saved by the merits of another. Yet this is the great Scripture doctrine,—salvation by imputed righteousness. "By the obedience of One shall many be made righteous." Rom. v. 13. How can it be "unto children's children," but by God's gracious imputation of it to each of them personally, as they appear in their successive generations? This glorious doctrine, wherever we turn upon that perfect globe of truth, the Holy Bible, is to be seen shining with meridian brightness in both hemispheres—the Old and the New Testaments. In the Old Testament the Messiah is thus foretold: "Unto you that fear MY name shall the Sun of righteousness arise, with healing in His wings," or rays. Mal. iv. 2. And "This is His name whereby He shall be called, The Lord our Righteousness." Jer. xxiii. 6. And therefore, of each of His believing people it is affirmed, "Surely shall one say, In the Lord have I righteousness and strength." Isa. xlv. 24. In the New Testament it is expressly written, that "The righteousness of God which is by faith of Jesus Christ, is unto all, and upon all, them that believe." Rom. iii. 22. And therefore, who can sufficiently describe the "blessedness of the man, to whom the Lord imputeth righteousness without works"? Rom. iv. 6.

This "blessedness" is freely bestowed on all who fear and obey God. Those who do not fear to offend Him, who regulate their lives only by their own wishes and desires, having no design to please their heavenly Master, possess neither part nor lot in this imputed and everlasting righteousness. Those, however, who by grace, retain a reverential remembrance of the Omnipresent God, who fear to act contrary to His holy will, and who entertain a child-like desire to please Him as a Father in all things, through Jesus Christ, such obedient believers have full warrant to appropriate, and to enjoy, the mercy and the righteousness of the Lord, as their present portion and their everlasting inheritance.

The believer possesses the happy assurance that these blessings are free, not only to his own soul, but also to the souls of his children after him. The covenant which God made with Abraham, was thus secured to his descendants in the Jewish Church: "I will be a God unto thee, and to thy seed after thee." Gen. xvii. 7. This covenant was ratified in Christ with equal fulness to the Gentile Church: "The promise is unto you and to your children." Acts ii. 39. Great is the joy which this assurance imparts to the believing parent. His children, he learns, are graciously included in the same covenant with himself. He therefore feels emboldened to plead on their behalf before that gracious God who has said, "I will pour my Spirit upon thy seed, and my blessing upon thine offspring." Isa. xliv. 4. Therefore, he feels intensely solicitous to train up his children in the nurture and admonition of the Lord; and longs and labors assiduously that both he himself, and all who belong to him, yea, and "his children's children," may be such as "keep His covenant, and remember His commandments to do them."

This declaration proves that the "fear" here spoken of by the Psalmist, is not an idle, inoperative, sentiment in the breast, but a powerfully influential, and active principle in the life. Those who "fear God," not only know, but "keep His covenant;" they not only remember His commandments to repeat them,but they "remember His commandments to do them." True believers both sincerely desire, and earnestly endeavor to please God. They strive to yield an unremitting obedience to all His injunctions. They love the Lord their God with all their heart, they delight to serve Him with all their soul. The words which He commands them they teach diligently to their children; and by their example, as well as by their precepts, they labor to train up every one of them in the way in which they should go.

The encomium pronounced upon Abraham by God Himself was this: "I know him that he will command his children and his household after him, and they shall keep the way of the Lord, to do justice and judgment." Gen. xviii. 19. And to the obedience of some of his "children's children," this remarkable testimony is given in the case of Moses and of Joshua: "As the Lord commanded Moses his servant, so did Moses command Joshua, and so did Joshua; he left nothing undone of all that the Lord commanded Moses." Josh. xi. 15.

"All the paths of the Lord are mercy and truth unto such as keep His covenant and His testimonies." Psa. xxv. 10. The promise is as gracious as it is explicit: "Train up a child in the way he should go: and when he is old, he will not depart from it." Prov. xxii. 6. It is to be expected that children will walk in the ways of their fathers, as said our Lord: "If ye were Abraham's children, ye would do the works of Abraham." John viii. 39. Therefore the promises are given, with a similar condition to David's: "If thy children will keep my covenant and my testimony that I shall teach them, their children shall also sit upon thy throne for evermore." Psa. cxxxii. 12. God said unto Abraham, "Thou shalt keep my covenant, thou and thy seed after thee, in their generations." Gen. xvii. 9. With peculiar emphasis did God re-deliver this covenant on Mount Sinai, saying unto Moses, "Thus shalt thou say to the house of Jacob, and tell the children of Israel: Ye have seen what I did unto the Egyptians, and how I bare you on eagle's wings, and brought you unto myself. Now, therefore, if ye will obey my voice indeed, and keep my covenant, then ye shall be a peculiar treasure unto me above all people: for all the earth is mine: and ye shall be unto me a kingdom of priests, and an holy nation. These are the words which thou shalt speak unto the children of Israel. And Moses came, and called for the elders of the people, and laid before their faces all these words which the lord commanded him. And all the people answered together and said, All that the Lord hath spoken we will do. And Moses returned the words of the people unto the Lord."—Exod. xix. 4—8. We learn also, when the first sacrifices were offered, after Moses came down from the mount of communion, that one half of the blood was sprinkled on the altar, and one half on the people, and a solemn covenant was thus ratified between God and them: "And he took the book of the covenant, and read in the audience of the people: and they said, All that the Lord hath said will we do, and be obedient. And Moses took the blood, and sprinkled it on the people, and said, Behold the blood of the covenant, which the Lord hath made with you concerning all these words." Exod. xxiv. 7, 8. The covenant of Grace, on God's part, is as free and simple as words can make it. The security thereof is as great as the promise and the oath of an immutable God can render it: "Know therefore, that the Lord thy God, He is God, the faithful God, which keepeth covenant and mercy with them that love Him, and keep His commandments, to a thousand generations." Deut. vii. 9. The covenant of obedience also on the part of the people, is as directly and universally binding as can possibly be conceived: "And thou shalt love the Lord thy God with all thine heart, and with all thy soul, and with all thy might. And these words, which I command thee this day, shall be in thine heart: And thou shalt teach them diligently unto thy children, and shalt talk of them when thou sittest in thine house, and when thou walkest by the way, and when thou liest down, and when thou risest up." Deut. vi. 5—7.

The religion of the Bible is eminently practical. Even in Eden, amid all the sweets of Paradise, there was no idleness, no unproductive sentimentalism. "The Lord God took the man and put him into the garden of Eden, to dress it and to keep it." Gen. ii. 15. In the heavenly paradise, the redeemed, we read, shall "*serve*" God day and night; and in the fulness of their love, and in the universality of their obedience, they will "follow the Lamb whithersoever He goeth." Rev. xiv. 4. The Scriptures of truth calls us to a religion of holy living, and of active benevolence. The blessings of peace and of joy promised in the gospel, are not bestowed on the talkative professor, but on the obedient and diligent disciple. "If ye know these things, happy are ye if ye do them," said our blessed Lord. John xiii. 17. And David, to past generations, had given his testimony to the same effect: "In the keeping of Thy commandment there is great reward." Psa. xix. 11. Blessed as did the women of Israel regard it, to be the mother of the Messiah, that Messiah himself declared that all His faithful disciples are far more blessed in the nearness of their spiritual relationship, than even the Virgin Mary in the closest bonds of the flesh. "He said, Yea, rather blessed are they that hear the word of God and keep it." Luke xi. 28. And that this was no solitary statement, no passing sentiment, on the part of our Lord, we learn from various passages of His life, and from none more emphatically than from the following most gracious declaration, by which He again brings all His true disciples into a nearer and more blesssed union with Himself, than even that which His mother and His brethren enjoyed. "Then one said unto Him, Behold, thy mother and thy brethren stand without, desiring to speak with thee. But He answered and said unto him that told Him, Who is my mother? and who are my brethren? And He stretched forth His hand toward His disciples, and said, Behold my mother and my brethren! For whosoever shall do the will of my Father which is in heaven, the same is MY brother, and sister, and mother." Matt. xii. 47—50.

If there be one truth, the necessity of which should be more extensively stamped than another upon the minds of men, it is that of sincere and continual OBEDIENCE. It is self-evident, even to the heathen, that there must always exist a correspondence between the professions of the mouth and the transactions of the life. It was the complaint of God against Israel of old, "they hear my words, but they will not do them." Ezek. xxxiii. 31. "This people draweth near to me with their mouth, and with their lips do honor me, but they have removed their heart far from me." Isa. xxix. 13. And Jesus spake plainly to them that followed Him, "Why call ye me Lord, Lord, and do not the things which I say?" Luke vi. 46. Therefore St. James thus warns all professing Christians, "Be ye doers of the word, and not hearers only, deceiving your own selves. For if any be a hearer of the word, and not a doer, he is like unto a man beholding his natural face in a glass. For he beholdeth himself, and goeth his way, and straightway forgetteth what manner of man he was. But whoso looketh into the perfect law of liberty, and continueth therein, he being not a forgetful hearer, but a doer of the work, this man shall be blessed in his deed. If any man among you seem to be religious, and bridleth not his tongue, but deceiveth his own heart, this man's religion is vain. Pure religion and undefiled before God and the Father is this, To visit the fatherless and widows in their affliction, and to keep himself unspotted from the world." James i. 22—27.

Of all the transgressions that are to be found upon this sin-laden world, none is more truly odious than that of the Antinomian—who "continues in sin, that grace may abound." Rom. vi. 1. The word and example of such, "eat as doth a canker." 2 Tim. ii. 17. "These are spots in our feasts of charity: they are clouds without water: they are trees without fruit: they are raging waves of the sea, foaming out their own shame: wandering stars, to whom is reserved the blackness of darkness for ever." Jude 12, 13. To all such let it again and again be declared, "if any man have not the Spirit of Christ, he is none of His." Rom. viii. 9. "He that saith, I know Him, and keepeth not His commandments, is a liar, and the truth is not in him." 1 John ii. 4. The Apostles reiterate most anxiously their emphatic warnings on this important point. St. John says, "Little children, let no man deceive you: he that doeth righteousness is righteous, even as He (Christ) is righteous. He that committeth sin is of the devil." 1 John iii. 7, 8. St. Jude declares that it was needful for him to exhort believers to "contend earnestly for the faith, which was once delivered to the Saints, because there were certain men crept in unawares" into the Church, "ungodly men, turning the grace of our God into lasciviousness." Jude 3. St. Peter declares that it would have been better for such, "not to have known the way of righteousness, than after they have known it, to turn from the holy commandment delivered unto them." 2 Pet. ii. 21. St. James asks this plain question, "What doth it profit, my brethren, though a man *say* he hath faith, and have not works? can faith save him? For as the body without the spirit is dead, so faith without works is dead also." James ii. 14, 26; and adds, "Therefore to him that knoweth to do good, and doeth it not, to him it is sin." (iv. 17.) St. Paul gives this most earnest injunction, "Let no man deceive you with vain words: for because of these things cometh the wrath of God upon the children of disobedience. Be not ye, therefore, partakers with them." Eph. v. 6, 7.

To comfort himself, together with the then existing, and all future, ministers and members of the Christian Church, under the bitter blightings of this moral pestilence, St. Paul instructed Timothy in this ever-memorable truth: "Nevertheless, the foundation of God standeth sure, having this seal, The Lord knoweth them that are His. And, let every one that nameth the name of Christ depart from iniquity." 2 Tim. ii. 19.

The universal law over all intelligent beings whom the

Lord hath made, is this: "Be ye holy, for I am holy." From the High and Holy One that inhabiteth eternity, no contrary command could possibly emanate. The fundamental law which His unchangeable word has recorded, is this: "without holiness, no man shall see the Lord." Heb. xii. 14. And that this law might be accomplished in us, we are taught in Scripture, that the Lord God "sent His Son to bless us in turning away every one of us from our iniquities." Acts iii. 26.

We must receive this freely-gifted Saviour whole and entire, or we do not receive Him at all. The security cannot be separated from the sanctity of His salvation. The title to heaven must be accompanied by the meetness for it. Both of these are vouchsafed to us in Christ with equal freeness and with equal fulness. Christ is given to us in fourfold and perfect measure—"He is of God made unto us wisdom, and righteousness, and sanctification, and redemption," 1 Cor. i. 30;—"wisdom," that we may know the things that are freely given unto us of God; 1 Cor. ii. 12; —"righteousness," that we may possess a title to the blessings thus freely given;—"sanctification," that we may be made meet to join with God in their present and continual enjoyment;—and "redemption," that we may fully and for ever be delivered from all decays which would bedim our knowledge; from every enemy who would dispute our title; from every polluting thing which would defile our souls; and from every form and manner of weakness, oppression and captivity, that would fetter our free, and joyous, and perpetual, intercourse with our Lord and Saviour in His prepared mansions, amid the unsearchable and everlasting treasures of heaven.

Reader, Christ, with all His blessings, is freely given to thee by God. Accept Him, with them all, as freely as He and they are given. Dost thou wish to possess the "everlasting righteousness" which He has brought in? Behold it freely given to thee in Christ! Receive of that "gift of righteousness." Accept it immediately and gratefully. Take it as your only title to heaven, renouncing all other, and thou shalt "reign in life by Jesus Christ." Rom. v. 17. Dost thou wish to "keep God's covenant," and to "do His commandments"? Behold Christ is thy "sanctification." Ask Him, and He will by His Spirit, "work in you to will and to do of His good pleasure." Every thought of your mind, Christ by His Spirit will purify. Daily will you be "renewed after the image of Him that created you." As a living branch in the living Vine, you will "have your fruit unto holiness, and the end everlasting life." The prayer of the Apostle for the Colossians will be fulfilled in the experience of your soul—"you will walk worthy of the Lord unto all pleasing, being fruitful in every good word, and increasing in the knowledge of God:" yea, and his thanksgiving unto the Father will also be the grateful acclamation of your heart—that He "hath made you meet to be a partaker of the inheritance of the saints in light." Col. i. 9—12.

The everlasting righteousness of the Redeemer, ensures the everlasting happiness of His redeemed. The Lord Jesus is their "ALL IN ALL." In every want He is their Friend. In every danger He is their Defence. In weakness He is their Strength; in sorrow, their Joy; in pain, their Peace; in poverty, their Provider; in sickness, their Physician; in hunger, their Bread; in trouble, their Consolation; in perplexity, their Counsellor; in the furnace, their Refiner; in the floods, their Rock; in assaults, their Refuge; in accusations, their Advocate; in debt, their Surety; in slavery, their Ransom; in captivity, their Deliverer; in the day, their Sun; in the night, their Keeper; in the deserts, their Shepherd; in offering prayer, He is their Priest; in rendering obedience, their King; in obtaining knowledge, their Prophet; in life He is their Hope; in death, their Life; in the grave, their Resurrection; and in heaven, their Glory.

The Lord Jesus is thus all in all to His people now, and He is all in all to them for ever and for evermore. It is His love which draws them toward Himself, and it is "everlasting love." Jer. xxxi. 3. It is His way on which they walk, and it is "the everlasting way." Psa. cxxxix. 24. It is His light which guides them therein, and it is "an everlasting light." Isa. lx. 19. It is His strength which helps them thereon, and it is "everlasting strength." Isa. xxvi. 4. His arms they are which bear and embrace them, and they are "the everlasting arms." Deut. xxxiii. 27. It is His consolation which encourages them to persevere, and it is "everlasting consolation." 2 Thess. ii. 16. It is His kindness which pities and supplies them, and it is "everlasting kindness." Isa. liv. 8. It is His righteousness in which they are arrayed, and it is "everlasting righteousness." Psa. cxix. 142. It is His mercy which surrounds them, and it is "everlasting mercy." Psa. c. 5. It is His joy which gladdens them, and it is "everlasting joy." Isa. xxxv. 10. It is His salvation which saves them, and it is "everlasting salvation." Isa. xlv. 17. It is His kingdom into which He receives them, and it is an "everlasting kingdom." Psa. cxlv. 13.

Let CHRIST, therefore, be thy ALL IN ALL, for time and for eternity. With the faithful Martyr say, while living, "None but Christ." When dying, say, "None but Christ." Through all eternity say, "None but Christ." Let this triumphant name, "THE LORD OUR RIGHTEOUSNESS," settle every difficulty, solve every doubt, and silence every accusation. When the Law cries, "Thou hast disobeyed my enactments," answer thou "Christ for me has obeyed them all." When conscience tells thee thy sins are both many and great, answer thou, "Christ's blood cleanseth from all sin." When reminded of your natural ignorance of the way to heaven, say, "Christ is my wisdom." When your ground and title to that kingdom are demanded, say, "Christ is my righteousness." When your meetness to enter within its sacred gates is challenged, say, "Christ is my sanctification." When sin, and the law, when death and Satan claim thee as their captive, reply to them all, "Christ is my redemption." "The Law saith, Pay thy debt. The Gospel saith, Christ hath paid it. The Law saith, Thou art a sinner; despair, for thou shalt be condemned. The Gospel saith, Thy sins are forgiven thee; be of good comfort, thou shalt be saved. The Law saith, Make amends for thy sins. The Gospel saith, Christ hath made it for thee. The Law saith, The Father of heaven is angry with thee. The Gospel saith,

Christ hath pacified Him with His blood. The Law saith, Where is thy righteousness, goodness, and satisfaction? The Gospel saith, Christ is thy righteousness, goodness, and satisfaction. The Law saith, Thou art bound to me, to the Devil, and to the hell. The Gospel saith, Christ hath delivered thee from them all.—*Patrick Hamilton's Disputation between the Law and Gospel Martyr.* 1527.

XV.

Everlasting Benefits.

THE PREPARED THRONE.

The Lord hath prepared His throne in the heavens.—Verse 19.

AMID the sins and the fluctuations of the world—the collision of armies—the fall of kingdoms, and the fading away of generations—it is an unspeakable comfort to know that "the Lord hath prepared His throne in the heavens." The history of the world is but a record of its evanescence. Fame informs us only of men and things that were. The busy stage of life presents to view a long funeral procession, where the whole multitude of the living are following after the dead. First in the line appear Antediluvian Patriarchs, followed by the descendants of Noah, who pass onward in the pageant before us by successive generations as time rolls on. Then were kingdoms established and empires founded, and the voice of adulation was heard vainly saying to each successive monarch, "O King, live for ever!" But where now are the flattered and their flatterers? All alike have crumbled into dust. Behold the splendor of the golden kingdom of the Chaldeans—the softer and silver brightness of the Medo-Persians—the stronger and more extensive kingdom of the Macedonians or brazen-coated Greeks—the mighty and universal kingdom of the Romans, breaking in pieces and subduing the whole earth with its iron sceptre. Where are all these now? Where are their royal founders? Where is Nebuchadnezzar? Where is Cyrus? Where is the mighty Alexander? Where are the illustrious Cæsars? Who now bear their names? And where dwell their descendants upon the earth? All is emptiness. Nothing but their history remains to informs us that they were and are not. How solicitious was each of these monarchs to found his kingdom on an indestructible basis. How anxiously did they prepare their thrones that their name and their power might remain. But they prepared them on the earth. The Lord likewise has prepared His throne, but He has prepared it in the heavens. It is a prepared, but not yet a manifested throne. Its power, however, is a present reality. Even now it possesses authority over all: yea, it has possessed authority over all from the beginning. Those four great monarchies were ruled and overruled by it, alike in the period of their origin, in the splendor of their progress, and in the circumstances of their decline. They came into being, not by the will, neither by the power, of their human founders, but according to the determined purpose and by the almighty power of the Lord our God. They have stood successfully upon the earth for centuries, and yet appeared long ago in vision to the King and to the Prophet as forming only one huge image. We now are privileged to behold the ten kingdoms of its feet partly strong and partly broken; and we stand in living expectation to see "the Stone that was cut out without hands," smite the image upon its feet and break them to pieces. It is our happy lot to live in the period when all these monarchies have filled up their respective parts in history; and it is our joyful anticipation that, "in the days of these kings" that are now, or that may shortly arise, upon the earth, "the God of heaven" will bring forth His prepared throne, and "set up a kingdom which shall never be destroyed, and which shall break in pieces and consume all these kingdoms, and which shall stand for ever." Dan. ii. 44.

There is, to the eye of sense, much apparent confusion in the past history, and in the present aspect, of our fallen world. There are sufferings and sorrows, disorders and discords, on every side. The impetuous passions of fallen men appear to be symbolized by the very elements around them. The winds, the storms, the fires of heaven from above—volcanoes, earthquakes, and pestilential vapors from the earth beneath—plagues, fevers, and infections in the air around—form a large pictorial alphabet, an illuminated elemental index, of the evil thoughts, the rapine, crime, and murder that proceed from within.

The aspect of society presents the same confusion to our view. The virtuous and honorable are not always the most successful. The vicious and the profligate do not invariably receive an adequate or immediate punishment. Neither prosperity nor adversity are regulated by an unvarying law. So manifest is this confused state of things, that the Psalmist warns us not to be troubled at the sight: "Fret not thyself because of evil doers; neither be thou envious at the prosperity of the wicked." Psa. xxxvii. 1. *Cranmer's version.* And Solomon declares, that "Because sentence against an evil work is not executed speedily, therefore the heart of the sons of men is fully set in them to do evil." Eccles. viii. 11.

Amid all this change and confusion to the eye of man, there has been no change, and no confusion, to the eye of God. All has been precision and regularity in His sight. One kingdom has but followed another in the order of His appointed course. Sorrow and suffering, indeed, have marked their progress. Pride and ambition paved their way, and war and bloodshed followed in their track. Men were either dazzled by the vain glory of their advance, or buried beneath the ruins of their decline. They beheld nothing further than their fellow men striving against each other for the mastery: and involved, as they felt themselves to be, against their wills, they could only groan, and bleed, and perish, in the universal struggle. But God seeth not as man seeth. All these things are permitted and overruled by Him. The breaking of sceptres; the overthrow of thrones; the fall of monarchs; and the change of dynasties, are the visitations of nations for their sins, and are visible preparations for His kingdom. "Thus saith the Lord God, Remove the diadem and take off the crown: for this shall not be the same: exalt him that is low, and abase him that is high. I will overturn, overturn, overturn it: and it shall be no more, until HE come whose right it is, and I will give it HIM." Ezek. xxi. 26, 27.

To the man of the world fortune is indeed pictured with

a smile of kindness upon her face, but with the fold of blindness upon her eyes. To the believer, however, there is no blind fortune. His eye of faith pierces the troubled elements of nature, and beholds a calm sunshine beyond. He looks through the vapory ebullitions of human passion, and discerns a heavenly King, causing the very wrath of man to praise Him, and ordering all things for His own glory. The believer can calmly survey the confused aspects of society and of the world. He feels certain that the prosperity of the wicked is but for a moment. And though, by the convulsions and oppressions that surround him, he may be borne down in the flesh, yet will he be lifted upward in the spirit by the assured knowledge of this blessed truth, "The Lord hath prepared His throne in the heavens."

Observe that word "prepared,"—not preparing, but prepared. It has been thought of, designed, determined, yea, set up. Whatever may be seen or felt, whatever may be thought or said, there is no lack of government, there is nothing wrong in the administration of the Most High. His sceptre is a right sceptre—a sceptre of righteousness. His throne is a prepared throne, but at present it is *in* the *heavens.* Beyond these visible clouds the throne of God is established. A thin veil of atmosphere conceals it from our mortal view; but still it is as really there as if we beheld it with our eyes. But it is now a throne of mercy, and not of judgment. God has appointed a day for His prepared throne to be set up on the earth, and now He forbears with the children of men, and gives them time, and promises, and warnings, and gracious invitations to return to their allegiance before that day arrive.

In some province of our empire should rebellion arise, our gracious Sovereign would neither cause, nor approve, nor assist that rebellion. But should faction increase, sedition multiply, and lawless men commit depredations throughout the land, would this confusion and these evils be justly chargeable on the Royal Person, while she prepared her throne, and made ready her power to remove them? And suppose, that in the exercise of a Sovereign's mercy to the misguided people of that province, instead of giving them over instantly to the sword, she should issue an amnesty inviting every rebel to lay down his arms before an appointed day? Should we not applaud the grace and the wisdom which would thus seek to convert the rebels into loyal subjects by an act of mercy, rather than to exterminate them at once by martial law? And while that amnesty—that day of grace—continued, however violent might be the acts of some portion of the rebels, and however severe might be the temporary trials of a part of her loyal subjects, who could, with any justice, lay these to the charge of the Royal clemency?

So is it with ourselves, and with the King of heaven. This earth on which we tread is the rebellious province. We ourselves are the rebellious subjects. Our life is spared under the act of amnesty, under the day of grace. "Behold, now is the accepted time; behold, now is the day of salvation." To-day, while it is called to-day, we are invited to lay down our arms. The Gospel is the royal proclamation of mercy. Whosoever comes, in the appointed way, and before the appointed time, shall in no wise be cast out.

If, however, confusion meanwhile exist, evils prevail, and anarchy predominate over government, in our rebellious province, are these to be charged upon our lawful Sovereign, and not rather on our own lawless rebellion? And what is the consolation which every loyal heart experiences?—Is it not the assurance that a day is appointed to put down evil, and to introduce order? Is it not the very declaration of the Psalmist, "The Lord hath prepared His throne in the heavens?" Yes, the believer fixes his eye continually on the sovereign, and overruling, power of God. And whatever may be the trials and the confusion that prevail for the present, "this is the victory that overcometh" the whole "world" of trouble and perplexity—"even our faith!" Meanwhile, we believe in the clemency of our King. We accept the amnesty. We lay down the weapons of our rebellion. And we rejoice to know that "His throne is prepared in the heavens," and that "He hath appointed a day in the which He will judge the world in righteousness by that Man whom He hath ordained." Acts xvii. 31.

Justly might the Lord have given up our rebellious race to condign punishment; but, in His mercy, He sent His Son into the world not to condemn, but to save. God declares that He has no pleasure in the death of the wicked. He is not willing that any should perish; and He graciously extends the sceptre of mercy, that we may turn from our rebellion and live. The Apostle warmly expostulates with all who would abuse this clemency of the King of heaven;

who continue in their rebellion, though mercy be proclaimed to them. "Despisest thou," he demands, "the riches of His goodness, and forbearance, and long-suffering: not knowing that the goodness of God leadeth thee to repentance. But after thy hardness, and impenitent heart, treasurest up unto thyself wrath against the day of wrath, and revelation of the righteous judgment of God?" Rom. ii. 4, 5.

Jesus is now sitting on His Father's throne, and in due time He will be seated on His own. Rev. iii. 21. As a "Priest" at the right hand on high, He now carries on the blessed work of mediation; but ere long as a "King" on His "throne," specially "prepared" for Him as the God-Man, He will appear Supreme, the Reigning Sovereign of our world. His heavenly sceptre will put "down all rule and all authority and power" (1 Cor. xv. 24) in Satan and the wicked, and introduce love and harmony, holiness and joy over the whole earth. Then our long-offered prayer will at last be answered. Christ's kingdom will come. The prepared throne of the God-Man will be set on high. The thin veil of atmosphere will no longer conceal the great Sovereign of the universe from our view. The Lord Jesus will come forth crowned King of kings and Lord of lords. The day of grace will be past. The act of amnesty will have ceased. The sword of justice will be unsheathed. Every rebellious subject will be destroyed. Every loyal subject will be honored. And a joy inexpressible and everlasting will pervade the breasts of all the members of the Redeemed Family, when they behold their Elder Brother seated on His prepared throne.

Dear Reader, have you seriously thought of that solemn day? The Lord has prepared His throne; have you prepared your heart? Not more certainly do you read these words of the Psalmist, than you shall assuredly behold this prepared throne. Are you preparing to stand before it? Is your trust based wholly on Christ? Do you renounce all sin? Have you given yourself to Jesus to be saved as a sinner through His righteousness? As He assumed your name to take the curse, do you use only His name to obtain the blessing? Do you renounce your own name and fancied merit before God—and do you plead only Christ's name and Christ's merits at His footstool? Do you see and know that you can have no righteousness of your own, and have you determined, with the Psalmist, to say, "I will make mention of Thy righteousness, even of Thine only?" Since God accepted Christ's work, do you likewise accept it for your own soul? Do you give your entire consent to it? In Christ's obedience as a Surety, do you believe that, in the eye of the law, you have obeyed?—that in His sufferings you have legally suffered?—that in His death you have legally died?—and that in His resurrection you have been legally acquitted? If you had obeyed the law in your own person, and suffered its penalty for your own guilt, and by the power of God had been made alive again, would you not believe that the sentence once executed would not again be enforced? —And do you now believe this—most blessedly and most certainly believe it—through such a Surety's obedience—through such a Surety's sufferings? Oh! thus *give* yourself to Christ, I beseech you. Cast yourself in this manner upon

His merits. Realize your oneness with Him. "PUT ON the Lord Jesus Christ" by this argument, and say, "He stood for me—He answered for me—He obeyed for me—He died for me—He rose again for me—and in the eye of the law therefore I stood in Him—I answered in Him—I obeyed in Him—I died in Him—I rose again in Him." Thus "reckon yourself to be dead indeed unto sin, but alive unto God, through Jesus Christ your Lord." Thus "yield yourself unto God, as one that is alive from the dead, and your members as instruments of righteousness unto God." Rom. vi. 11—14. Thus "let not sin reign in your mortal body," but let "grace reign through righteousness unto eternal life by Jesus Christ our Lord." Rom. v. 21. Thus "set your affections upon things above, not on things on the earth: for ye are dead, and your life is hid with Christ in God. When Christ, who is our life, shall appear, then shall ye also appear with Him in glory. Mortify, therefore, your members which are upon the earth." Col. iii. 3—5. This, this, will be a most blessed preparation for your soul to stand before the prepared throne: and unlike the men of the world, who will "call upon the rocks and the mountains to fall upon them and to hide them from the face of Him that sitteth on the throne and from the wrath of the Lamb," you will now be enabled to say, and then be enabled to realize, what a believing poet has sung:

"Jesus, thy robe of righteousness
My beauty is, my glorious dress
'Midst flaming worlds, herein array'd,
With joy shall I lift up my head.

When from the dust of death I rise,
And crave a mansion in the skies,
E'en then shall this be all my plea—
'Jesus hath lived and died for me.'"

XVI.

Everlasting Benefits.

THE UNIVERSAL KINGDOM.

And His kingdom ruleth over all.—Verse 19.

The Son of Jesse at this part of the Psalm reaches the climax of his enumerated blessings. From the third and onward through every succeeding verse, he had specified a great variety of benefits as subjects of thanksgiving to his God and Saviour. He now sums up all by giving utterance to a most comprehensive truth, and by placing on record that one grand blessing which imparts fulness and security to every other—"His kingdom ruleth over all."

In the preceding verses the Psalmist had spoken of the Lord as his Benefactor, his Forgiver, and his Physician—as his Deliverer and his Preserver—as his Teacher, as his Friend, and as his Father, and now he speaks of Him as the Universal King. What joy does this truth infuse into the heart! What stability does it impart to all our blessings! To have a Benefactor and a Forgiver is truly delightful; but when we can add that our Benefactor and our Forgiver is a Potentate whom no circumstances can baffle, and whom no adversaries can control, what language shall express the measure of our delight? To hear that we have a Physician

11*

and a Deliverer, a Preserver and a Teacher, is indeed "glad tidings;" but to learn that He is also an Everlasting King, whose Almighty skill and wisdom are invariably, and shall be unceasingly, exerted for our benefit, is "GLAD TIDINGS OF GREAT JOY." To possess a Friend and a Father is a blessed cause of thanksgiving; but to know assuredly that this Friend and this Father is also the Universal King, the love of whose heart and the power of whose hand will rule and overrule all things for our good in time and in eternity, oh, this is transporting knowledge, and fills the soul with over-flowing gratitude, and the mouth with over-flowing praise.

Such is the last and crowning benefit with which David completes his catalogue of mercies received from his Redeemer, and which He would not that his soul should ever willingly forget—"Bless the Lord, O my soul: and all that is within me, bless His holy name. Bless the Lord, O my soul, and forget not all His benefits"—for "His kingdom ruleth over all."

Deeply and indelibly let this truth be impressed upon our minds. Throughout the ages that are past, when kingdoms were born, lived their appointed time, then died, and were forgotten amid the multitude of their successors, this kingdom of the Lord was ruling over all. Amid the diversity of nations, and the multiplicity of governments that now exist on the more widely inhabited surface of the globe, this kingdom of the lord is ruling over all. Whatever may be the principles of the governed, or the powers of the governors, whatever may be the overturnings of thrones, the assumptions of monarchs, or the devastations of nations in the periods that are yet to come, this kingdom of the Lord shall rule over all for ever.

Unspeakable is the joy and thankfulness of the believer to know that the kingdom of his Lord ruleth over all. The kings of the earth may war, and the nations be agitated to their centre—men's minds may fail them for fear—and havoc and cruelty and death may threaten on every side: the lust of conquest and the pride of power may set the strong against the weak, and deadly struggles for the mastery may mark the progress of their conflict: the passions and the principles of men may be enlisted against all established order, and the limited tyranny of the Ruler may be displaced by the unlimited tyranny of the multitude—losses may be sustained and untold hardships be endured, yea, life itself may be tortured from the frame of the believer under the rule of man; but this is his consolation, this his triumph, that these are all working together for his good, because the kingdom of his Lord ruleth over all.

Unspeakable is the joy and thankfulness of the believer to know that the kingdom of his Lord ruleth over all. The church of Christ may be overrun with error. The worship of the Saviour may be cast into the shade by idolatrous devotions presented to His mother, and offered to the bread of His own sacrament. The "power of the keys" may be boasted as superior to the power of the sword, and she who bears them may say in her heart, "I sit a queen, and am no widow, and shall see no sorrow." Rev. xviii. 7: the false prophet may extend his faith by the sword, and wave his green banner over lands held sacred in the history of the past: the midnight of heathen superstition and idolatry may envelope the great majority of the human race—the whole earth may be debased and prostrated under the rule of the "god of this world," 2 Cor. iv. 4; but still the believer looks to the working of that mighty power which hath put all things under the feet of Jesus, Eph. i. 19—24, and he assuredly knows that the idols shall be utterly abolished, and the power of the Mohametan superstition be overthrown, and the city on the seven hills be burnt up with all her pomp and power; yea, Satan himself shall be cast down, and the "earth be filled with the knowledge of the Lord," for His kingdom ruleth over all.

Unspeakable is the joy and thankfulness of the believer to know that the kingdom of his Lord ruleth over all. The reign of sin, of Satan, and of the world, had often vexed his soul, and many an earnest conflict had he waged against them. The dominion which they maintained over his flesh, his judgments, and his affections, he had often in vain attempted to subvert. Pierced by many a wound he had groaned, and, borne down by combined assaults, he had looked anxiously round for aid or refuge. "Oh wretched man that I am," he has been heard to exclaim, "who shall deliver me?" And then, like a joyous conqueror, he has been known to add, "I thank God through Jesus Christ my Lord," Rom. vii. 24, 25—sin shall not have dominion over me, Rom. vi. 14—He will bruise Satan under my feet shortly, Rom. xvi. 20—He will deliver me from this present evil world, Gal. i. 4—their triple tyranny shall be stripped of power, for "God's kingdom ruleth over all."

"O God, whose blessed Son was manifested that He might destroy the works of the devil, and make us the sons of God and heirs of eternal life; grant us, we beseech Thee, that having this hope, we may purify ourselves, even as He is pure; that when He shall appear again with power and great glory, we may be made like unto Him in His eternal and glorious kingdom, where with Thee, O Father, and thee, O Holy Ghost, He liveth and reigneth ever one God, world without end. Amen."

The present generation may go, like their fathers, to the tomb, while they behold the kingdom of God come with grace; but one day there will be some living on the earth, who shall not taste of death till they have seen that "kingdom come with power." To mortal ken that day and that hour have never been revealed. We cannot, therefore, assert that it will be in our own day, neither can we affirm that it will not be in the lifetime of the present generation. All that we can say with certainty is this, that it becomes us all to "watch and to pray, because we know not when the time is." "Watch, therefore, for ye know not what hour your Lord doth come." Matt. xxiv. 42. The lapse of 1800 years gives us emphatic warning that this grand event is by so much nearer to ourselves. And every passing hour seems to call upon us to watch and pray, that we may be counted worthy to stand before the Son of Man. Luke xxi. 36. Oh, thrice happy will be that holy expectant disciple, who shall be caught up to meet his Lord. Unlike the departed believer, his soul will not be unclothed by the hand of death, but clothed upon by the power of Jesus with his new body, or house, which is from heaven. 2 Cor. v. 1—4. In a moment, in the twinkling of an eye, the mortal will become immortal—the weak powerful—and the natural, a spiritual body. He who was kneeling under the fig-tree in secret prayer, will be translated into the presence of His Lord. He who was singing the praises of Jesus in the earthly sanctuary, will be caught up, like Elijah, to join the worship of heaven. Happy the man who, without seeing corruption, will thus inherit incorruption, and who, without tasting death, will thus be ushered into life. But this happiness shall not be his till the prisoners of the tomb are liberated. "The dead in Christ shall rise first." Sleeping in Jesus, their bodies will be raised, and changed into the glorious likeness of Christ's body. "Then we that are alive and remain, shall be caught up together with them in the clouds, to meet the Lord in the air: and so shall we ever be with the Lord." 1 Thess. iv. 13—18.

"Blessed and holy is he that hath part in the first resurrection." Rev. xx. 6. Abel, the first believer who entered into rest, and all who have followed him in the faith, will be there together. The last shall be as the first, and the first as the last. The living will obtain no precedency over the dead, nor the dead over the living. Oh, blessed time when "the Lord our God shall come, and all His saints with Him." Zech. xiv. 5. Then will the voice of the great multitude be heard, saying, "Alleluia: for the Lord God Omnipotent reigneth. Let us be glad and rejoice, and give honor to Him; for the marriage of the Lamb is come, and His wife hath made herself ready." Rev. xix. 6, 7. This glorious period was thus prefigured to Daniel in visions of the night: "Behold, One like the Son of Man came with the clouds of heaven, and came to the Ancient of Days, and they brought Him near before Him. And there was given Him dominion, and glory, and a kingdom, that all people, nations, and languages, should serve Him; His dominion is an everlasting dominion, which shall not pass away, and His kingdom that which shall not be destroyed. And the kingdom and dominion, and the greatness of the kingdom under the whole heaven, shall be given to the people of the saints of the most High, whose kingdom is an everlasting kingdom, and all dominions shall serve and obey Him." Dan. vii. 13, 14, 27.

This is the "glory" that was to "follow." This is "the joy" that was set before the Redeemer on the cross; and soon shall it be set before the universe. The "glorious majesty of His kingdom" shall be revealed to men. Jesus, "in His own glory, and in the glory of His Father, and of the Holy angels," Luke ix. 26, shall come forth wearing "many crowns." Angels and archangels, cherubim and seraphim, shall throng around Him in allegiance. Thrones and dominions, and principalities and powers, shall do Him homage. "The kingdoms of this world shall become the kingdoms of our Lord and of His Christ." All kings shall fall down before Him: all nations shall serve Him. "Every knee shall bow, of things in heaven and things in earth, and things under the earth: every tongue shall confess that Jesus Christ is Lord to the glory of God the Father." Phil. ii. 10. He who is "The Truth" will ascend the "prepared throne," and every false religion shall flee, and all diversities of opinion shall cease; the Father of lies shall be destroyed, and all who believe him shall be condemned. "The Lord our Righteousness" will reign, and sin and iniquity shall prevail no more—transgression and disobedience shall be excluded for ever. "The Prince of Peace" will wield the sceptre, and wars shall cease unto the ends of the earth, variance and contention shall be brought to an end for ever. Jesus, the God of Holiness and Love, will be King over all the earth, and impurity and selfishness and malevolence shall never again be found within its borders. Oh what a glorious King, and therefore what a glorious kingdom! "The Desire of all nations," and "the Light of the world," will be on His throne. His kingdom will rule over all—a kingdom of universal truth, of universal righteousness, of universal peace, and of universal purity and love!

Oh joyous period,—oh longed-for time, when the "head that once was crowned with thorns, will be crowned with glory,"—when the hand that held the reed, shall wield the sceptre,—when the ear that heard the accusations of false witnesses, will listen to the Hosannas of adoring multitudes, singing, "Blessed is He that cometh in the name of the Lord;"—when He who was nailed to the cross, with this title contemptuously affixed, "King of the Jews," will be seated on the throne of the universe, and have on His vesture and on His thigh this title written, King of kings, and Lord of Lords. Rev. xix. 16. Amen. Even so, come, Lord Jesus. Come quickly. Come and reign.

If we would welcome Jesus then in His kingdom of

glory, let us welcome Him now in His kingdom of grace, which is "righteousness, and peace, and joy in the Holy Ghost." Rom. xiv. 17. The human heart is the territory over which this kingdom of grace reigns, and this threefold blessedness is the result. Oh, Reader, is Jesus the King of your heart? Is His throne established there? Has your rebellious will been made loyal and obedient? Does "His kingdom rule over all" your thoughts and affections, over all your desires and motives? Are you His loyal subject? —His faithful soldier?—His devoted servant? His kingdom of power ruleth over all the universe, and yet He condescends to ask you to let Him set up the kingdom of His love in your heart. "Behold, I stand at the door, and knock: if any man hear my voice, and open the door, I will come in to him, and will sup with him, and he with me." Rev. iii. 20. "Let" His "grace reign" in your soul. Rom. v. 21.; "let" His "peace rule" there. Col. iii. 15. Let the kingdom be with power—a hidden life within you. Submit to the sovereignty of Jesus. Yield up all you love to be dealt with as He pleases. Oh, if you but knew the love of His royal heart, you would never withhold anything from Him. None of us really know it. The strongest faith does not give Him sufficient credit—the most glowing gratitude comes far short of His benefits—the most ardent love is but as taper-light to the burning brightness of His love. Meditate much on the freeness, the fulness, the tenderness, the self-sacrificing of the love of Jesus. Try to get enlarged views of His character and excellency. Jacob served seven years from love, and they seemed to him but a few days.

Gen. xxix. 20. Jesus served thirty-two years from love to your soul; and as if that were a small thing, He died from love to you; and now He has risen from the tomb, and asks you if there was ever love like unto His love? or any one, therefore, to be preferred before Him? Oh, what an adamantine heart must beat within us, if it respond not to such a love as this—if we "yield not ourselves unto God, as those that are alive with Him from the dead;" our members as the subjects of His "righteousness," our hearts as the subjects of His "peace," our spirits as the subjects of His "joy." Thus will His kingdom of grace be established in our souls; and with all loyalty and love we shall be brought to say, "Whom have I in heaven but Thee, and there is none upon earth that I desire in comparison of Thee."

How blessed is the reign of love, when Jesus sits enthroned on the affections of the heart. Christ bears rule, and all is peace and harmony. Hardship seems nothing for the love we bear to Him. A whole lifetime spent in His service appears "but as a few days." Religion is no longer a task, a monotony, a dulness. It becomes a liberty and a delight. We hail the Sabbath-day with welcome. We joy when it is said to us, Let us go into the house of the Lord. The chapter that we read is not now selected for its brevity; and the prayers we offer are no longer mere formal repetitions. At one time we may have been accustomed to say, "I must read a chapter. I must say my prayers. I must go to church. I must try to be good." Now, under the reign of grace, the spontaneous utterance of the heart is this: "I will continually try to please my God in all things.

I will diligently read His word, that I may learn His will regarding me. I will earnestly and thankfully present my petitions in the closet and in the sanctuary." And then the commandments are regarded as royal commands, as gracious invitations, as welcome messages; as courtiers regard theirs from their beloved Sovereign, and count themselves honored to receive them; so in regard to the Ten Commandments, the imperative becomes the optative mood, by this logic of loyalty and affection; and when the King of heaven says "THOU SHALT," the believer joyfully replies, "I WILL love the Lord my God with all my heart, and with all my soul, and with all my mind, and with all my strength;" and as Jesus said, so we in measure are enabled to say, "I delight to do Thy will, O my God, yea, thy law is within my heart."

With David we are enabled by grace to rejoice and thank our God unfeignedly, that His kingdom ruleth over all. With gladness and with gratitude we place ourselves under His rule. In fervency of desire we say, "Come, Lord Jesus, come and reign in my heart. Let me be wholly Thine. Let no other Lord have dominion over me. Reign over me in body, soul, and spirit, in time, and throughout eternity. Regulate my motives and desires. Rule over my judgment, my imagination, and my affections. Set up Thy prepared throne upon the province of my will. Yea, over my soul and all that is within me, extend Thy sceptre; and come, the Lord of all, and take possession of this world, that Thy dominion may be from sea to sea, and from the river unto the ends of the earth (Psa. lxxii. 8); then will my soul bless Thee, O Lord, and all that is within me will magnify Thy holy name, because Thy kingdom ruleth over all."

XVII.

Call to Universal Gratitude—Angels.

Bless the Lord, ye His angels, that excel in strength, that do His commandments, hearkening unto the voice of His word.—Verse 20.

HAVING summoned all his faculties, enumerated all God's benefits, and soared in gratitude to the highest point, the Psalmist finds, by the Spirit, that all he had desired is not half accomplished. He finds his faculties inadequate, his enumeration incomplete, and his gratitude imperfect. His intention in composing this Psalm, had been to "BLESS the Lord." He had proposed to himself, herein, the noblest object that can occupy the mind; and, to aid him to attain it, he had collected the most ample materials that could possibly be reached. All he knew, and all that he could think of, in the past and in the present, were adduced to help. The Spirit had led him from thought to thought, from mercy to mercy. His soul becomes enlarged with most exalted conceptions of Divine goodness. And the Spirit vividly impresses these two truths upon his mind, that God is worthy of infinite blessing, and that all blessing is unworthy of His infinite excellence—"His praise is above heaven and earth." Psa. cxlviii. 12. *Cranmer's version.* The benefits of the Lord stand before and around him as mighty mountains that cannot be covered by the highest tide of praise. The abounding goodness, the pardoning mercy, and the everlasting love of his Redeemer can never be sufficiently extolled. The longer he meditates on His mercies, the more wonderful, and undeserved, and innumerable, and inestimable do they appear. He longs for some one to aid him in his praises. All earthly gratitude seems too gross, too selfish, too cold, too transient. His own gratitude appears to be scarcely worthy of the name; and yet poor and feeble as it is, he feels that it cannot be repressed. Bless God I must. Bless God I will. Everything within me shall praise His name. All the members of my body shall subserve His glory. For ever will I bless the Bestower of my benefits, the Pardoner of my sins. His goodness is inexhaustible; His love is ineffable; His benefits are immeasurable; His mercy is everlasting; His kingdom ruleth over all. Angels are my fellow-subjects. Every created thing is indebted to my King. Raise then your songs all ye in heaven and earth. Join me in this glorious work of praising God. "Bless the Lord, ye His angels, that excel in strength, that do His commandments, hearkening unto the voice of His word." "Bless ye the Lord, all ye His hosts; ye ministers of His, that do His pleasure. Bless the Lord, all His works in all places of His dominion: bless the Lord, O my soul."

How natural is this address of the Psalmist. When the heart is full, either of joy, or of sorrow, we long for sympathy, for fellow-feeling, for enlarged, and prolonged, and united utterances. The believer cannot be satisfied to praise God alone. He longs that every creature should do Him homage. He knows that God is worthy to be praised—so worthy that if every man, and angel, and intelligent being that ever existed, should speak His praise, His praise could not sufficiently be spoken. The believer knows that it is the duty of every created being to glorify the Lord. He feels it also to be his own bounden duty—his one grand duty upon earth. He feels it not only to be his duty, but also, by grace, to be his supreme delight. Not by nature, but by the visitations of God's Spirit, the love within his heart becomes at times so fervent, and his gratitude so strong, that he knows not how to give it utterance. His thoughts are too feeble, his voice too weak, his words too poor. If he had a hundred tongues he could more than occupy them all in this glorious theme. And so enlarged does his heart become with thankfulness and joy, that he exclaims "I will extol Thee my God, O King; and I will bless thy name for ever and ever. Every day will I bless Thee, and I will praise thy name for ever and ever." Psa. cxlv. 1. And oh! when this pent-up heart, this faltering tongue, these sinful lips, this languid body, shall be transformed on the resurrection morning, then will the full burst of joy and gratitude be heard; and then will the poor believer love without wavering, and rejoice without mourning, praise without sinning, and bless without ceasing; then will the voice of each ransomed sinner help to swell the tide of thanksgiving, as it flows toward the Triune Jehovah from the whole multitude of the redeemed, never again to ebb; and then will men and angels unite in the interchanges of unceasing hallelujahs, blessing together their Eternal Benefactor, and each aiding the other to ascend the height of everlasting gratitude.

David here anticipates that reunion of praise. He knew that there had been a time when the angels rejoiced over and with man, praising God for his creation. And he believed that a time would come, when angels and men should again praise Jehovah with, and for, each other. And now, therefore, he calls upon these high and holy beings, during the present period of human weakness and alienation, to continue and to increase their songs of gratitude. We have sinned and fallen; they stand steadfast in their original postion. We cannot rise to the high note of an unfallen joyous angel. He cannot descend to the deep note of a once fallen, but restored, and joyous, man. The harmonies of heaven are perfected by their united song. Sing, then, O sing, ye angels; and sing, ye rescued men. Let heaven and earth be one in praising God. Fly swift, ye heavy years of time, and bring in the glad New Year of Eternity, when the universal Jubilee shall burst upon our ear, and when the hosannas of believers shall be in unison for ever with the hallelujahs of angels.

It is an unspeakable consolation, under the painful consciousness of the imperfection of our praises, to know that there are others who worship the Thrice Blessed Jehovah with perfect hearts, with faultless lips, with untiring devotion, and with unceasing song. Every created being is under infinite obligations to the Most High. Angels owe a debt of everlasting gratitude. Angels are continually attempting to discharge that debt. They delight to do so. They know no opposite emotions to those of joy and gratitude. Every new mercy gives them new happiness; and every attempt to acknowledge it, gives them fresh pleasure. Their whole life is praise. Service is joy. Obedience is gladness. They live, they move, they have their being in God.

Angels are incalculable in numbers. Daniel, in night visions, beheld the "Ancient of Days," and records, that "thousand thousands ministered unto Him, and ten thousand times ten thousand stood before Him." vii. 10. St. John "heard the voice of angels round about the throne, and the number of them was ten thousand times ten thousand, and thousand of thousands." Rev. v. 11. St. Paul informs us, that it is our privilege to have come, through union with Jesus, "to an innumerable company of angels." Heb. xii. Thus we know these two facts, that angels exist, and exist in countless numbers; but of angelic nature, and of angelic life, we can form no adequate conception. The pen of inspiration discloses to our view several interesting points, which we might have supposed, but could not otherwise have known. The Psalmist gives us a threefold description of angels in this verse. He sets before us their characteristic endowment, their outward life, and their inward spirit. He says that the angels "excel in strength," that they "perform God's commandments," and that they "hearken to the voice of His word."

The power of angels is largely exhibited in Scripture, and

universally admitted in the common maxims of all nations. It is their characteristic endowment, that they "excel in strength." Their various manifestations in the sacred History, are marked by a swiftness of motion, and by a display of power, beyond all human calculation. Gabriel came from heaven in the short space of Daniel's supplication. ix. 21, 23. In one night the angel of the Lord smote in the camp of the Assyrians an hundred and eighty-five thousand persons. 2 Kings xix. 35. Their physical or bodily strength does not surpass their moral or spiritual power. We read that when our blessed Redeemer was passing through His agony in Gethsemane, "there appeared an angel unto Him from heaven, strengthening Him." Luke xxii. 43.

Angels "excel" men in strength of person, in strength of will, in strength of affection, and in strength of judgment. No effort exhausts their powers; no passing consideration turns them from their purpose; no secondary object allures them from their "first love" to God; and no fair appearances, or specious arguments, beguile them to a false conclusion. With clear intellects, they apprehend God's messages; with loving hearts, they hasten to fulfil them; with steadfast determination, they pursue each particular to its completion; and with irresistible power, they successfully execute the whole will of God.

Such is the characteristic endowment of angels: "they excel in strength:" the Psalmist also informs us that "they do God's commandments." Of the outward life of angels, and how they are engaged, we know nothing more than this verse inform us. One word expresses it all; and that word is OBEDIENCE—a word engraven on the hearts of angels. Oh, that it had never been obliterated from the hearts of men! Angelic life is an unvarying obedience. Their will is pliant with the will of God. They do nothing of their own motion; and yet they do everything with their full consent. When they rest, it is in obedience,—God has bid them rest. When they wait, it is in obedience,—God has bid them wait. He says to one, Go; and he goeth: to another, Come; and he cometh. Their songs of praise are rendered, not only in gratitude, but also in obedience. That "God wills it," is their grand motive, the powerful mainspring of all their actions. Their outward life is a continual and perfect doing of the will of Him who is holy, and just, and good. No murmur lurks in an angel's breast. No questioning rises upon an angel's lips. No hesitation or short-coming is visible in an angel's act. All is loyalty and readiness within. All is acquiescence and cheerfulness on his tongue. All is promptitude and performance in his hand. Man either does not, or half does; but the angels DO God's commandments thoroughly and constantly, willingly and joyfully, perseveringly and universally.

Such is the outward life of angels; "they do God's commandments." They spend their existence in a perfect circle of obedience. And why? Because, adds the Psalmist, they "hearken to the voice of His word." This precious declaration gives us an insight into their inward spirit. It is not said: "who hear the voice of His word;" but, "who hearken to the voice of His word." The angels are eager to catch the slightest intimation of the Divine will. They listen. They watch. "They hearken." They listen, because they love. They watch, because they wish to obey. They hearken, because they desire to learn. It is no indifferent matter to an angel whether God is obeyed or not. He is not regardless whether he hear correctly and fully what his Lord has uttered. It is to him a matter of the most intense and absorbing consideration, that God should be obeyed—obeyed universally by all His creatures, and obeyed especially by himself. The minutest point—the smallest jot and tittle in His law, obtains an angel's full and perfect attention. Therefore his position is that of one who "harkens to the voice of His word"—who desires to know what his Lord is saying—who is eager to learn all His holy will. An angel hearkens not only to His word, but to the "voice" of it; that is, to the sound and meaning of it. He does not listlessly wait, like a heartless earthly servant, till the word fall so loud and strong upon his ear, as to leave him no excuse for pretended misapprehension and consequent inaction; but on the contrary, the moment that the slightest sound is heard, that instant, in reverent attention, the entire faculties of an angel are turned to hearken—suffering not the slightest syllable to escape; and anxious to ascertain the precise, and the entire meaning of "every word that proceedeth out of the mouth of the Lord."

Such is the inward spirit of an angel. He is willing, and ready, and eager to obey; and therefore he "hearkens" that he may learn what his Lord requires him to perform. An angel is all inward, as well as outward obedience. And thus in the inward spirit joyfully, and in the outward act completely, the angels do the commandments of God in the world above. And our blessed Saviour has, as it were, commanded us never to take any lower standard, any inferior example, by thus teaching us to pray, "Thy will be done on earth as it is done in heaven." These blessed beings assume no merit, and claim no reward. There is no self-righteousness among angels. They intuitively say after they have done all, "We are unprofitable servants, we have only done that which it was our duty to do." God Himself is their joy—His favor their highest honor, and the keeping of His commandments their great reward. Angels are upheld by Divine grace. They are "elect angels," 1 Tim. i. 21—they are kept by the power of God. Not by their personal holiness, but by their union with, and dependence upon, God, they overcome the power of temptation, and fall not into the abyss of the angels that sinned. It is these elect and holy, these humble and obedient angels, whom our Redeemer sets before us as our pattern, and whom the Psalmist here calls upon to bless their Creator: "Bless the Lord, ye His angels, that excel in strength, that do His commandments, hearkening to the voice of His word."

That example shall be attained—the Lord's prayer shall be answered. Angels excel men in strength, and, in that respect, will be pre-eminent over man for ever; but, thank God, there is a time coming when they shall not excel the redeemed in obedience, or in willingness of spirit. We shall love as the angels. We shall serve as the angels. We shall do God's commandments as the angels. And when the world is filled with the knowledge of the Lord, then shall the will of our Father be done on earth, as it is done in heaven. And in the new heavens and the new earth, wherein dwelleth righteousness, angels and men will mingle together in their service and their song, and the one shall not outstrip the other in loyalty or love, or excel in readiness, or in constancy, or in universality of obedience.

Angels are "fellow-servants" with men. They stand the highest in the form of creature being, with which we are acquainted. Jesus made them: "they were created by Him, and for Him." Col. i. 16. The Psalmist, therefore, in contemplating the great duty which universal being, and universal nature, owe to Him as the Glorious Creator, appropriately begins at the highest point. Jehovah-Jesus must be adored. And surely if, when man "hold their peace, the very stones would cry out," how much more should angels, when the highest note of saints falls infinitely below His praise. The Spirit saith, "Let all the angels of God worship Him." The Psalmist cannot himself express all the praises of his Redeemer; but he goes in thought to those who will express them for Him. He cannot raise an universal song; but he will do all that in him lies to get it raised by others. Therefore, he here calls upon the angels to "bless" the Lord. "The less is," indeed, "blessed of the better;" but when THE BEST condescends to accept of the blessing of the least, how honored does the creature become in the bestowment! God honors angels by allowing them to praise Him; and angels bless themselves by blessing God:

"Blessing and blest—sweet honor, sweet employ!
Happy, and filling every heart with joy!"

Gratitude abounds in heaven. Let it abound for ever; and let it eternally increase. Angels are the chief of God's servants—let them be the chief of God's worshippers. Let them set the example to the whole universe. It was one, formerly of their number, who struck the harp out of man's hand, and broke all its strings. It is, therefore, but right that they should now sing for us, as well as for themselves. Our best strings are not entire, but only mended. The melody that we produce, must consequently be imperfect through all the years of time. Ere long, a perfect harp will be given to us by the Divine Hand; its strings entire—its melody sublime. That harp will never be unstrung, never be broken, never be dashed from our grasp. Till then, we call upon the angels to take up our part. The song must not be stopped—the choir must not be silent, because man has lost his powers. Never, for an instant, let our Creator and Redeemer be robbed of His due praise. And if we may say, "Sing, O ye heavens; shout, ye lower parts of the earth; break forth into singing, ye mountains, O forest, and every tree therein," Isa. xliv. 23; surely we may also say: "Bless the Lord, ye His angels. Praise Him, ye archangels that surround His throne. Let seraphim to cherubim respond His praise; and all ye sons of God who have never fallen, shout for joy, and laud, and praise, and magnify for ever that gracious Lord who evermore upholds you."

Not that in thus addressing angels, the Psalmist conceived that his voice could reach their ear, or that the beings of another world can be affected by the words of men. But there is a spirit in man which feels its affinity with that higher world, and which soars often toward it. Our spirit finds itself pent and circumscribed by the body of flesh; and while it can only speak by the human tongue, and see by the natural eye, and hear by the outward ear, it has yearnings which outstrip the voice, and thoughts more rapid than the rays of light, and impressions more delicate than the sounds of earth. The human spirit feels itself imprisoned. It can enjoy no actual converse with angel spirits. Yet still it feels as if it *could*, but for this heavy clay:—it knows that it *shall*, when it leaves this tenement of flesh. And this is what its yearnings inwardly say; yea, this is what it would actually say to angels, could it reach them: "Bless the Lord, ye His angels, that excel in strength, that do His commandments, hearkening to the voice of His word." And as the cherubim cry one to another as they fly around the throne of glory, so we may suppose will the spirits of redeemed men, and the spirits of unfallen angels, incite each other in heaven above, to raise new themes of praise, to bless with greater fervency of blessing, and to adore with ever-increasing adoration.

But it is not the mere human spirit of David that is here addressing the angelic beings, it is the Spirit of God—it is "the Lord the Spirit." 2 Cor. iii. 18. *Margin.* The various addresses to the heavens and to the earth, to animated beings and to inanimate things, which the Psalms and the books of the Prophets contain, are not mere bursts of impassioned feeling, mere figures and apostrophes of human eloquence: they are the sober and the deliberate utterances of that Mighty Spirit, by whose creative energy they were all brought into being, and who, when resisted by men, takes heaven and earth to witness against human ingratitude, Isa. i. 2; Jer. ii. 12; xxii. 29; Micah. vi. 1—3, and who, when man is silent, calls upon every part of the creation to take up the hymn of praise. Psalms cxlviii. cl. It is this Divine Spirit who here calls all created things and beings to the high duty and privilege of thanksgiving. The Father glorifies the Son—the Eternal Son glorifies the Father—and the Holy Spirit glorifies both—by whom, and with whom, He is likewise glorified. The Spirit of God who "moved upon the face of the waters," has a right to move His influences when and where, upon whom and upon whatsoever, He pleases. He has a right to call upon the highest and the lowest intelligences to glorify Jehovah; and by His own power to summon them, and all created things, saying, "Fulfil the end of your creation!" "The Lord the Spirit" has a right to publish this call by any, and by every, means in the whole universe, which He may condescend to employ. He may send it directly by His own voice, or by the medium of angels, or, as in this Psalm, by the instrumentality of man. He may cause it to be engraven on a rock, or printed in a book, to be made visible to the eye, if He so pleases, as well as audible to the ear.

We must remember also that these addresses were not written merely for the time then present, nor for the time that now is, but also for that which is to come. The Book of Inspiration is the Bible of the future, equally as of the past and of the present. The mind of the Spirit went beyond the mind of David and of Isaiah, when He used their pens. HE wrote for all ages. Thus, for instance, speaking of the great coming struggle in the day of the Lord, it is said, " He hath bid His guests." Zeph. i. 7. The invitation was written also by St. John, as heralded by an angel hundreds of years ago in these terms, " To all the fowls that fly in the midst of heaven, Come, and gather yourselves together unto the supper of the great God: that ye may eat the flesh of kings, and the flesh of captains, and the flesh of mighty men, and the flesh of horses, and of them that sit on them, and the flesh of all men, both free and bond, both small and great." Rev. xix. 17. Those very kings, though not yet reigning upon earth, are addressed and forewarned by the mercy of the same Spirit in the second Psalm, " Be wise, therefore, O ye kings; be instructed, ye judges of the earth: serve the Lord with fear, and rejoice with trembling. Kiss the Son lest He be angry, and ye perish from the way, when his wrath is kindled but a little."

In like manner as these " guests" are invited beforehand for the " day of the great slaughter," so all creation is preengaged in this Psalm, by the same Spirit, for the day of praise. The complete fulfilment of this invitation from the Spirit of God, is reserved to that future period. These words are recorded, not as David's but as " the Lord the Spirit's" public, perpetual, and standing invitation; fulfilled, fulfilling, and to be fulfilled—gloriously going on to its grand and universal accomplishment. Then all the " angels," " all the hosts," and " all the works" of the Lord, will be heard sweetly and harmoniously, powerfully and unceasingly, blessing His great and glorious name.

Reader, do you feel interested that angels should bless their Lord? Having lost the ability to pay the tribute of perfect praise, are you the more anxious that it should be paid by others? Or have you so little love for your Lord, that it matters not to you whether angels bless Him or not? Cold-hearted ingrate! *you* will never call on others, oh that God would call on you to praise Him. Tremble for yourself, lest Satan's wail may become your only note. If not one in spirit with the angels of light, you must become one with the angels of darkness, except you repent. Oh haste you to your closet. Fall upon your knees. Cry mightily to God for pardon. Ask Him to warm, to soften, to enlarge, your cold, hard, selfish heart. Ask Him to fill you with His own Spirit—the Spirit who will unite you to Jesus, and through Him to all who are good and holy in heaven and earth—the Spirit who will harmonize your spirit with the worship of saints and angels, constraining you to rejoice, and to thank God, that their notes are not like your own, but clear and full and sinless and unceasing.

Reader, the angels are blessing God day and night! What are you doing? Are you often praising, or oftener sighing? Bless God, I beseech you, night and day—in trouble and in sunshine; your trouble *might* be greater, your sunshine *might* be less. Job blessed God in the midst of calamities. Angels are blessing God in the midst of joys. Job had an angel's spirit, and his soul has long attained to an angel's position. Be like Job in heart now, that you may be like an angel in happiness hereafter. Bless God with the Patriarch through the dark night of time, that you may bless God with the angels throughout the bright day of eternity.

XVIII.

Call to Universal Gratitude.

ALL THE HOSTS OF THE LORD.

Bless ye the Lord, all ye His hosts: ye ministers of His, that do His pleasure.—Verse 21.

The preceding verse presented the angels before us as in a time of peace, each individually engaged in attending to his own particular duty—fulfilling the commands of God, and hearkening to His voice. This verse appears to present the angels to view—at least a large proportion of them—as in a time of war, as assembled and marshalled together in a collective capacity, ready, with united energy and power, to execute the pleasure of their Lord. Having addressed angels as moral and spiritual agents, the Psalmist now addresses them as ministering and instrumental agents. There he viewed them as he "messengers" of the Most High; here he regards them as the "armies" of His empire.

The Scriptures plainly indicate that there are various ranks and orders of beings included under the general title of "angels." St. Peter, however, makes a threefold distinction, when he says that "angels, and authorities, and powers, are made subject unto Christ." 1 Pet. iii. 22. St.

Paul speaks of "principalities and powers in the heavenly places," Eph. iii. 10, and also of "thrones and dominions." Col. i. 16. The term "angel" comprehends them all; but strictly signifies "messenger," "one who is sent;" and, in harmony with the classification by St. Peter, we would consider "angels" as peaceful messengers, to be specially addressed by the Psalmist in the 20th verse; and angels, as "authorities and powers" assembled for action, to be more immediately intended in the verse before us, as "the hosts of the Lord."

Of these "hosts," the Lord Jesus, in His human nature, is appointed chief. When the Second Person in the ever-blessed Trinity appeared as a "Man" to Joshua, He appropriated to Himself this remarkable title—"Captain of the host of the Lord," and required Divine worship to be offered. Josh. v. 15, (compared with Exod. iii. 5.) And, again, when the same glorious Person revealed Himself to John, in vision, as going forth "in righteousness, to judge and to make war," we read that the "armies which were in heaven followed Him." Rev. xix. 14. And well may it be asked, "Is there any number of His armies?" Job xxv. 3. Our blessed Saviour had but to ask, and presently His Father would have given Him more than twelve legions of angels. Matt. xxvi. 53. In the great moral conflict for our redemption, when Jesus, on the cross, "spoiled" the "principalities and powers" of darkness, and triumphed over them; Col. ii. 15, and when "He ascended on high and led captivity captive," these hosts of angels were spectators merely. The "twenty thousand, even thousands of angels" who are as the chariots of God, Psa. lxviii. 17, 18, stood looking on, as did the hosts of Israel, when David, single-handed, slew Goliath. And when, returning from that glorious victory, The Conqueror appeared before the gates of heaven, and admittance at the everlasting doors was demanded for Him, as the King of glory,—not more certainly was the question asked, "Who is this King of glory?" than it was triumphantly and appropriately answered, "The Lord strong and mighty, the Lord mighty in battle: the Lord of hosts, He is the King of glory." Psa. xxiv. But in the coming struggle at the end of time, similarly as we suppose in the conflict before time began, the angels will be personally engaged. Speaking of the vision of the future, which he saw, St. John says, "There was war in heaven. Michael fought, and his angels; and the Dragon fought, and his angels." Rev. x. ii. 7.

These angels, under Michael, are the "hosts of the Lord." Nor these alone. "Host" is a military term; it has a most comprehensive signification in earthly warfare. The men of all arms, and of all nations, whoever are found marshalled together in one army, to fight on one side, and in one cause, are called "the host." And as the Psalmist uses the plural number, and the comprehensive monosyllable "all," we must fix our attention not only upon the conspicuous leaders of the van, but likewise on all those who follow in the rear; and on everything that is summoned by the glorious Jehovah to execute the purposes of His almighty will. By the words, "all the hosts," we therefore understand the Psalmist as presenting before us the various assemblages of animated beings, and, in a subordinate sense, of inanimate things, that have been known at any time, to be marshalled on the Lord's side, and that may be called forth in His service to punish sinners, or to destroy His enemies. To all such, we consider the Spirit as virtually saying by the Psalmist: "Stand ready and loyal. Be prepared to act on the Lord's side—and bless your Creator by your prompt, unswerving, and perfect execution of His pleasure."

It is delightful to know that there are hosts of conscious, and of unconscious, agents, who, as "ministers," that is servants, do God's pleasure. Accustomed as we are in this rebellious province of His empire, to feel so much opposition in our fallen nature to His laws, and to see so many engaged only in the performance of their own pleasure, it is refreshing to turn to the contemplation of these faithful hosts. Even on our earth there is more obedience to our God in the unintelligent, than there is in the intelligent creation: "The winds and the seas obey Him." God calls the locusts and other insects, "My great army." Joel ii. 25. David testifies of the "fire and hail, snow and vapor, and stormy wind, as fulfilling His word." Psa. cxlviii. 8. And regarding "hail," we read that there "were more" of the enemies of the Lord in the battle at Gibeon, "who died with hailstones, than they whom the children of Israel slew with the sword." Josh. x. 11.

Everything praises and blesses God by fulfilling, first, the general object of creation, and secondly, the special service to which it is appointed. This rule applies equally to the animate as to the inanimate, alike to the mightiest principalities and powers, and to the most insignificant things that fulfil the great purposes of Jehovah. All these are arranged and appointed by God, and are liable to be called any moment into active service by Him. The Psalmist therefore addresses them as His ministers or servants, and calls on them to bear their part in the universal worship due, of praise and of obedience: "Bless the Lord, all ye His hosts, ye ministers of His that do His pleasure."

The "angels" being all intelligent agents, are capable of "doing God's commandments." They can receive and understand an order, and they can knowingly and intentionally set themselves to perform it. But "the hosts of the Lord," being not all intelligent agents, are here appropriately spoken of as "doing His pleasure." They are capable of executing what He requires, or He would never require it of them; therefore, let them fulfil it—let them at all times, and on all occasions, and in every variety of circumstances, bless their Great Creator, their Almighty Ruler, by uniformly, and perseveringly, and unitedly, doing His pleasure in heaven above and on earth beneath.

These addresses of the Spirit by the Psalmist, say in effect: "Let there be harmony in the universe!" Rebellion commenced in heaven. It has extended to our globe. We trust that no other world than our own, has been involved in its guilt. This much, however, we know, that on this globe it is to be terminated. Thank God that we know this fact. The devil, with every one who kept not his first estate, is to be cast into the lake of fire, which is the second death. Rev. xx. 10, 14. That foul rebellion—that unnatural civil war in heaven—though it commenced on high, and whithersoever it may have extended, is to be crushed, and concluded here below. Satan's lies and artful misrepresentations of his Maker, will be sifted to the bottom ere the sands of time run out. Every insinuation will then stand exposed—every aspersion disproved—every calumny refuted. Ample time and opportunity have been granted him to solve his problem, and to prove his several points of accusation. That problem he can never solve. Those accusations he can never prove. And when the GRAND EXPLANATION DAY arrives, he will be covered with everlasting shame, and God with everlasting glory. He will then be demonstrated to the whole universe to be, what "The Faithful Witness," whom he put to death, declared, "The Father of Lies—in whom there is no truth." John viii. 44. By one lie, he deceived a portion of his brother angels. By another lie, he seduced our first parents; and for well-nigh six thousand years, he has been whispering falsehood by his agents into the ear of every human being. His object is to misrepresent the character of God—to make us believe that He does not really care for us—that he would keep us in ignorance, and deny us many things that are really good for us. The poor creature who believes this calumny, feels and says, "I must take care of myself. I must do what I judge to be most conducive to my own advantage. And as to touching this, or not taking that, I must be overruled by no restrictions, but those which appear right to my own mind." Thus is fought over again, in every human breast, that fatal battle which the principles of good and evil waged within the heart of Eve as she gazed at the forbidden tree. Even in her pure mind, *self* rose uppermost—her own supposed interests gained the ascendency—the calumny was believed—God was distrusted—and disobedience to Him, and obedience to her own dictates, were the immediate results. This victory gained over such a mind, makes Satan vaunt that he can conquer easily her fallen children.

God wishes to impress the truth of His real character upon our minds. Satan desires to impress his own misrepresentations of that character. Truth says, God is love. Satan says, God is not love to you. Truth says, God careth for you. Satan says, God careth only for Himself. Truth says, Love and serve God. Satan says, Love and serve yourself. The reception within the heart, of either of these opposite statements, produces its natural effects in the life and action. He who believes that God is love, and that He careth for him, will love and serve God in return, will praise and bless His name. He who believes that God is not love, and careth not for him, will love and serve himself. God knows that this will be the immediate and necessary result, and therefore He demands our faith. Satan also knows that this will be the inevitable consequence, and therefore he stirs up our belief. And is Satan to be credited in preference to the Most High?—Is the calumny against their Creator to be universally believed by the creatures He has made? No. By the Divine grace we answer, No. A host of witnesses from the beginning have denounced the falsehood, disowned the calumny, rejected the misrepresentation. In every age, and in every generation, God has "reserved to Himself" some "seven thousand," who believed in His true character, and who loved, and served, and blessed Him with their whole souls. The Psalmist was one of these. His loyal heart beat strong with desire for victory over sin and Satan, over falsehood and misrerepsentation. He knew that God had been calumniated in heaven above, and on earth beneath: therefore he calls on all the hosts of the Lord to reject the calumny, and to wage war with the calumniator: therefore he calls upon his own soul, and upon the whole universe, to praise and bless The Good, The Wise, The Just, The Holy, whose heart is love, whose laws are right, whose character is spotless.

Oh! rise, ye hosts of the Lord, and "bless His holy name." Declare that ye are for ever on His side, and "bless His holy name." As ministers and servants, do His pleasure in preference to your own, and "bless his holy name." "Oh all ye powers of the Lord, bless ye the Lord, praise Him and magnify Him for ever. O all ye servants of the Lord, bless ye the Lord, praise Him and magnify Him for ever."

There shall be harmony in the universe. The lie of Satan will be disproved, and the liar himself will be silenced. All who believed the lie will be "convinced" at last of its falsity—and all who took part with its framer will be made partakers of his punishment. Both men and devils will be forced to acknowledge that God is holy, and just, and good. The sentence will not only be pronounced upon the wicked by the mouth of the Judge, but it will also be pronounced within each of them by his own conscience. The lie will have become transparent, and the truth transparent also:

and throughout the long eternity, no lost spirit, no ruined man, will be heard any longer finding fault with God; but each will then find fault with himself, and throughout the depths of his own consciousness there will resound this bitter aggravation of his never-ending misery, "I deserve all I suffer—I deserve all I suffer."

There shall be harmony in the universe. God will be acquitted, even by His enemies, and "justified by all His children." The recoil of falsehood will be universal before the advance of truth. "Every eye shall see" Jesus seated on His glorious throne. Those who heard of Him only by "the hearing of the ear," will then, too late, abhor themselves, and unavailingly repent in fire and ashes. The devils, who now "believe and tremble," in anticipation of their doom, will then be overwhelmed under its terrible realization.

There shall be harmony in the universe. No opposing sentiments will be uttered—no disobedience manifested—no self-will exhibited. A time is coming, when an angel may fly round the universe, and no one will gainsay his testimony for God. He may visit every different nation on our globe, and find every one of its inhabitants loving Jesus, and doing the will of God on earth as it is done in heaven. The elements will not strive. The brute creation will not quarrel. Every man will love his brother. And the whole universe will show forth the glorious attributes of Jehovah. Heaven will declare that God is *love*. Hell will attest that God is *just*. Creation will demonstrate that God is *strong*. Time will have manifested that God is *wise* and *good*. Angels will assert that God is *holy*. Devils will confess that God is *unchangeable*. The redeemed will exclaim that He is *true* to His promises. The lost will declare that He is *faithful* to His threatenings. Thus all God's attributes will be irradiated and glorified. Eternity will display them all in their individual fulness and perfection, and in their perfect union and harmony of operation.

Before that glorious calm can be witnessed, there must be heard the storm of war. Not more certainly will the material elements contend against each other, and the foundations of the earth be shaken, Isa. xxiv. 18, than the angels of light will wage war against the angels of darkness: "It shall come to pass in that day that the Lord shall punish the hosts of the high ones that are on high, and the kings of the earth upon the earth. And they shall be gathered together as prisoners are gathered in the pit, and shall be shut up in the prison; and after many days shall they be visited. Then the moon shall be confounded, and the sun ashamed, when the Lord of hosts shall reign in Mount Zion, and in Jerusalem, and before His ancients gloriously." Isa. xxiv. 21—23.

The instruments of God in this warfare, are here addressed by the Lord the Spirit through the mouth of David, "Bless ye the Lord, all ye His hosts: ye ministers of His that do His pleasure." The contest now is against the principles, then it will also be against the persons, of devils. Michael will right and his angels; and the Dragon and his angels. The progress of the war will be from victory to victory, and every enemy shall be subdued for ever. In His own good time the "Captain of our salvation" will lead on the hosts of the Lord, to take possession of the earth, Rev. xix. 11; and then will the "great voices be heard in heaven, saying, 'The kingdoms of this world are become the kingdoms of our Lord, and of His Christ; and He shall reign for ever and ever.'" Rev. xi. 15. "All the hosts of the Lord" will "bless the Lord" by executing His pleasure on the usurper of His throne, and the calumniator of His character. The very elements, as subordinate agents, will "bless the Lord" by doing His pleasure against the enemies of their Creator; fire will torment them for ever and ever. Rev. xx. 10.

Reader! are you on the Lord's side? Are you blessing God by contending against sin, and the world, and the devil? Can your fidelity be reckoned on, in the day of battle? When *unbelief* presents itself to take possession of your heart, do you resist it? When *cares* would gain the mastery, do you cast them down? When *riches* would entice you, do you refuse to become their slave? When your *besetting sin* returns to assail you, do you wrestle hard against it in secret prayer? When *impatience, fretfulness,* and *irritable tempers,* rise within, do you indulge, or do you try to master them? When *coldness* and *ingratitude* steal upon your heart, are you vigilant to assault them as the enemies of your Lord? Oh "be faithful unto death, and Christ will give you the crown of life." Call not these small sins. Goliath despised David as a stripling, yet he fell by his hand. Perhaps you think "lukewarmness" or indifference, a small sin; but so abhorrent is it to your God, that He would rather have you altogether "cold." Rev. iii. 15. An open enemy is better than a lukewarm friend. Reader, your battlefield is in your own heart. If you have no warfare there, you are not a true soldier of Christ. More difficult is it to fight against self, than against all the hosts of darkness. Yet fight we must, against both the one and the other, in the name of our Lord and by the Spirit of our God. It is "to him that overcomes" that all the promises are made. Rev. ii. 7, 11, 17, 26; iii. 5, 12, 21; xxi. 7. And *how* we are to overcome, we are graciously informed, "They overcame him by the blood of the Lamb, and by the word of their testimony; and they loved not their lives unto the death." Rev. xii. 11. Bless God therefore, and be blessed of Him in contending against every sin within, and every enemy without. Take heed that you never act the coward and the traitor in the day of battle. Take heed that you incur not wrath, by refusing to fight for God. "Curse ye Meroz, said the angel of the Lord, curse ye bitterly the inhabitants thereof: because they came not to the help of the Lord, to the help of the Lord against the mighty." Judges v. 23.

Take courage, Christian soldier. Greater is He that is for you, than all they that can come against you: "Be strong in the Lord, and in the power of His might. Put on the whole armor of God, that ye may be able to stand against the wiles of the devil. For we wrestle not against flesh and blood, but against principalities, against powers, against the rulers of the darkness of this world, against spiritual wickedness in high places. Wherefore take unto you the whole armor of God, that ye may be able to withstand in the evil day, and having done all, to stand. Stand therefore, having your loins girt about with truth, and having on the breastplate of righteousness; and your feet shod with the preparation of the gospel of peace; above all, taking the shield of faith, wherewith ye shall be able to quench all the fiery darts of the wicked. And take the helmet of salvation, and the sword of the Spirit, which is the word of God: praying always with all prayer and supplication in the Spirit, and watching thereunto with all perseverance and supplication for all saints." Eph. vi. 11—18. Bless God with all His faithful hosts by fighting the good fight of faith, "doing His pleasure" continually, in preference to your own. The time is at hand, when you will be made "more than a conqueror." Fear no enemy but sin, and you will have no other enemy to fear. Sin is the only foe that can separate us from the Captain of our salvation. Strive, therefore, against all sin, and you will be enabled to say with the Apostle, "I am persuaded, that neither death, nor life, nor angels, nor principalities, nor powers, nor things present, nor things to come, nor height, nor depth, nor any other creature, shall be able to separate us from the love of God, which is in Christ Jesus our Lord." Rom. viii. 38, 39.

XIX.

Call to Universal Gratitude.

ALL THE WORKS OF THE LORD.

Bless the Lord, all His works, in all places of His dominion.—Verse 22.

HAVING called on all the "angels" and the "hosts" of the Lord, to bless their King, the heart of the Psalmist is raised by the Spirit with yet more enlarged and intense desires for his God and Saviour to be glorified. The thought is abhorrent to his mind that any part of creation should be silent in the universal chorus of praise. Jehovah is worthy to be magnified, and to be had in everlasting honor. "He inhabiteth eternity." His presence pervadeth the universe. His voice called creation out of nothing. His power preserves it in existence every moment. Let it all therefore show forth His praise. Let not a spot be found in heaven or earth where God is not acknowledged. And whatsoever animate or inanimate portion of the wide universe may not have been included in these two previous invitations, the inspired Psalmist here calls upon it to bless and to glorify its Divine Creator. He carefully selects the most comprehensive language that can possibly be found; and in few but forcible terms he embraces the whole circle of the created universe, saying, "Bless the Lord, all His works, in all places of His dominion.

Every created thing blesses its Maker by occupying the place, and accomplishing the purpose, which He has appointed for it. "All God's works, in all places," are here cited to loyalty and obedience. The universe does not consist of the single planet on which we live. "The King Eternal, immortal, and invisible," possesses dominions far beyond the ken of man. The Divine Spirit, therefore, while here speaking with human words, is not to be limited by human ignorance, but is to be considered according to His own omniscience as calling all the created universe to the performance of its highest and most incumbent duty, in fulfilling the will and showing forth the glory of the Great Creator. While therefore we daily bless our God for His redeeming love toward our fallen race, let us not forget to send our loyal thoughts, our ardent aspirations, through the realms of space, and say, "Wheresoever the King of kings possesses a dominion, there let Him possess loyal subjects. How many soever may be the worlds which the Creator has made, throughout them all for ever, let Him find loving hearts. In every part of the wide universe which He has filled with matter or with mind, let Him receive the homage of gratitude and obedience: 'Bless the Lord, all His works, in all places of His dominion.'"

Never let us lose sight of this revealed truth, that all Creation is the work of the Triune Jehovah. The Father created all things by The Word, through the Eternal Spirit. "The High and Holy One that inhabiteth eternity," has made Himself known to us in Christ Jesus, and in recognizing and honoring Him as the Creator, we recognize and honor the Father also. John v. 23; and xiv. 7. Oh how it magnifies creation in the eyes of a believer, and endears it to his heart, when he remembers that his gracious Redeemer formed it.

JESUS IS THE CREATOR: "All things were made by Him: and without Him was not anything made that was made." John i. 3. Therefore of Jesus it is written, that "He hath made the earth by His power. He hath established the world by His wisdom; and hath stretched out the heavens by His discretion." Jer. x. 10. All things "do whatsoever He commandeth them upon the face of the world in the earth." Job xxxvii. 12. JESUS IS THE CREATOR: "For by Him were all things created, that are in heaven, and that are in earth, visible and invisible, whether they be thrones, or dominions, or principalities, or powers: all things were created by Him and for Him: and He is before all things, and by Him they all consist." Col. i. 16. "In the beginning was the Word, and the Word was with God, and the Word was God." John i. 1. "In the beginning God created the heaven and the earth." Gen. i. 1. It was God the Word "who spake and it was done: who commanded and all things stood fast." Psa. xxxiii. 9. A time has come to Jesus in the world above, when, as The God-Man, "all the angels of God worship Him," Heb. i. 6; a time is coming on this earth when "all nations shall call Him blessed, and when all kings shall fall down before Him." Psa. lxxii.; and a time is coming in the wide universe, when "at the name of Jesus every knee shall bow, of things in heaven, and things in earth, and all things under the earth: and when every tongue shall confess that Jesus Christ is Lord, to the glory of God the Father." Phil. ii. 10.

How glorious, on the sixth day, must have been the scene when Jesus, the great Creator, looked on every thing that He had made, and behold it was "very good." Light had sprung out of darkness at His command, and order had arisen out of confusion. Waters were divided by His word, the vital air was expanded, the habitable earth was consolidated. Rich foliage and sweet fruits adorned the trees that never grew; creatures that had sprung from no parents, roamed in air and earth and sea; and man, without knowing childhood, rose, full-formed, from dust to manhood,—a living image of his Maker. Oh how "very good" was our God and Saviour to give them being—how "very good" was the being which He gave. How glorious was creation; when the earth was fresh, and the sea was young; when the wind first spread its new-made wing; and man and all the creatures, lived and moved and had their being in God. The Creator was glorified throughout the entire creation. All His works blessed Him in all places of His dominion.

Our eyes behold creation now, only under the curse. God saw it in its primeval bloom; and the Spirit of God in the Psalmist here fervently desires its restoration. Satan has usurped authority over the globe. He could take Adam's kingship and gain dominion over the creatures; but he could not take the Lord's; "His kingdom still ruleth over all." The Bible is a recorded protest against Satan's

USURPATION. Every subject is reminded of his duty. The whole creation is thus expressly summoned to give in its tribute of adoration to the Only True God, the Universal King—"Praise ye the Lord from the heavens: Praise Him in the heights. Praise ye Him, all His angels. Praise ye Him, all His hosts. Praise ye Him, sun and moon. Praise Him, all ye stars of light. Praise Him ye heavens of heavens, and ye waters that be above the heavens. Let them praise the name of the Lord: for He commanded, and they were created. Praise the Lord from the earth, ye dragons, and all deeps: Fire and hail; snow and vapors; stormy wind fulfilling His word: Mountains, and all hills; fruitful trees, and all cedars: Beasts, and all cattle; creeping things and flying fowl: Kings of the earth, and all people; princes, and all judges of the earth: Both young men, and maidens; old men, and children: Let them praise the name of the Lord: for His name alone is excellent; His glory is above the earth and heaven." Psa. cxlviii. In one comprehensive sentence, the Divine Spirit, by the Psalmist, here calls all creation to the discharge of its high duty, saying, "Bless the Lord, all His works, in all places of His dominion." And again, elsewhere, he specifies several parts of creation, saying, "Let the heaven and earth praise Him, the seas, and everything that moveth therein." Psa. lxix. 34.

How marvellous is our world—created out of nothing with its immeasurable fulness—and hung upon nothing with its enormous bulk. Deep calleth unto deep, and one mountain peak to another, that "great is the Lord, and of great power, and His understanding is infinite." The very elements are but as shadows of His attributes :—fire, or light, of His glory : air of His omnipresence : earth of His beneficence : and the ocean of His power.

"The heavens declare the glory of God, and the firmament showeth His handiwork. Day unto day uttereth speech, and night unto night showeth knowledge." The brilliant luminaries in the vault of heaven invite the regard of man; in every region they awaken and repay his admiration; they are calculated to elevate his soul with impressions of grandeur and beneficence, and to illuminate his mind with this grand truth that "the Hand that made them is Divine."

How glorious is the sky by day; how magnificent by night! The dawn of morn proclaims God's presence; the close of evening displays His power: "He clothes Himself with light as with a garment. He stretches out the heaven as a curtain." The Sun, in his golden splendor, the Moon, in her silvery brightness, and the studded firmament of Stars, have a voice, more eloquent than human words, to glorify the Lord : "There is no speech nor language where their voice is not heard," (Psa. xix.) proclaiming "His eternal power and Godhead," His benevolence and love.

The precise movements of the heavenly bodies—unvarying for ages—glorify the Great Creator, inculcate the lesson of order, regularity, and obedience, and present to man, that great gift from God, a standard of time. Even the erratic comets, those lights that appear but at intervals in the heavens, testify for God, put every Atheist to shame, and prove how false and blasphemous is his doctrine of Chance. Sudden and brief in their appearance, and unequalled in the velocity of their movements; inexplicable in their nature, and surpassing observation in the depths they traverse; yet so exact and obedient to their Creator's law, are these creatures of His hand, that man rejoices to predict the period of their return; and, where it was least to have been expected, receives this all-important lesson, never to deviate from the path of duty which his Maker has prescribed.

How marvellous is the element of light—simple, yet complex—mysterious in its nature, yet revealing mysteries in others—apparently colorless, yet coloring all things with the most different hues—imparting freely of itself, and yet losing nothing—so swift in motion, as to be really in appearance motionless! Light blesses God by its minute and universal obedience to His will, in giving brilliancy to the diamond, verdure to the leaf, tints to the flowers, and flavor to the fruits. But not more marvellous is light, than useful, and beautiful, and indispensable. Our globe without the Sun would become a wide circle of death—no light over its whole circumference—no warmth in air, or land, or sea,—no life, no growth, in seeds or plants, in man or animals. But, thanks be to God, at His command it shines through every particle of the atmosphere, pervades every drop of the ocean, beams on every part of the earth's surface, and guides and gladdens every living thing.

Who shall describe the various offices by which the element of Air glorifies its Creator! Present everywhere, yet seen nowhere, it is a universal remembrancer of the Omnipresent God. Air is at once the representative of man's spirit, and the supporter of man's life. It is necessary not only to his breathing, but also to almost every function he performs. Its gentle, but powerful and supporting, pressure on every part of his frame, is an emblem of that all-surrounding but unseen Hand which continually upholds him,—for without the air he cannot move or act; he can neither speak, nor see, nor hear. The atmosphere is not only universally necessary to our globe, but Jesus, at creation, made it universally suitable to all that the globe contains; and the air glorifies its Maker by universal and ready subservience to the continual and varied demands that are made upon it on land and sea. It permeates the waters of the ocean, and penetrates the recesses of the earth: and yet diffuses the most delicate fragrance of the flowers, and conveys the softest notes of the birds. The fowls of the heaven fly therein, and the fish in the sea swim thereby. Air, how simple is it, yet how compound. Though more soft and yielding than any other element, yet the Almighty Word made it His "firmament" to divide the waters from the waters, and most faithfully has it obeyed Him unto this day.

How wonderful and varied are the works of the Lord in the region of the Earth! His people at the contemplation of them exclaim, "O Lord, how manifold are Thy works! in wisdom hast Thou made them all: the earth is full of Thy riches." Psa. civ.

How fair and fertile are the plains—how beautiful the valleys, how magnificent the mountains. Every season of the year bears its peculiar testimony to the ever-watchful, ever-gracious care of its Creator. Winter gives rest and strength for the activities of Spring: Summer fosters to maturity what the Spring has produced, and Autumn completes the tribute of their praise. Her trees, loaded with blessing, seem to bend their branches in acknowledgment of the Giver; and her fields, undulating with profusion for man and beast, appear as if presenting their wave-offering to the Lord ere the hand of man can sully it.

"The works of the Lord are great; sought out of all them that have pleasure therein." The telescope reveals a part of their magnitude, and the microscope of their minuteness. A mountain declares the glory of God, and a grain of sand displays His creative power. Man exults that he is the chief of God's works, and yet the Great Creator has "so clothed the lilies of the field, that even Solomon, in all His glory, was not arrayed like one of these." Matt. vi. 29. Man is, indeed, the chief glory of God's earthly workmanship, and richly and freely has He given all things to him to enjoy. In His considerate benignity, He adorned and replenished the earth before He created man to be its inhabitant. And in its various parts, what a store of happiness has He laid open to rich and poor alike!

"Not the rich nursery's costly toys
Such wealth of bliss can yield,
As childhood's simple, priceless joys,
Of Tree, and Rock, and Field.

"The music of the singing birds,
The fragrance of the flowers,
The valley streams, the mountain herds,
The woodland's leafy bowers.

"The sunset hues, the starry sky,
The groves, the pebbly shore,
The chasing clouds, the cliffs on high,
The stormy ocean's roar.

"The sweet hoards of the honey-bee,
The fruits that fenceless grow,
Wild winter's magic tracery
Of frost and fleecy snow.

"The cottage Child, these treasures all,
By birthright doth possess;
Free is to him the Palace-Hall
Of Nature's loveliness.

"God's beauteous earth is surely rife
With good in every part;
With blessings for the outer life,
With lessons for the heart.

"And when that life is tun'd to praise,
That heart to Him is given,
Earth, e'en with all its sorrowing days,
A foretaste is of heaven." F.

What a mirror of its Great Creator is the mighty Ocean, —in resources inexhaustible, in depth unfathomable, in breadth immeasurable,—in appearance ever changing, and yet unchangeably the same: in divisions innumerable, and yet in unity how perfect and entire throughout the globe; never wearied, never old; unsullied in purity, and fresh as at creation. In its simplicity and its diversity; in its beauty and its bounty; in its power and in its playfulness; this mighty element is indescribable. The silvered waters of the sleeping ocean, form a vast visible image of God's hidden peace—the Divine repose of soul; and the loudest storm that rises on its surface, is but as a mighty orchestra of winds and waves celebrating His praise. The very saltness of its waters praises Him, who has thereby made them healthful; and their perpetual motion sounds a perpetual thanksgiving to Him, who thereby preserves them from stagnation.

Nothing throughout our globe appears more fluctuating than water, or, in its various movements, more extraordinary and irregular: yet in no department can we trace more visibly the laws of harmony and of order. The great water-wheel of Nature shows forth the glory of its Creator by the regularity and the constancy of its rotation—dispersing blessings throughout the entire circuit of its revolution. Behold its working in the endless variety of water-forms;—commencing its movement in springs, or advancing slowly from fountains, then trickling downward in rills, pouring forward in streams, rushing onward in rivers, moving powerfully in oceans, rising upward in vapors, rolling over us in clouds, and then descending in the mist and the rain, in the hail and the snow, to commence again in springs its perfect circle of drink-bearing distribution to parched soils and drooping foliage, to thirsty man, and bird, and beast, and insect. Thus, "unto the place whence the rivers come, thither they return again" Eccles. i. 7; and bless their Maker by the music of their unceasing flow.

Not more wonderful are the elements of air, and earth, and water, than is the life with which they teem: some creatures showing forth the glory of God, and blessing their Creator, by their magnitude, some by their magnificence, some by their minuteness, and all together by their uncounted myriads.

Man himself, the chief inhabitant of the globe, is its chief wonder,—three mysteries in one, each surpassing the other with its tribute of glory to the Divine Creator. Whether we consider man in his bodily parts, his mental powers, or his spiritual capacities, ineffably glorious does that Divine Mind appear which could originate the idea of such a being as man, and that Divine power which could give it living reality in a body, soul, and spirit. Man—the creature of yesterday, the child of the dust—is furnished by his God with a bodily eye that can pierce millions of miles through space to distant stars—the finite gazing on the works of the Infinite—he is endowed with a mental eye that can survey in thought the whole globe on which he treads, the mighty system to which it belongs, the heaven of heavens, the hosts of angels, the throne of the Eternal, and God Himself seated thereon,—and he is endowed by grace with a spiritual eye that can look through Jesus, by faith, to "Him who is invisible," and behold an Almighty Creator, a reconciled Father, and a God of Love.

Nor man alone, all creatures bless their Creator by displaying His power in their existence, His wisdom in their design and adaptation, His resources in their number and variety, His beneficence in their food and their enjoyments, His all-pervading presence in their continual preservation. Some praise Him by the velocity of their motion, some by their energy and strength, some by the elegance of their forms, some by the beauty of their colors, and some by the sweetness of their notes. From the huge Leviathan to the smallest animalcule, all glorify their Maker by occupying the place He has assigned them in Creation. Not one of all the myriads in air and earth and sea, breathes or moves, or acts, or dies, without the knowledge of God. They "all wait" on Him for their daily sustenance, (Psa. civ. 27,) and derive from Him their entire strength, their every breath. What glory redounds to the Almighty Giver, from that marvellous energy of existence, with which He has endowed even the smallest tribes of animated matter. What an amount of happiness has His beneficence comprehended in a living atom. What a century of joy has His love summed up in the tiny creature that bursts into life with the sun's warmth, sports itself in his meridian beams, and sinks into death before the sunset. Even death itself, mysterious absorber, produces life, and praises the wonder-working God. Decay and mould are but His seed-plots of new forms of existence. Disruptions place themselves at His feet as stepping-stones to order. Instability in one form, paves the way for permanence in another; and every change blesses God by leading onward to improvement and perfection.

The Lord is glorified in every part of His creation, and accomplishes vast designs by the most apparently inadequate instrumentality. The wind at His command becomes the planter of a portion of His seeds; a feeble insect the architect of His coral islands; and a warbling bird, His messenger of life to an immortal soul. "What are these birds doing?" said a fisherman to himself as he awoke in his boat; "Late last night, and here again early this morning:

what are they always singing?" a voice within him replied, "They're praising their Maker." And deep was the conviction stamped upon his conscience, that all creatures praised God but himself. Day and night the song of the birds was in his ear, and the lesson of the Spirit accompanying it in his conscience. He became a new man in Christ Jesus; and was often heard to say, "Who could have thought that the songs of a few little birds, should be the instruments of my salvation?" All God's works give Him glory; if we had only spiritual eyes to see it, and spiritual ears to hear it, the universe would be found full of praise. All God's works would be heard blessing "Him in all places of His dominion."

"All power is given unto Jesus in heaven and on earth," (Matt. xxviii. 18;) and "all things are put under His feet," though as yet "we see it not." Heb. ii. 8. The whole creation lies under the curse, and its voice of praise is consequently imperfect. But the time is coming, when Jesus will "take to Himself His great power;" and then shall the prophecy of the Psalmist be fulfilled, "ALL THY WORKS SHALL PRAISE THEE O LORD, AND THY SAINTS SHALL BLESS THEE." Psa. cxlv. 10. Jesus, the Creator, will come forth as the Re-Creator, and say, "Behold, I make all things new." Then in the new heavens and the new earth, all His works, in all places of His dominion, will bless the Triune Jehovah. God the Father will be worshipped. God the Son will be adored. The Divine Spirit will be divinely honored. The thanksgiving of the universe will be offered. The twofold homage for Creation and for Redemption will be paid. Oh, transporting thought! thrice happy prospect: most glorious period! Who shall describe the triumph of that hour? Who can conceive the grandeur of that scene?—A universe of voices; a choir of worlds; the music of eternity; all creatures worshipping; all creation praising; Jesus acknowledged as "God over all, and blessed for ever."

In preparation for this glorious consummation, the Divine Spirit here calls on "all God's works, in all places of His dominion, to bless His name." What though discordant sounds grate upon our ear during the period of this Tuning time,—the instruments will soon be perfected, and then what a burst of harmony will break upon us in Eternity! Angels and archangels, cherubim and seraphim, thrones and dominions, principalities and powers, all the hosts and servants of the Lord, all the members of His redeemed family, and "all His works in all places of His dominion," will join in one melodious choir to sing the song of universal gratitude and praise. Hymns of Creation and of Redemption will be sung responsive; and the voices of the created will chant "Amen" to the symphonies of the redeemed. The SERAPHIM, as representatives of the angels, will be heard worshipping the Trinity in Unity as they cry one to another, "Holy, Holy, Holy, is the Lord of hosts—the whole earth is full of His glory." Isa. vi. 3. The four LIVING CREATURES, as representatives of the Church, will never rest, day nor night, worshipping the Unity in Trinity, "Holy, Holy, Holy, Lord God Almighty, which was, and is, and is to come." The four-and-twenty ELDERS, on behalf of the redeemed, will not be slow to raise the praises of the Creator: "Thou art worthy, O Lord, to receive glory and honor and power: for Thou hast created all things, and for Thy pleasure they are and were created." Rev. iv. Then "the voice of HARPERS" will be heard "harping with their harps, before the throne, that new song" of Redemption, which no man can learn, but the hundred and forty and four thousand which are redeemed from the earth. Rev. xiv. "And, lo, a GREAT MULTITUDE, which no man can number, of all nations, and kindred, and people, and tongues, standing before the throne, and before the Lamb, clothed with white robes, and palms in their hands," will cry "with a loud voice, saying, Salvation to our God which sitteth upon the throne, and unto the Lamb." To this grateful song of the redeemed, the angels will immediately and joyfully respond "Amen! Blessing, and glory, and wisdom, and thanksgiving, and honor, and power, and might, be unto our God for ever and ever. Amen!" Rev. vii. Again the high praises of the Redeemer will be raised by those who "have every one of them harps and golden vials full of odors;" falling down "before the Lamb," they will sing this "new song," "Thou art worthy to take the book, and to open the seals thereof; for Thou wast slain, and hast redeemed us to God by Thy blood, out of every kindred, and tongue, and people, and nation: and hast made us unto our God kings and priests: and we shall reign on the earth." In full harmony with this song of the redeemed, and in direct adoration of the Redeemer, the "innumerable company" of the ANGELS, "the number of whom is ten thousand times ten thousand, and thousands of thousands," will be heard praising him, and saying, "Worthy is the Lamb that was slain to receive power, and riches, and wisdom, and strength, and honor, and glory, and blessing." Then, like the mighty sound of many waters, the light voices of all the created, and of all the redeemed—"all His works, in all places of His dominion"—"EVERY CREATURE WHICH IS IN HEAVEN, AND ON THE EARTH, AND SUCH AS ARE IN THE SEA, AND ALL THAT ARE IN THEM," will be heard "blessing God" in this harmonious, universal, and everlasting song of gratitude and praise,—"BLESSING, AND HONOR, AND GLORY, AND POWER BE UNTO HIM THAT SITTETH UPON THE THRONE, AND UNTO THE LAMB FOR EVER AND EVER." Rev. v.

XX.

Call to Universal Gratitude.

THE PSALMIST'S OWN SOUL.

Bless the Lord, O my soul.—Verse 22.

HAVING addressed the whole universe of intelligent beings, animated creatures and inanimate things, the Son of Jesse sums up his addresses and his Psalm together, by calling upon his own soul to unite with them in the glorious work of praise. He would not suffer it to come behind even the angels in blessing God. He knows how good the Lord is. He had long and largely experienced the freeness of His forgiveness, the fulness of His forbearance, the richness of His benefits, and the tenderness of His love. "All that was within him" glowed, under the Divine Spirit, with intense gratitude to his Redeemer. Not more ardently, therefore, did he long to hear the praises of his Divine Benefactor sung by the entire creation, than he desired that he himself should bear a high and holy part in the universal and everlasting song.

The Royal Psalmist commenced this beautiful hymn of gratitude with a special address to his own soul, and now he closes it with a similar self application. In the course of it he had called on others to bless the Lord, and here, with redoubled earnestness, he calls upon himself. He had made it his first duty, and now he makes it his last, to bless his Creator and his Redeemer.

It is this heart application that we need in all our readings of Scripture, in all our hearings of sermons, and in all our experiences of God's goodness. The doctrines we learn must all be reduced to practice. The instructions we give to others must all be laid also upon ourselves. The mercies we receive must all be specially acknowledged. The truths of the Bible and the blessings of Providence should not be entertained as mere external verities; they should come home to the heart—they should be real, living, abiding sources of thought and feeling, and motives of action. Here is a pattern in David. These concluding words bear the stamp of reality upon them. The Psalmist was in deep earnest; and without earnest heart application there can be no true religion. Every one must be made to feel that it is with his own soul that he has to do. Angels may be praising God in heaven; the question for us is this—"Are we praising God on the earth?" All His works may be fulfilling His will; the consideration for me is—"Am I similarly serving my Redeemer?" My fellow men may, some of them, be loving Jesus, and others of them loving the world: their love to Him will not save me,—their rejection of Him will not ruin me. My own soul is to be the grand object of my solicitude. Others are better than I am; their goodness will not make up for my deficiency. Others may be worse than myself; their vileness will not excuse my sinfulness. Every one of us stands before the eye of Jesus as he inwardly is. We each personally receive his benfits: we should each personally give Him praise. We are each to stand individually before the throne of judgment. We must each personally take our place, on the right hand or on the left, of the Great White Throne. The question, therefore, for each of us is,—Am I preparing for that solemn day? What avail will it be to me though millions enter heaven, if I enter it not? As if David had said, Why should I write this Psalm for others? Why should I call upon the universe to glorify the Lord, if I call not upon myself? "Bless the Lord, oh MY soul." Whatever others do, let me do service to my God. Whoever others love, let me love my Redeemer. Whatever others glory in, let me glory only in the Lord. Let all my faculties be fixed on serving Him. Let all my powers be actively and continually engaged to show forth His praise. Home to my own heart let every duty come. Home to my own conscience let every threatening peal. Home to my own spirit let every promise press. Others, it is true, ought to praise God; but my soul ought also to praise Him. Others may forget; but let me not forget. All that is within me shall be effectually stirred up to celebrate the mercies of my God and Saviour. It is my first injunction upon myself, and it shall also be my last, "Bless the Lord, oh my soul."

What an instructive example is here exhibited for our individual instruction, and for our continual imitation! All our religious efforts should begin with our own hearts; next they should go forth to rouse the gratitude of others;

and then unfailingly return with increased energy to reanimate our own spirits. This is our first and our last duty. It testifies our sincerity; it quickens our progress; and it increases our joy. Blessings multiply as we use them; graces increase as we call them into exercise; and, both together, endow the heart with a continually enlarging circle of praise. Blessings impart gladness and awaken gratitude; gladness and gratitude increase love; love enlarges obedience; obedience obtains blessings; and renewed blessings redouble our gratitude and our gladness, our love and our obedience, in endless succession. Thus the soul becomes fitted for heaven and for eternity. It feels itself put in possession of powers and of materials for unceasing praise—the finite creature becomes capable of blessing for ever the infinite Creator—and thus onward and onward through time—from the day of his conversion onward through eternity—the soul of the believer is still rising, gratitude increasing, and thanksgiving abounding. The new birth of the soul introduces it to a life of everlasting gratitude. It is born of God's Spirit, and is made, by His teaching, increasingly conscious of its infinite obligations to creating power, preserving care, providing beneficence, and redeeming love. By the same Spirit it is endowed with everlasting gratitude for these blessings, and with everlasting love for their glorious Giver;—it is furnished with spiritual powers to praise Him immediately and unceasingly;—and it will be provided with a spiritual body to serve Him unweariedly throughout eternity.

The Scriptures uniformly testify that all true religion begins, continues, and ends with grace and gratitude—grace from God and gratitude from man. From first to last it is all on God's part GRACE—and from first to last it should be all on man's part GRATITUDE: "What have we, that we have not received?" Our very thankfulness is of the Lord, and in giving praise we only give Him back His own. We cannot make the Lord our debtor by our services or by our praises: "What can we render unto the Lord for all His benefits towards us?" Nothing, literally nothing. We can only take something further from His ever-giving-hand: "I will take the cup of salvation, and call upon the name of the Lord." Psa. cxvi. 12, 13. God is first in everything —first in love, first in the reconciliation. 1 John iv. 19; 2 Cor. v. 19. Man originates no movement towards the Most High. God's grace certainly, invariably, and everlastingly goes first, and our gratitude ought certainly, invariably, and everlastingly to follow.

Gratitude is an elevating sentiment. It raises us nearer to God. It unites the Receiver with the Giver. It refines and enlivens his heart. It fortifies his spirit against anxieties and dejection. And it prepares him to enter and to enjoy the high, and holy, and eternal state of being; for love is the grace, gratitude is the duty, and praise is the employment of heaven. True gratitude is a fruit of faith. All human systems of religion, ancient and modern, come short in the inculcation of thanksgiving. The Bible alone teaches us both to see God in all things, and thankfully to acknowledge Him as the suggester of thought, the prompter of word, the director of action, and the bestower of blessings. Ingratitude hardens the heart, but gratitude softens it. Ingratitude drives us further and further from God, but gratitude draws us nearer and nearer to Him in time, and makes us near for ever. Gratitude makes the believer now a willing worshipper at the throne of grace, and it will make him for ever a joyful worshipper at the throne of glory.

Every professing Christian should pray earnestly for the grace of gratitude; and honestly examine himself as to its sincerity, fervency, and progress. We are all prone to "forget." We need "line upon line, and precept upon precept," lest we go "backward, and be snared, and be taken," by the great adversary of our souls. Daily should we stir up "all that is within" us, to praise and to magnify our God. To be slow to pray is sinful: to be slow to praise is likewise base and odious. Murmuring is a heinous sin. Shall we set our will above the Lord's, and rebel against the appointments of His government? Shall we think, and speak, and act, as if we were wiser and better, more tender and generous than God? Shall we harbor that monster of ingratitude in our breasts—which says, in effect, "It is not kind; it is not well done. I would have done it better"—which thus virtually sets God aside, that it may become its own adviser, its own disposer, its own God? Never let us be so presumptuous as to conceive that the government of the universe is to obey our will, and be regulated by our convenience. Never let us sit in judgment upon the ways of God; repine against His providences; and find fault with His arrangements. "Who art thou that repliest against God?" Dost thou proudly deem thyself worthy of all that has been done for thee, of all that has been given to thee, yea and of far more besides? Wilt thou deliberately indulge this unthankful murmuring spirit, and permit it to say before God, within thy rebellious heart, that His gifts are not needed, nor their continuance cared for? Is it all the same, whether God smite, or smile upon thee? Dost thou neither fear His frown, nor desire His favor? Because one thing is not as thou wouldst have it, are all other mercies to be overlooked and despised? Flee, my soul, from ingratitude, as from a serpent. A murmuring spirit will bring thee to destruction. The unthankful can find no admission to heaven. For "murmurers and complainers" is "reserved the blackness of darkness for ever," Jude 13—16. Therefore, O my soul, bless thou thy God continually. Be thankful for His withholdings, as well as for His bestowments. Repine not at any allotment, "neither murmur as some have murmured, and were destroyed of the destroyer," 1 Cor. x. 10. Most offensive is ingratitude. Most dishonest is it, and unjust, defrauding God and men of their due acknowledgments. An earthly benefactor repents of having given his labor, love, and kindness; and feels his heart closed against the ungrateful recipient of his former favors. Be grateful, O my soul! I charge it upon thee as thy first and as thy last duty—Be grateful to thy God. Let me give Him the glory of all the blessing I enjoy on earth. Never let me attribute one of them to my own good management, or to blind chance, or to any second causes whatsoever. Let me not be guilty on the one hand of idolizing, or on the other of undervaluing, a single blessing which my God and Saviour condescends to bestow. For His glory, as the Giver, let me employ them all, and not for my own sinful gratifications, continually remembering and acknowledging how unworthy I am even of the least of His mercies. Let holy gratitude for the past and the present, lead me to humble confidence in His wisdom and love for the future, through time and through eternity; and let the sweet sense of obligation be an "easy yoke." to bind me most willingly and unreservedly to His service.

If we pursue the downward path of complaint, where shall we end but in the abyss of woe? If we follow the upward path of gratitude, whither shall it lead us but to the mansions of joy? All our earthly mercies have a heavenly origin. They bid us continually ascend. They teach us to rejoice as created and redeemed, as rational, and responsible, and grateful beings. They invite us to a spiritual thankful ness, to a holy joy. God desires our happiness. He gives unnumbered blessings to make us cheerful, contented, and thankful. Our memories ought to be registers of God's mercies. We should often recount them, one after another, and take delight in bringing all His goodness to remembrance. From time to time we set apart a day for fasting and prayer; so ought we to set apart a day for rejoicing and thanksgiving.

We should often hold our "Jubilee" of entire gladness, recapitulating the gracious acts of the Lord with glowing gratitude. We should enumerate the averting of evils that we feared, the unexpected turnings of affairs that revived our hopes, the hair-breadth escapes that surprised and gladdened us, and the answers to prayer that put our unbelief to shame. The various *circumstances* by which mercies have been distinguished and accompanied, should be carefully remembered; the *seasonableness* of their *supply*, the *tenderness* of love, and the *wisdom* of adaptation with which they were brought to our need and suited to our case; and the *greatness* of evils prevented, and of the blessings bestowed; the *health*, and *food*, and *raiment*, with which God has provided us; the *friends* raised up to us in the hour of difficulty; the *light* which has arisen upon us in seasons of darkness and perplexity, and the *peace* which has sustained our souls under bereavement, should all be specially and thankfully acknowledged.

Go back, O my soul, to the days of earliest remembrance. Gather together in review as many as possible of the various blessings of childhood, of youth, and of manhood, or now also it may be of old age. See life preserved, dangers averted, wants supplied, and comforts continued by the God of love. Try to recollect all the mercies and blessings, the deliverances, alleviations, and consolations bestowed by the Lord. Were they not as so many varied and lovely flowers adorning my onward path? Did they not render fragrant many an otherwise wilderness spot in my earthly pilgrimage? Let then a lively gratitude be ever as an ornament of grace around my neck, and appear as a coronet of gladness upon my brow? and let me ever be ready to bear grateful testimony to the goodness of my God and Saviour in all His dispensations. "Bless the Lord, O my soul," for he has dealt well with me. Well, in sickness, because He designed my good; well, in trials, because they were less than I deserved; well, in mercies, for they were all as unmerited on my part, as on His they were rich and free, continual and everlasting. Oh, my God, let me "abundantly utter the memory of thy great goodness." "Let me publish with the voice of thanksgiving, and tell of all Thy wondrous works."

Reader! this hundred and third Psalm, inspired by the Holy Ghost, yields spiritual "benefit" both in sorrow and in joy. When you feel sad and dejected, read over this Psalm, and it will relieve and sanctify your sorrow. When you feel happy and joyful, read over this Psalm, and it will increase and sanctify your joy. May the Holy Spirit write its every word upon your heart, to your "great and endless comfort." David, taught by the Spirit, has here both set the example of a grateful worshipper, and furnished "acceptable words" of praise. Imitate that example. Adopt these words. Be diligent in cultivating a grateful spirit. Seek for opportunities of praise. In your going out and your coming in, give thanks unto God. In your lying down and in your rising up, give thanks unto your God. Let it be your daily duty, and your hourly privilege, to "speak to yourself" in this or some similar, spiritual song. Lay up verses of Scripture, and hymns of thanksgiving, in your memory, with which to make sweet melody in your heart, repeating them to the Lord. Let every moment as it flies, bear onward a note of praise. Let every breath, as it rises, bear upward the incense of thanksgiving. Like the Psalmist, enjoin it upon your soul, as its first and as its last duty, to "bless the Lord." "In everything," says the Spirit, by the Apostle, "in everything give thanks, for this is the will of God in Christ Jesus concerning you." 1 Thess. v. 18.

So unceasing is His kindness, that there is no part of the day or of the night that may not have its peculiar theme—its appropriate subject of thanksgiving. Every hour, every circumstance, brings some lesson, some benefit, from God. Every hour, every circumstance, therefore, should carry with it some tribute of our gratitude. Peculiar mercies should receive peculiar acknowledgments. Every morning's comforts should draw forth every morning, praise. Every evening's mercies should excite every evening, gratitude. Every day should be a thanksgiving-day. Our whole life should be a life of praise. What a blessed sight to God, to angels, and to every holy being, is a grateful believer! The song of a sinner, sensible of his own vileness and of his Saviour's love, is the sweetest music in their ears. He has become a new man in Christ Jesus; the garment of righteousness is around him; the Spirit of Holiness is within him; humility has taken the place of pride; happiness has superseded heaviness; praise has put aside repining; joy has eclipsed all sorrow in his breast; and he is "singing and making melody in his heart to the Lord."

If our consideration of this Psalm has been attended with no other benefit, let us at least hope that it has convinced us of our ingratitude, and awakened us to thankfulness. The Lord grant that it may thus have proved as a "two-edged sword" in the hand of the Spirit, and then our labor shall not have been altogether in vain. Little indeed is that mind to be envied which can pass, from the perusal of this beautiful hymn of thanksgiving, to its wonted indifference. Cold and dead must be that heart which it does not constrain to say, "I fear, yea, I feel that I have not been sufficiently sensible of my mercies. How ungratefully have I requited my Divine Benefactor, my gracious Saviour, my holy Comforter." If such be the conviction produced in our breasts, surely it will have called forth an earnest cry for greater thankfulness of heart. Cherish that conviction. Give daily utterance to that cry. And to the very close of life let this be the fervent petition of your soul, "Lord, increase my gratitude." There are higher and lower notes of praise. Seek to rise: "Let the high praises of God be in your mouth." "Praise Him according to His excellent greatness."—Every gift, every mercy, increases our debt to God. Our thanksgivings *ought* to be proportioned to His blessings. David earnestly desired that his should become so, more and more, by the Spirit of grace. His were no listless praises: "All that was within him" blessed his God.

Reader! are you in earnest? Turn not from the question as superfluous, and say that it may be taken for granted that you are. I beseech you, in the great matter of your salvation, take nothing for granted. Make sure work for eternity. Be all alive with reality. Let your thanksgivings be real. Again, therefore, we ask, Are you in earnest?—in earnest, not merely to go to heaven; not merely to be safe when you die—but to bless God while you live, and to glorify him on earth? Are you really grateful? Do you try to be so? Do you earnestly desire to increase in gratitude? Do you strive against all murmuring and ungrateful thoughts? Do you pray to be enabled to take trials unrepiningly; to bear disappointments patiently, rebuffs meekly, and discomforts not moodily but cheerily; believing that a kind and tender Lord is moulding you by these tender touches, that sharper may not be required? Again, then, we ask, Are you in earnest? Is your whole soul engaged in thanking God? Is your life a reality of praise? Does it "bless" God? Does it "bless" your fellow men? Is it a "blessing" to yourself? Is it preparing you by thanksgivings on earth, for the everlasting thanksgivings in heaven! God wishes you to be happy in praising Him, and do you take pleasure in the discharge of this joyful duty? Is it the first thing you say to yourself—is it the last, "Bless the Lord, O my soul"? Do you often stop yourself on the pathway of forgetfulness, and say, "FORGET NOT:" Oh, my soul, thou hast forgotten many, but I charge thee "forget not all God's benefits!" FORGET NOT thy Benefactor; FORGET NOT His benefits. FORGET NOT thy sins; FORGET NOT the blood that obtains their pardon. FORGET NOT thy duty to praise; FORGET NOT thy privilege to bless; and FORGET NOT that Spirit who alone enables thee to be thankful. Say "Sooner will my right hand forget her cunning, and my tongue cleave to the roof of my mouth," than I will forget Thee, O my Saviour, and Thy redeeming love. I will prefer Thy glory before my chiefest earthly joy: "Whom have I in heaven but Thee, and there is none upon earth that I desire beside Thee." "O Lord my God, I will give thanks unto Thee for ever."

Reader! stir up your soul after the example of the Psalmist. Try to remember one mercy more, then another, then still another. One mercy at a time mark down, then add a special thanksgiving; next note another benefit, and then add another offering of praise. God is continually giving gifts: be you continually giving thanks. Not by words without feeling; not by feelings without deeds; but by each and all of these, out of a sincere and fervent heart. Get into the habit of praise. Recapitulate blessings. Look back on former deliverances. Try to remember, and not to lose sight of God's great benefits. Keep an enumeration of them beside you. Let new mercies recall old benefits. Let even the dark cloud of your sorrow for sin, reflect a bright rainbow of God's mercy. Look always at your transgressions through the wounds of Jesus, then your sorrow will become "godly," and every bitter confession will be sweetened with this thanksgiving - that such a sinner should have such a Saviour. "By Jesus offer the sacrifice of praise to God continually, that is the fruit of your lips, giving thanks to His name." Say, like Chrysostom of old, though suffering by disease and persecution, "Glory be to God for everything that happens." Be satisfied with God thy Saviour, and sit loose to all creature comforts. "A believer can lose nothing of importance, unless he can lose God: but God is his 'portion for ever,' Psa. lxxiii. 26, and therefore his complaints are childish." The Scripture bids thee "rejoice in the Lord alway." It has nowhere bid thee to mourn always. You would not ask the Great High Priest to present your murmurings to the Lord, why, then, do you present them yourself? Trials are sent to do you good, not to do you harm. Why, then, should losses and bereavements make you fretful, and fill you with repinings? "Shall present evils make us either insensible of, or unthankful for, past mercies? Shall present troubles be a grave wherein to bury the memory of all our former comforts?"—*Caryl.* You trust that you are planted in the garden of the Lord; seek, therefore, to be one of His incense-breathing flowers —a lily of the valley—humble, pure, and fragrant. Beware of that morbid melancholy which, like a biting frost, nips gratitude in the bud. "All unbelief and dejection should be ashamed of itself, and be put to shame, which does not give God the glory of interesting Himself in His creatures, and of feeling for their misery."—*Hengstenberg.*

It is not of your own spirit that you can be thankful, or bear up with a patient mind under all the trials and disappointments of this mortal life. It is alone the Spirit who wrote this Psalm, who can enable you to sing it. Jesus gives that Spirit freely, and the Apostle exhorts you, "Be filled with the Spirit; speaking to yourselves in psalms and hymns and spiritual songs, singing and making melody in your heart to the Lord: Giving thanks always for all things unto God and the Father, in the name of our Lord Jesus Christ," Eph. v. 19. Pray, therefore, earnestly to be "filled with the Spirit." His presence will give you society in loneliness, light in darkness, and joy even in a dungeon. "At midnight, in the inner prison," though their backs were bleeding with many stripes, and their feet made fast in the stocks, yet "Paul and Silas prayed and sang praises unto God," Acts xvi. 23—25. Pray for the spirit of praise. God heard Paul and Silas, and He will hear you. In answer to prayer, the Comforter will be sent to gladden your dreariest hour. The presence of the Spirit will awaken every faculty and lighten every thought; revive every feeling and warm every affection; sanctify every imagination, brighten every hope, and guild every word with gratitude. Your whole life, under that Spirit, will become praise, and every act an offering of incense. Earnestly, therefore, make this your prayer,—Oh God the Father, God the Son, and God the Holy Ghost, three Persons and one God, forget me not, and never suffer me to forget Thee. Be always present with my soul, that my soul may be always present with Thee:

> "THY PRESENCE has a wondrous power:
> The sharpest thorn becomes a flower,
> And breathes a sweet perfume.
> Whate'er look'd dark and sad before,
> Now bright with light shines silver'd o'er,
> And life has lost its gloom!"

Pray for the spirit of praise. Earnestly desire that your soul may be as a well-tuned instrument in the hand of the Divine Spirit. Let every faculty, yea, "all that is within you," be ready harmonized to sing God's praise. Let *conscience* "bless the Lord," by unvarying fidelity. Let *judgment* bless Him, by decisions accordant with His word. Let *imagination* bless Him, by pure and holy musings. Let the *affections* praise Him, by loving whatsoever He loves. Let *desire* bless Him, by seeking only His glory. Let *memory* bless Him, by not forgetting any of His benefits. Let *thought* bless Him, by meditating on His excellencies. Let *hope* praise Him, by longing and "looking for the glory that is to be revealed." Let every *sense* bless Him by its fealty, every *word* by its truth, and every *act* by its integrity. Bless God by trusting Him at all times; cleaving to Him under chastisements, and resigning yourself to Him under bereavements. Bless God by patience under adversity, and by humbleness under prosperity. Bless your Saviour in heaven by imitating His example on earth—in meekness and gentleness, in charity and long-suffering, and in the God-like act of returning good for evil. Bless God by diligence in your calling, by prudence and integrity in all your dealings, and by owing no man anything but love. Bless God by not forgetting earthly benefactors, and by an ever-living remembrance of your Great Benefactor in heaven. Say again and again to yourself, "Bless the Lord, O my soul; and all that is within me bless His holy name." Be continually blessing God. The Scripture, four times in one verse, thus enjoins thee, "Sing praises to God, sing praises. Sing praises unto our King, sing praises." Psa. xlvii. 6. Say from the very heart with the Psalmist, "I will bless the Lord at all times, His praise shall continually be in my mouth." Psa. xxxiv. 1. "While I live, I will praise the Lord. I will sing praises unto my God while I have my being." Psa. cxlvi. 2. "I will extol Thee my God, O King; and I will bless Thy name for ever and ever. Every day will I bless Thee, and I will praise Thy name for ever and ever." Psa. cxlv. 1, 2. "I will sing unto the Lord as long as I live. I will sing praise to my God while I have my being. My meditation of Him shall be sweet. I will be glad in the Lord." Psa. civ. 33. "My soul shall be satisfied as with marrow and fatness: and my mouth shall praise

Thee with joyful lips, when I remember Thee upon my bed, and meditate on Thee in the night watches." Psa. lxiii. 5.

That *your* days and nights may be thus blessed, dear Reader, *your* soul satisfied, and *your* lips made joyful, meditate much on the excellencies of your God in His own nature, and on the blessed relationships in which He has revealed Himself, Father, Saviour, Comforter, and on the boundless benefits which in all these He has bestowed. Think of SPIRITUAL BLESSINGS—personal, domestic, and social, and say, "Blessed be the God and Father of our Lord Jesus Christ, who hath blessed us with all spiritual blessings in heavenly places in Christ." Eph. i. 3. Think of TEMPORAL BLESSINGS—mental, and corporeal—circumstantial, national, and universal. Think of PROVIDENTIAL BLESSINGS, private and public—of providential deliverances known and unknown—of enlarging providences to the good, and of restraining providences upon the wicked. Think of these innumerable temporal and providential benefits, and say, "Many, O Lord my God, are Thy wonderful works which Thou hast done, and Thy thoughts which are to usward; they cannot be reckoned up in order unto Thee: if I would declare or speak of them, they are more than can be numbered." Psa. xl. 5. Impress upon your mind that you have not deserved the very least of any of these mercies, and then think of the Lord, in the richness of His goodness, adding EVERLASTING BLESSINGS: freely giving, in Christ Jesus, everlasting pardon, eternal life, never-ending salvation, an immortal soul, a spiritual body, purity and perfection for ever, a kingdom without end, and joys that never fade.

Think of the praises of the UNIVERSAL BENEFACTOR sung by the universal choir of all His angels, and all His hosts, and all His works, in all places of His dominion; think of yourself, by grace, uniting with them hereafter in their everlasting song; and surely, after such a survey of benefits, and in harmony with such a company of worshippers, you will delight with the Psalmist to present yourself before the throne of grace, and say, as long as life and breath shall last, "Bless the Lord, O my soul; and all that is within me bless His holy name. Bless the Lord, O my soul, and forget not all His benefits. Bless the Lord for SPECIAL KINDNESSES. Magnify Him for MANIFOLD MERCIES. Praise Him for IMMEASURABLE BLESSINGS. Glorify Him for EVERLASTING BENEFITS. Bless the Lord, ye His angels. Bless the Lord all ye His hosts. Bless the Lord all His works, in all places of His dominion. BLESS THE LORD, O MY SOUL."

THE END.

The Pastor's Family.

18mo.

A sweet little story, full of interest and instruction.

Female Scripture Characters.

By the Rev. William Jay. Royal 12mo. $1.

"By all sincere Christian women the world over, this volume will be regarded as a spiritual treasure."—*Presbyterian.*

"They will be found unusually interesting in style and spirit, as well as in the skill and beauty of their portraiture, wise in their counsel, and excellent in their influence—worthy the fame of the distinguished author."—*Evangelist.*

"They bear all those characteristics of both mind and heart which have rendered all his productions at once so popular and so useful."—*Argus.*

Jay's Morning and Evening Exercises.

A new edition, in large type, in *four* volumes, royal 12mo.
Price $1 per volume.

"This is a new edition of an excellent practical work, beautifully printed on large and fair type, and bound in cloth. The execution of this volume is in the best style, entitling it to a preference before all other editions. As the work is highly appreciated on both sides of the Atlantic, it is sufficient to say that we know of nothing more pure and scriptural in sentiment, nothing more elevated and devotional in spirit, nothing more simple and beautiful, than the reflections on the lessons from the Bible contained in this book."—*Christian Observer.*

"We doubt whether any work of modern times has been more blessed to the edification of God's people than Jay's Exercises. It has been the closet companion of tens of thousands of earnest Christians in all parts of the world, kindling anew within their hearts, with each day, the flame of devotion; instructing, cheering, and comforting them on their heavenward way."—*Presbyterian.*

A New Edition of the

Life and Times of John Calvin.

By Paul Henry. 2 vols. in one. Price $2.

Africa and America Described.

By the author of the "Peep of Day," &c; 16mo. 75 cents.

"This is a capital book for young readers, and one that we can recommend as suitable to be placed in their hands. It interweaves descriptions of countries, people, morals and manners, with anecdotes and illustrations so appropriately, that it cannot fail to interest the mind of the reader."—*Courier and Journal.*

Discourses and Sayings of our Lord Jesus Christ.

Illustrated in a series of Expositions. By John Brown, D.D. 2 vols. 8vo. $4.

"Where several conflicting opinions of the learned are detailed, his discrimination is admirable; when his own interpretation is given, it is set forth with so much clearness, and appears so reasonable, that the reader will seldom feel disposed to withhold his assent. As an able expositor—clear, candid, comprehensive—Dr. Brown is unrivalled among British divines."—*Kitto.*

The Right of the Bible in the Common Schools.

By George B. Cheever, D.D. 16mo. 75 cents.

"It is a question which in its decision is to influence the happiness, the temporal and eternal welfare of one hundred millions of human beings."—*Daniel Webster.*

By the same Author,

The Powers of the World to Come, and the Church's Stewardship, as invested with them.

12mo. Price $1.

"He makes the realities of the invisible world take on a living and substantial character. We seem to be in contact with the sublime scenes of the judgment, to breathe the air of the upper Paradise, and to listen to the wailings of the reprobate. If we were to characterize this work in a single word, we would say that it is a work of power."—*Puritan Recorder.*

"This is a solemn and stirring book. Many of the pages sparkle with gems of the richest lustre."—*Watchman and Observer.*

By Dr. John Brown,

Sufferings and Glories of the Messiah;

An Exposition of Psalm xviii. and Isaiah lii. 13; liii. 12.

"It is the ripe fruit of thirty years study of the deeply interesting passages on which it is founded. The learned author has spared no pains to make his examination thorough and satisfactory."—*St. Louis Presbyterian.*

Abbeokuta;

Or, Sunrise in the Tropics. An Outline of the Origin and Progress of the Yoruba Mission. By Miss Tucker, author of "The Rainbow in the North." Illustrated. 16mo. 75 cents.

Infidelity;

Its Aspects, Causes, and Agencies. By Thomas Pearson, Eyemouth, Scotland. 8vo. $2.

"He writes like one thoroughly familiar with his ground; he has the confidence of one who has examined well the strength and manœuvrings of the enemy; who also knows well his own resources, and has no hesitation as to the side toward which victory will finally turn. He shows an uncommon degree of judgment and strong common sense. We feel assured that ministers and intelligent laymen generally, will read this work with no common interest."—*Presbyterian.*

"This work is written in a masterly style of argument, and with a beauty, as well as power of language, which makes it an eminently readable book."—*Observer.*

"We have no hesitation, without knowing anything of the author except from this work, in assigning to him a place among the most philosophical and discriminating minds of the age."—*Puritan Recorder.*

Jaqueline Pascal;

Or, A Glimpse of Convent Life at Port Royal. With an Introduction by W. R. Williams, D.D. 12mo. $1.

"Jaqueline Pascal, the younger sister of the renowned Blaise Pascal, was a woman of surpassing powers, of remarkable feminine attractions, and intellect and disposition in no respect inferior to her celebrated brother. The work before us gives a most delightful picture of this wonderful woman—of her sister, their eminent brother, and the members and connections of the family.

The Young Woman's Friend and Guide through Life to Immortality.

By the Rev. John Angel James. 16mo. 75 cents.

"The sphere of woman and the value of piety in the discharge of her duties, are unfolded and enforced in a most attractive and impressive manner. Let every one of the sex purchase and read this invaluable book."—*Pbn. Herald.*

* The Self-Explanatory Bible.

The Holy Bible: the Authorized Version, with Parallel References printed at length. 1 vol. 8vo. Half calf, $4 50; Turkey morocco, $6; morocco gilt, $6 50.

While the importance of parallel and illustrative passages, in elucidating the meaning of Scripture, is generally admitted, it cannot be denied that their utility is very much impaired by the time and labor required in turning to the numerous passages. With a view to remedy this defect, the present edition has been prepared. Its peculiar object is to set before the reader, at a glance, the very words of those passages which are best fitted to illustrate the text, or to throw satisfactory light on its meaning.

285 Broadway, New York,
May, 1854.

ROBERT CARTER & BROTHERS'

New Publications.

Vara; or, the Child of Adoption.

12mo. Price $1.

"We would give something to know who is the author of this delightful book. It is the work of no novice, of no dreamer, of no tyro in the feelings, passions, and errors of the human heart, and the temptations, ordeals and reverses of this shifting life of ours. The mind in which it originated is opulent in experience—perhaps in suffering experience—and the hand that penned its sentences was guided by truth and soberness.

"It is the history of an adopted child, and such a history as must soften the heart and awaken the pity of every reader. It is a story, and yet a sermon. Taking the little Vara by the hand, and leading her through the corridors of an eventful life, it leaves upon the mind a genial and lasting impression which will prove of service. We hope to see it circulated widely."—*Buffalo Express.*

"It is indeed written with an aim—the intent to show the self-abnegation of the missionary, to correct some wide-spread calumnies against his saintly character, to interest all in the cause of missions; but although this is the thread that runs through the whole, it is invisible to the careless, while its influence is felt.

"We predict for it an immense sale, and venture to announce the author as a worthy addition to the few distinguished American authors.

"As a work of art, we place it high. Independently of any aim of plot, the language is both chaste and ornate, frequently pathetic, often humorous. The characters are drawn with great skill, and we can find originals in our mind who seem to be here carefully pictured."—*Newark Daily.*

Quarles' Emblems.

Emblems, Divine and Moral. By Francis Quarles. Illustrated.
16mo. $1.

"The quaint, suggestive, and beautiful emblems of Quarles are here produced in a handsome volume, full of wisdom and sanctified wit, and impressive with the most spiritual and earnest views of Divine truth."—*Evangelist.*

"We are pleased to see an American edition of this volume of quaint and rich old poetry."—*Christian Intelligencer.*

"The author of this work was successively cup-bearer to Elizabeth, Queen of Bohemia, Secretary to Archbishop Usher, and Chronologer to the city of London. With the quaintness of the age to which he belonged, he unites a vigorous imagination, keen wit, and uncommon skill in delineating the human character and probing the human heart."—*Puritan Recorder.*

The Woodcutter of Lebanon and the Exiles of Lucerna.

By the author of "Morning and Night Watches. 18mo.

Mabel Grant.

A Highland Story. By Randall Ballantyne. 18mo. 50 cents.

Charles Roussel; or, Honesty and Industry.

By the author of "Three Months under the Snow." 18mo. 40 cents.

The Eternal Day.

By the Rev. Horatius Bonar. 18mo. 50 cents.

"This book is written and published for the joy and strength of those who are looking forward to an eternal day in heaven. The discussion is scriptural and full of unction and power. Many a weary pilgrim will read it with intense interest, and receive a new impulse in his journey toward that better land."—*Ch. Chronicle.*

Is it Possible to make the Best of Both Worlds?

By the Rev. T. Binney. 16mo. 60 cents.

"We wish that all apprentices, and young men entering on business, could be induced to procure and study this book. The happy results of future years would be the reward of attending to its counsels."—*Banner.*

Also a supply of the London edition of

Sir Thomas Fowell Buxton.

A Study for Young Men. By the same author. 16mo. 50 cents.

The Words of Jesus.

By the author of the "Morning and Night Watches." 16mo. 40 cts.

"They are like the precious words that introduce them, of a most tender and consolatory character, and especially adapted to strengthen the heart of the weary pilgrim."—*Puritan Recorder.*

Daniel, a Model for Young Men.

By the Rev. W. A. Scott, D.D. 8vo. $1 50.

The Law and the Testimony;

By the Author of the "Wide, Wide World," &c. 8vo, second thousand. Cloth, $3; half calf, $4.

"This is a great book, and manifestly the result of labor, patient and long continued. It is a complete collection, or at least a very extensive one, of all the passages in the Bible having a bearing upon particular specified subjects or points of doctrine, such as the Divine Nature, Divinity of the Saviour, God's Omniscience, Sovereignty and Justice, Christ's Office, Office of the Holy Spirit, Man's Freedom and Fall, Nature and Consequences of Sin, Nature of Faith, Repentance, Salvation, Judgment, Heaven and Hell, &c. . . . . A remarkable book, one that will take the shelf by the side of the most elaborate tomes and learned works of distinguished divines. The author has already acquired a wide reputation by two works of lighter literature, 'Queechy' and the 'Wide, Wide World;' but the 'Law and the Testimony,' we imagine, will be her most enduring work."—*U. S. Journal.*

"We welcome it as a fresh and worthy aid to the examination of the pure word of God."—*Watchman.*

"A delightful handmaid to the perusal and right understanding of the meaning, force, fulness, and harmony of the sacred text."—*Spectator.*

"A most valuable aid to all those who revere and study the Scriptures, as the only rule of faith and practice."—*Pbn. of West.*

"We commend this volume with all our heart. The Sabbath School Teacher needs it. Parents may well lay it on the table of the new married daughter. And aged Christians, as they follow on through these clear and well printed pages, will rejoice to find the foundation of their hope standing so strong."—*T. L. C.*

"We can commend it as a volume of great convenience in the study of the Sacred volume, and especially to the Ministers of the Gospel in their preparations for the pulpit."—*Pbn. Herald.*

Now completed, by the publication of the eighth and last volume,

Daily Bible Illustrations:

Being Original Readings for a Year on Subjects from Sacred History, Biography, Geography, Antiquities, and Theology. Especially designed for the Family Circle. By John Kitto, D.D.

Morning Series:—Vol. I. The Antediluvians and Patriarchs, Fourth Edition; Vol. II. Moses and the Judges, Second Edition; Vol. III. Samuel, Saul, and David, Second Edition; Vol. IV. Solomon and the Kings, Second Edition.
Evening Series:—Vol. I. Job and the Poetical Books; Vol. II. Isaiah and the Prophets; Vol. III. Life and Death of our Lord; Vol. IV. The Apostles and Early Church.

Each Volume is sold separately, price $1 each.

"One of the best books of the kind. Dr. Kitto brings to each reading curious learning, real information, and close argument, conveyed in a solid style."—*Spectator.*

"The series is admirable."—*Evangelical Christendom.*

"For family reading, these Illustrations are inestimable."—*Baptist Magazine.*

"We should wish to see this most useful work in every house."—*Church of England Magazine.*

Scotia's Bards.

Comprising the choicest productions of Scottish Poets, Illustrated with more than fifty elegant engravings in the highest style of the art, with Frontispiece and Vignette by Ritchie. 8vo. Cloth, $3; full gilt, $4; Turkey Morocco, $6 50.

"Scotland, rich in the treasures of Theology, History, and Philosophy, here stands before us with their long array of Poets, such as any country might be proud to acknowledge as its own."—*Watchman and Reflector.*

"An elegant volume, in the very best style of execution."—*Chrs. Intelligencer.*

"It is enriched with the most brilliant and costly poetic gems, from the mines of that land, which has been as fruitful in minstrels as in metaphysicians, heroes, and martyrs."—*Presbyterian.*

"This fine large octavo volume, printed in beautiful style, and enriched with many choice engravings, containing, we believe, the first extended collection of the best productions of the Scottish poets, that has ever been made. It cannot fail to be acceptable to all who can appreciate the finest creations of genius."—*Argus.*

"We predict that as 'Scotia's Bards' is one of the most superb books of the season, so it will be one of the most popular also."—*T. C. L.*

"A most excellent taste and judgment are displayed in the selection of this volume, and the biographical and critical notices prefixed to the poems, are happily written, in a chaste and simple style; the illustrations of the work will combine with its intrinsic value, to render it one of the most attractive of the season."—*Independent.*

Family Prayers.

By the Author of "Morning and Night Watches." 75 cents.

These prayers are conceived in a truly evangelical spirit, and are remarkable for the appropriate introduction of Scripture language. Besides morning and evening prayers for four weeks, there are a number of prayers designed for, and well adapted to as many different occasions. Those who are accustomed to use forms of any kind, will find this an excellent auxiliary to their family devotions.

Memoir of Richard Williams.

Surgeon. Catechist to the Patagonian Mission. By James Hamilton, D.D. 16mo. 75 cents.

"In all the history of Gospel Missions there is nothing that possesses such a fearful interest as that of the English Missionaries to Patagonia, the terrible sufferings and starvation of a portion of whom created such a shock a year or two ago. The subject of this memoir was the surgeon and catechist of that devoted band, and it is chiefly made up of his journal, which was continued by his own hand so long as he was able to put pen to paper. The annals of martyrdom contain few stories of a Christian heroism more noble than his and that of his associates."—*Bulletin.*

Christian Progress.

A sequel to the "Anxious Enquirer." By the Rev. John Angel James. 18mo. 30 cents.

www.ingramcontent.com/pod-product-compliance
Lightning Source LLC
LaVergne TN

LVHW020214110826
845151LV00003B/716
* 9 7 8 1 4 2 5 5 3 3 8 3 0 *